THE WISDOM OF
ANDREW CARNEGIE
AS TOLD TO
NAPOLEON HILL

By Dr. Napoleon Hill

Author of

THINK AND GROW RICH

LAW OF SUCCESS

HOW TO SELL YOUR WAY THROUGH LIFE

MASTER KEY TO RICHES

SUCCESS THROUGH A POSITIVE MENTAL ATTITUDE
Co-Authored with W. Clement Stone

GROW RICH WITH PEACE OF MIND

YOU CAN WORK YOUR OWN MIRACLES

PMA SCIENCE OF SUCCESS COURSE

The books written by Dr. Napoleon Hill have inspired millions of people in all parts of the world, and the principles Dr. Hill discovered are as practical today as when he had his first interview with Andrew Carnegie in 1908.

Reading this book will inspire you to understand the great benefits from Hill's conversations with the great industrialist Andrew Carnegie, who came to the United States from Scotland and began working as a thirteen year old lad at wages of $1.20 per week.

The success formula presented in *The Wisdom of Andrew Carnegie As Told To Napoleon Hill* will prove to you that "Whatever the mind can CONCEIVE AND BELIEVE, the mind can ACHIEVE."

Published by

THE NAPOLEON HILL FOUNDATION
PO Box 1277
Wise, Virginia 24293
Don M. Green, Executive Director

Published by:

The Napoleon Hill Foundation
P. O. Box 1277
Wise, Virginia 24293

Website: www.naphill.org
email: napoleonhill@uvawise.edu

ISBN-13: 978-0-937539-45-3
ISBN-10: 0-937539-45-7

Distributed by:

Executive Books
206 W. Allen Street
Mechanicsburg, PA 17055

Telephone: 800-233-2665
Website: www.executivebooks.com

CONTENTS
of
THE WISDOM OF
ANDREW CARNEGIE
AS TOLD TO
NAPOLEON HILL

*"The famous success formula of a great American
industrialist who taught thousands of people
how to increase their incomes"*

PUBLISHER'S INTRODUCTION
The story behind this volume

Napoleon Hill gives you in—"THE WISDOM OF ANDREW CARNEGIE AS TOLD TO NAPOLEON HILL"— all seventeen Principles of Success *IN A SINGLE VOLUME* just as they were taught to him in person by Andrew Carnegie and other successful men who gave freely of their time and experience.

Napoleon Hill tells you the secret of *How to win riches . . . power . . . prestige.* He tells how the average man may learn to use the secrets of America's greatest and richest men.

In this book you will discover the answer to all of your problems, whether you are seeking to increase your income or searching only for peace of mind . . . happiness . . . harmony in your home or place of occupation. You have here not only the means of making more money but a philosophy of success through which *you may set your own goal in life and achieve it,* just as thousands of others have done.

Read the probing questions Dr. Hill asked of Andrew Carnegie. Profit by the philanthropist's frank, illuminating statements *HOW HE MADE HIS MONEY.* This inspiring writer made it his life's work to trace these answers. He found that other men agreed! At last Napoleon Hill knew he had made a sensational discovery: *THAT THE APPLICATION OF CERTAIN FUNDAMENTAL PRINCIPLES WOULD INSURE SUCCESS TO EVERY ONE WHO MADE USE OF THEM.* The entire secret of success is written down in "THE WISDOM OF ANDREW CARNEGIE AS TOLD TO NAPOLEON HILL." This edition has been revised and modernized.

With illuminating pen and purpose, Dr. Hill writes from his intimate knowledge of and association with the world's wealthiest men. He found and gives you the true philosophy upon which all lasting success is built.

In the Steel King's own words, Napoleon Hill records his personal interviews with Carnegie, setting down each question and answer. The entire law, consisting of seventeen steps, is condensed in this volume, and gives a master plan to win success.

The theory that the road to wealth is hard and narrow is dead-as-a-doornail. You'll know it for the broad, smooth paved highway it is for those who apply the seventeen principles in the Science of Success. That promotion will look easy. That top job will not look so far away.

If you, like thousands of other men and women, have dreams of retiring some day but find your goal as far away as it was five . . . ten . . . fifteen years ago . . . ACT NOW! Start by deciding *how much money you need . . . for retirement . . . for a new house . . . a car . . . son's education.* We take you now to the private study of Andrew Carnegie, where Napoleon Hill is taking his first lesson on success.

THE NAPOLEON HILL FOUNDATION
W. CLEMENT STONE

REMEMBER

That the quality of service you render, plus the quantity, plus the mental attitude in which you render it determines the sort of job you hold and the amount of pay you receive.—NAPOLEON HILL

Chapter One

Develop Definiteness of Purpose

HILL: Mr. Carnegie, I would like to have you go back to the beginning of your career and describe to me, step by step, the principles of achievement through which you began, without money, without great influence and with but little schooling, and lifted yourself into a position of great affluence and wealth. Inasmuch as I am requesting this information in behalf of men and women who have neither the time nor the opportunity to acquire knowledge of the rules of success from those who have been successful, I ask that you forego all formalities and speak to me plainly and frankly, in terms that any person of average intelligence may understand.

CARNEGIE: Very well, I shall describe the rules of personal achievement which have been responsible for my own accomplishments, but I do so on condition that you organize these rules of human relationship into a philosophy that will be available to every person who has the ambition to master and use it.

What I am asking you to do is one of the constructive means I have for the distribution of my fortune. The money I have accumulated I will give away, in due time, through sources that will do the least amount of harm and the greatest possible good; but my real wealth—that portion of it which I wish to donate for the good of mankind—consists of the principles of personal achievement which I am entrusting to you.

In lending you my aid in the organization of the rules of personal achievement, I do so with the understanding that you will carry on a continuous research until you shall have compared my own experiences with the experience of other men who have been recognized as successes in many fields of endeavor, in order that you may give the world a success philosophy of sufficient flexibility that it will serve the needs of all people, regardless of their calling or purpose in life. A sound philosophy of individual achievement must present a clear understanding of the principles that bring success and those that lead to failure.

HILL: Your conditions are accepted, Mr. Carnegie, and you may rest assured, Sir, that I will never stop until the job has been finished, regardless of the time required. Your faith in my ability to do the job is all the inspiration I need to insure my carrying on until I finish. Will you begin, now, and give me an understandable analysis of all the principles of success which you have used in your personal advancement?

CARNEGIE: To begin with, let me state that there are seventeen major principles of success, and every person who attains the objective of his major goal, in any undertaking, must use some combination of these principles.

We shall name, first, the most important of these principles. It stands at the head of the list of the seventeen principles of achievement because no one has ever been known to succeed without applying it. You may call it the principle of Definiteness of Purpose.

Study any person who is known to be a permanent success and you will find that he has a Definite Major Goal; he has a plan for the attainment of this goal; he devotes the major portion of his thoughts and his efforts to the attainment of this purpose.

My own major purpose is that of making and marketing steel. I conceived that purpose while working as a laborer. *It became an obsession* with me. I took it to bed with me at night, and I took it to work with me in the morning. My Definite Purpose became more than a mere wish; it became my *Burning Desire!* That is the only sort of definite purpose which seems to bring desired results.

Emphasize, through every means at your command, the vast difference between a mere wish and a *burning desire* that has assumed the proportions of an obsession. Everyone wishes for the better things of life, such as money, a good position, fame, and recognition; but most people never go far beyond the *"wishing" stage.* Men who know exactly what they want of life, and are determined to get it, do not stop with wishing. They intensify their wishes into a *burning desire,* and back that desire with continuous effort based on a sound plan. It is necessary that they induce other people to cooperate in carrying out their plan.

No great achievement is possible without the aid of other minds. Later on I will explain how successful men go about inducing others to give their cooperation.

HILL: Before you achieved the object of your *Definite Major Purpose* you had to have the use of money, a large amount of it, as operating capital. How did you manage to procure so huge an amount of money, starting, as you did, without money of your own? I wish you would answer this question in detail, Mr. Carnegie, because nearly every person arrives at the point, sooner or later, at which he might rise to great heights of achievement, if only he had the capital with which to make the right start.

CARNEGIE: The first step from poverty to riches is the most difficult. It may simplify my statement if I tell you that *all riches, and all material things that anyone acquires through self-effort, begin in the form of a clear, concise mental picture of the thing one seeks.* When that picture grows, or has been forced to the proportions of an obsession, it is taken over by the subconscious mind, through some hidden law of nature which the wisest of men do not understand. From that point on one is drawn, attracted or guided in the direction of the physical equivalent of the mental picture.

I shall come back to this subject of the subconscious mind many times before we finish, as it is one of the vital factors in connection with all outstanding achievements.

Speaking of my own experience in taking the first step toward the achievement of my major purpose in life, I can describe it very clearly, in a few words.

First, I knew that I wanted to go into the making of steel. I whipped up that desire until it became a driving obsession with me. By this I mean that my desire drove me day and night.

Then I took the next step in carrying out my major purpose, by selling my idea to another workman. He was a friend of mine who had no money, but he did have the mental capacity to recognize the value of my idea, and the courage to join with me in carrying it out. Between the two of us we induced two others—men with vision, courage and initiative—to become interested in our plan for the making and marketing of steel.

We four men formed the nucleus of a Master Mind group which we later increased until it consisted of more than twenty men—the men who helped me acquire my fortune, to say nothing of having made fortunes for themselves through our joint efforts. Through the combined enthusiasm of my Master Mind group, we induced other men to supply the money necessary to carry out our idea. I will explain the "Master Mind" principle in detail later on in our conversation. What we are concerned with now is the starting point from which I took off in pursuit of my major purpose.

HILL: Am I to understand from what you say, Mr. Carnegie, that Definiteness of Purpose gives one the benefit of a natural law in carrying out an objective?

CARNEGIE: I wish you to observe other men who have been successful, as you go about your task of organizing the philosophy of achievement, for you will learn from them that each of them began, as I did, with a definite purpose and a definite plan for carrying it out. And another thing you will observe in connection with successful men, if you look closely enough, is the fact that they are succeeding with effort apparently no greater than that being used by others who are not succeeding.

It has long been a mystery to some people why men with little or no schooling often succeed, while men with extensive schooling are failing all around them. Look carefully and you will discover that great successes are the result of understanding and the use of a *positive mental attitude* through which nature aids men in converting their aims and purposes into their physical and financial equivalent. *Mental attitude* is the quality of mind which gives power to one's thoughts and plans. Remember this fact, and stress it in organizing the philosophy of individual achievement.

HILL: How long does it require, Mr. Carnegie, for one's mental attitude to begin attracting the physical and financial requisites of one's major purpose?

CARNEGIE: That depends entirely upon the nature and extent of one's desires, and the control one exercises over his mind in keeping it free from fear and doubt and self-imposed limitations. This sort of control comes through constant vigilance, wherein one keeps his mind free of all negative thoughts and leaves it open for the influx and the guidance of Infinite Intelligence.

Definiteness of Purpose involving a hundred dollars, for example, might be translated into its financial equivalent in a few days, or even a few hours, or a few minutes, whereas, desire for a million dollars might call for considerably more time, depending to some extent on what one has to give in return for the million dollars.

The best way I can think of to describe the time necessary for the translation of a definite purpose into its physical or financial equivalent, can be accurately stated by determining *the exact time necessary to deliver the service, or the equivalent in value one intends to give in return for the object of that purpose.*

Before I finish describing the seventeen principles of achievement, I hope to be able to prove to you that there is a definite connection between *giving* and *getting*. Lack of understanding of this truth has brought many men to grief and failure.

HILL: Am I to understand, from what you say, that natural law does not favor an attempt to *get something for nothing?*

CARNEGIE: Everything connected with nature and natural laws is based upon cause and effect. Generally speaking, riches and material things that men get are the effect of some form of useful service they have rendered. My fortune did not come to me until I had delivered to others definite values in the form of large quantities of well-made steel. I wish you would emphasize this great truth when you take the rules of success to the world.

Do not merely state that all success begins in the form of a Definite Major Purpose, but emphasize the fact that the only known way of insuring that a definite purpose will be carried out to a full realization, through the forces of natural law working through the minds of men, is by first establishing a cause for such realization, through useful service, rendered in a spirit of harmony.

HILL: How should one go about expressing the nature of one's

Definite Major Purpose? Is it sufficient merely to choose a purpose and hold it in one's mind, or is there some better way of translating this dominant purpose into its physical equivalent?

CARNEGIE: That depends entirely upon the sort of mind one has. A well disciplined mind is capable of holding and acting upon a definite major purpose without any form of outside, or artificial aid. The undisciplined mind needs a crutch to lean upon while dealing with a Definite Major Purpose.

The best method to be followed, by one with an undisciplined mind, is that of writing down a complete description of one's major purpose and then adopting the habit of reading it aloud at least once every day. The act of writing down one's major purpose forces one to be specific as to its nature. The act of habitual reading fixes the nature of the purpose in the mind, where it can be picked up by the subconscious mind and acted upon.

HILL: Do you follow the habit of writing down your major purpose, Mr. Carnegie?

CARNEGIE: I followed that habit many years ago, while I was struggling to make the change from day labor to industrial management. Moreover, I went much farther than merely reading my written statement of my major purpose; I met with my Master-Mind group nightly and we entered into a detailed round-table discussion for the purpose of building plans to carry out the object of my major goal.

I heartily recommend this round-table habit. It is a habit I still follow. I believe you will find that all men of noteworthy achievement rely upon this habit of intimate discussion of their plans with their advisers and business associates.

I learned, years ago, that no single mind is complete. When we come to the discussion of the Master-Mind principle I will explain to you why two or more minds, working together in harmony toward a definite objective, have more power than a single mind.

You will find corroborative evidence of this great truth throughout the Bible, if you search carefully and understand that which you read. Jesus of Nazareth understood the principle of the Master-Mind and made effective use of it in His alliance with

His Disciples. That is where I got my first cue concerning this astounding law of Nature.

HILL: I hope you will pardon me for mentioning it, Sir, but I have heard you severely criticized because you have accumulated a great fortune, while thousands of men who work for you have remained comparatively poor. Some people feel that you gained your fortune at the expense of those who worked for you. Will you explain your conception of the reason for the great difference between your financial achievements, and those of the men who work for you?

CARNEGIE: I am very glad you asked that question. Many others have asked the same question. I will answer you as I answered them. First, let me explain that I expect to give away practically every dollar of wealth I possess before I pass on; but let me hasten to say that I am finding it very difficult to give money where it will do more good than harm.

It seems queer, but it is true, that *men seldom profit by money except that which they earn.* I would willingly give every dollar I have to the men who work for me if I could do so without doing them more injury than good. The good there is in money consists of the use to which it is put, and not in the mere possession of it. Generally speaking, the man who earns his own money, acquires, along with it, some of the necessary wisdom as to its constructive use.

You ask me to explain the reason for the great difference between my financial achievements and the financial status of those who work for me. I can only answer you by saying that I have accumulated great wealth because I was willing to assume great responsibilities and deliver service of a widespread nature.

Of the thousands of men who work for me, I hazard the guess that not more than a score of them would be willing to assume my responsibilities and work the hours that I work, if I gave them all the money I possess for doing so. A few of the men who work for me have been willing to assume such responsibilities, and it is significant that every one of these is as rich as he desires to be.

In a single year I have paid such men as Charlie Schwab as

much as a million dollars for their services, most of which was paid for services they rendered over and above that which was required of them in connection with the earning of their regular salaries. But before I paid out such huge sums to these men they had become practically indispensable to me, by their willingness to assume responsibilities and relieve me of the load I was carrying. Men with this sort of mental attitude have a way of fixing their own incomes, and there is but little anyone else can do to stop them from getting their own price.

I never set the wage scale of any man who works for me. Every man sets his own wage scale, by the sort of service he renders— the quality and the quantity of his service, plus the mental attitude in which he renders it. Understand this truth and you will know that there is no injustice in connection with the difference between the fortunes which men accumulate.

HILL: I take it, from what you say, Mr. Carnegie, that most of the men who work for you have no Definite Major Purpose in life, for if they had, they, too, would be as rich as you. Is this correct?

CARNEGIE: You are at liberty to talk with as many of my men as you please, but you will find out that the highest aim of a majority of them is to be able to hold the jobs they have. *They are where they are, and they are drawing the wages they receive solely because of the limitations they have set up in their own minds.*

Nothing that I can do will change this. Only the men themselves can change it. My men began in exactly the same station in life which I occupied a few years ago. They have had the same privileges for personal advancement that I had. We all live in the richest and freest country in the world, where no man is limited except by his own mental attitude and his own desires.

Take yourself, for example: I have placed in your hands the greatest opportunity any American writer has ever enjoyed. I am giving you free access to a life-time of practical experience in the accumulation of wealth, through the rendering of useful service.

Within the next few years I will open doors to you that will lead you into the rich store-houses of experience of some of the most successful men this country has produced. You will have a great wealth of knowledge at your disposal.

If you make the proper use of your opportunity you can occupy more space in the world than any other philosopher who has ever concerned himself with the problems of human beings.

HILL: Mr. Carnegie, many people believe that the opportunities available to men who wish to gain financial independence are fewer now than when you began your career. Some people believe that you and other men of wealth practically monopolize the field of opportunity; that you will not give others a chance. Would you mind telling me what you think of this theory?

CARNEGIE: I am glad you used the term "theory," because the belief that there is any scarcity of opportunities in a country such as ours is nothing but pure theory. The truth is this: We have more opportunities in America, for the making of fortunes in return for useful service than in all other countries combined. This is a new country. We are just now approaching an age in which we are destined to become the greatest industrial country on earth. Within the next few years we shall see stupendous developments in the field of industry.

Lack of opportunities in America? Why, man alive! Don't you see that our only lack is going to be a shortage of imagination, self-reliance, and initiative which will be needed to man the future of this country? I have but little patience with the short-sighted person who sees no future in America. If you will analyze those who cry "no opportunity" you will find that they are using this as an alibi for their own unwillingness to assume responsibilities and use their minds.

The time is at hand when the whole world will be turning to America for new ideas, new inventions, new opportunities, for skill and imagination. I see no less than fifty years of opportunity available to the young men of this country, every hour of which will give them far greater advantages than any I ever had.

Men who complain of lack of opportunity remind me of the Congressman who not long ago wanted to introduce a Bill in Congress providing for the closing of the Patent Office on the ground that there was nothing else to be patented. Now I sincerely hope you will not become a victim of this short-sighted belief that this country has run out of opportunities.

HILL: Mr. Carnegie, I'm sure your exceptional vision gives you still much more to say about the opportunities this great nation affords to the men and women willing to learn the rules of success, use them to play the game of life and claim the prizes as they go along.

You have expressed a strong, inspiring note of encouragement to the young men and women of this nation, if they only have the imagination, self-reliance, and initiative to see and take advantage of the opportunities which this country affords them. Do you now wish to add anything to your statement of the hope of future achievement in America?

CARNEGIE: Yes, right here I wish to lay down a challenge to you! I wish to impress upon your mind the fact that you have the greatest opportunity of any young man of this generation whom I know, because you are being coached and prepared to present to the people of this country a new philosophy of individual achievement which will inspire men and women in all walks of life to recognize and embrace this age of abundant opportunity.

Your mission in life is that of helping to inspire the people with a new birth of the spirit of Americanism. My greatest prayer is that you may catch this vision as I see it, and, in due time, that you may inspire others with the same vision.

The world of great opportunity is available now, as it has always been, only for those with great vision. If you lose yourself in an obsessional desire to make yourself useful to others, you will find yourself through the voluntary recognition of the good you are doing.

There is nothing new about this thought. It is as old as the world; it will remain as long as civilization endures. I am stressing the thought because it should run, like a golden cord, as a binding force throughout the philosophy of individual achievement.

HILL: I hope I have the strength of character to accept your challenge! I can only promise to use faithfully, such talents as I may possess, in carrying out your trust. I am only a young man, and my major asset is a keen thirst for knowledge and a willingness to pay whatever price is required to obtain it.

CARNEGIE: In one sentence you have described the greatest asset any young man can possess—*a desire for knowledge and the willingness to earn it!* If you write that sentence into your Definiteness of Purpose in life, and never overlook its value, you are sure to occupy more space in American life than any other writer of this generation.

Remember, that a man's achievements correspond, with unerring certainty, to the philosophy with which he relates himself to others. If you follow through your willingness to give something in return for the knowledge you desire, you are certain to make yourself so useful to the world that it will be compelled to reward you in terms of your own choice. This is the spirit of true Americanism.

HILL: Mr. Carnegie, you have made frequent reference to the term "Americanism." Will you please give me a detailed analysis of what you mean by this term? I believe that altogether too many people skip lightly over the word "Americanism" without having a clear conception of all it means.

CARNEGIE: That is an excellent suggestion, and I hope you will incorporate in the philosophy of achievement a full and complete analysis of Americanism, so that others who are seeking an opportunity to attain financial independence in this country may become acquainted with the foundation on which our nation rests.

All success begins with Definiteness of Purpose. Every person who seeks personal success in America should both understand and respect the fundamentals of Americanism. Those who neglect or refuse to give loyal support to the institutions of Americanism may unconsciously contribute to the downfall of these supporting pillars, thereby cutting the very foundation from under their own opportunities for personal success. It is obvious that no individual may enjoy permanent success if he is out of step with the forces which have given him his opportunity to succeed.

HILL: You refer to "supporting pillars" of American institutions. Would you mind naming and describing these, Mr. Carnegie?

CARNEGIE: I should be most happy to do so. The first of the major pillars which distinguish this country from all others is: *Our American form of government.* It was originally written into the Constitution of the United States, providing the fullest possible measure of the right to individual liberty, freedom of thought, freedom of speech, freedom of worship.

Above all, freedom of individual initiative that gives to every citizen the privilege of choosing his own occupation and setting his own price upon his knowledge, skill and experience. No other country in the world offers its citizens such an abundant choice of opportunities for the marketing of their services as those provided under our form of government.

HILL: Mr. Carnegie, you have named the first of the "pillars" underlying our great nation. Will you please go on now and tell me about number two?

CARNEGIE: Number Two is our *industrial system,* with its matchless natural resources of leadership and raw materials, co-ordinated as it is, with our American spirit of Democracy, and supported by our American form of Government. So long as there is harmony and understanding and sympathetic cooperation between leaders of industry and the officials of our government, every citizen will benefit, directly or indirectly, by our expanding industrial system.

This is definitely an industrial nation. Industry not only supplies a major portion of the income for men who work for wages, but it absorbs a major portion of the products of agriculture, and it is the major source of support for men and women who are in professional work. There is no way of separating "Americanism" from industry without destroying one of the strongest and most important of the pillars of Americanism.

HILL: I sincerely hope the time will never come when the leaders of government and the leaders of industry neglect or refuse to work in harmony toward a common end. It would impose economic difficulties on each and every one of us. What do you consider to be the next important "pillar," Mr. Carnegie?

CARNEGIE: Number Three is *our banking system,* providing as it does the life-blood which keeps our industrial system and our agriculture, and our business and professional systems active and flexible, at a cost that is not a burden to anyone. Understand the nature of the service being rendered by our banking system and you will be forever done with the ignorant few who cry out against the imaginary sins of "Wall Street."

Every well-informed person knows that in this country we have a twin-system of government, with a political division operating in Washington and a financial division operating in New York. When these two branches of our form of national life operate harmoniously, we have prosperous times. Moreover, we have the resources of both political and financial economy to compete successfully with any other country in the world.

The Banking Houses are just as essential to the successful operation of our system of living as are the merchandising stores and business offices. As a matter of fact, no form of merchandising or business could be carried on successfully without access to a ready supply of cash or credit which the banks supply.

HILL: Well, Mr. Carnegie, your explanation of the importance of our banks will give many of us a different opinion of them. Are the banks the only financial aid to our economic system?

CARNEGIE: No; there is another very important one. Number Four is *our life insurance system,* serving, as is does, as the people's greatest national institution of individual savings, and providing our economic system with a form of flexibility that would not be available through the banking system alone. No other American institution provides the people with a source of savings that gives the individual man protection for his family and at the same time releases his mind from worry in connection with the possibility of approaching old age and its economic uncertainties. The institution of Life Insurance is definitely a part of the fundamentals of America.

HILL: Your discussion of the four "pillars" you have mentioned, Mr. Carnegie, must give every American food for serious thought. Did you say there are six of these important differences between our nation and all others?

CARNEGIE: Indeed, there are two more. The fifth one is *our national spirit of love for liberty* and our demand for the privilege of self-determination, as expressed by the pioneers in industry and government, and the national love of freedom of speech, thought, and action, which were the distinguishing characteristics of the great leaders produced by America in the past.

HILL: And what is the sixth one, Sir?

CARNEGIE: The sixth is *our national sense of justice,* which inspires us to fight for the protection of the weak as well as the strong, and has never tolerated territorial annexation by conquest without adequate compensation.

Under these six headings you will find everything of major importance that distinguishes this country from all others. In presenting the philosophy of individual achievement, be sure to call attention to the fact that *anything which weakens any of the six pillars of Americanism, undermines correspondingly, the whole of our national life.*

Be sure to emphasize, also, that it is not enough for an individual to refrain from doing or saying anything that would weaken these pillars; but it is the duty of every loyal American to defend these fundamentals against all who endeavor to weaken or destroy any portion of them.

HILL: Mr. Carnegie, following your brilliant summary of the most distinguishing features of our nation, which guarantee our priceless individual liberties and freedom of opportunity for personal success, is there any special precaution you care to give concerning them?

CARNEGIE: There is a growing tendency in this country for men with a radical trend of mind to find fault with our form of government, our industrial system, our banking system, and about everything else that represents the typical portion of our Americanism. They should not be permitted to destroy the world's greatest nation merely because we preach and practice the right of free speech in this country.

The right of free speech does not carry with it a license to libel respectable men merely because they have been successful! Since the beginning of civilization wealth has found its way into the hands of men who think accurately, men with definiteness of purpose; men with keenness of imagination and the initiative to translate imagination into useful service. It is this very truth that has led me to the belief that *the very best method of distributing wealth is that of distributing the principles of achievement by which wealth is procured.*

HILL: Mr. Carnegie, you made mention of the great resources of this country. What do you consider to be the greatest of our national resources?

CARNEGIE: In speaking of the great resources of this country it should be kept in mind that the greatest of these is not the money in the banks, nor the minerals in the ground, nor the trees in the forest, nor the richness of our soil; but it is the mental attitude, and the imagination, and the pioneering spirit of the men who have mixed experience and education with these raw materials, thereby transferring them into various types of useful service for our own people and for the people of other nations.

The real wealth of this nation is not any material, tangible thing. Our real wealth consists of the intangible power of thought, as it is expressed by our leaders who understand and apply the philosophy of individual achievement. It reflects itself in broader vision, wider horizons, greater ambitions and initiative. Anyone who misses this truth will fail to understand why our country is the "richest and freest" in the world.

HILL: Why do you place the principle of Definiteness of Purpose at the head of the list of the 17 principles of achievement, Mr. Carnegie?

CARNEGIE: The principle of Definiteness of Purpose obviously is a necessity to all who succeed, since no one may achieve success without first knowing precisely what he wants. It may interest you to know that approximately ninety-eight out of every hundred people are totally without a major goal, and it is significant that approximately the same percentage of people are regarded as failures.

The principle of *Definiteness of Purpose,* to be of enduring value, must be adopted and applied as a daily habit. Absence of this habit leads to another habit that is fatal to success, and that is the habit of drifting.

HILL: Would you mind giving me your definition of the word "success"?

CARNEGIE: My definition of success is this: *"The power with which to acquire whatever one demands of life without violating the rights of others."*

HILL: Well, Mr. Carnegie, is it not true that success is often the result of "luck"?

CARNEGIE: If you will analyze my definition of success you will see that there is no element of luck about it. A man may, and sometimes men do, fall into opportunities through mere chance, or luck; but they have a queer way of falling out of these opportunities the first time opposition overtakes them.

A man may come in possession of opportunity by pull, but he can stay in possession of it only by push, and that calls for *Definiteness of Purpose!*

HILL: Mr. Carnegie, in your definition of success you used the word "power." You said that success is achieved through "the power with which to acquire whatever one wants."

CARNEGIE: Personal power is acquired through a combination of individual traits and habits, some of which will be explained in greater detail as we come to the other sixteen principles of achievement. Briefly, the ten qualities of personal power (which we call the ten-point rule of personal power) are these:

> The habit of definiteness of purpose
> Promptness of decision
> Soundness of character (intentional honesty)
> Strict discipline over one's emotions
> Obsessional desire to render useful service
> Thorough knowledge of one's occupation
> Tolerance on all subjects
> Loyalty to one's personal associates and faith in a Supreme
>   Being
> Enduring thirst for knowledge
> Alertness of imagination

You will observe that this ten-point rule embraces only the traits which anyone may develop. You will observe, also, that these traits lead to the development of a form of personal power which can be used without "violating the rights of others." That is the only form of personal power anyone can afford to wield.

Use the Master Mind Principle   *Chapter Two*

HILL: Mr. Carnegie, we now come to the second of these principles, which you have named the Master Mind. Will you please define what you mean by the term "Master Mind" so that we will all have a clear understanding of it?

CARNEGIE: The Master Mind is "An alliance of two or more minds, working together in the spirit of *perfect harmony,* for the attainment of a definite purpose."

HILL: Do you mean to say, Mr. Carnegie, that the mere choice of a major purpose in life is not, of itself, enough to insure success?

CARNEGIE: To achieve the object of one's major goal, *if it be of proportions above mediocrity,* one must so relate himself to the members of his Master Mind alliance that he will procure the full benefit of their brains, *in a spirit of harmony!* Failure to understand the importance of harmony and sympathy of purpose *in the mind of every member* of a Master Mind alliance has cost many men their chances of success in business.

A man may bring together a group of men whose cooperation he appears to have, and perhaps on the surface he will have it; but, the thing that counts is not surface appearances; it is the "mental attitude" of each member of the group. Before any alliance of men can constitute a Master Mind every man in the group must have his heart as well as his head in full sympathy with the object of the alliance, *and he must be in perfect harmony with the leader and every other member of the alliance.*

HILL: I believe I understand your point, Mr. Carnegie, but I do not see how a man can ever be sure of inducing his associates, in a Master Mind alliance, to work with him in complete harmony. Will you explain how this is accomplished?

CARNEGIE: Yes, I can tell you exactly how harmonious relationships are established and maintained. To begin with, remember that everything a man does has back of that action a definite motive. We are all creatures of *habit* and *motive*. We begin doing things because of a motive; we continue doing them because of both motive and habit; but there may come a time when motive is forgotten and we continue on because of established habit.

There are but nine major motives to which people respond. I will describe these, then you will see for yourself how men are influenced to work with others in a spirit of harmony.

At the very outset, in the organization of a Master Mind group, the leader must select, as individual members of his alliance, first, men who have the ability to do what is required of them; and secondly, men who will respond in a spirit of harmony to the particular motive held out to them in return for their aid.

HILL: I believe, Mr. Carnegie, that on previous occasions you have referred to these nine major motives for voluntary action as the "alphabet of success." I now begin to see why you thus describe them. Will you name them for me now?

CARNEGIE: Here are the nine motives, some combination of which creates the "moving spirit" back of everything we do:

(1) The emotion of LOVE
    (the gateway to one's spiritual power).
(2) The emotion of SEX
    (which while purely biological, may serve as a powerful stimulant to action, when transmuted).
(3) Desire for FINANCIAL GAIN.
(4) Desire for SELF-PRESERVATION.
(5) Desire for FREEDOM OF BODY AND MIND.
(6) Desire for SELF-EXPRESSION leading to fame and recognition.
(7) Desire for perpetuation of LIFE AFTER DEATH.
    The last two motives are negative, but very powerful as stimulants to action. They are
(8) The emotion of ANGER, often expressed as envy or jealousy.
(9) The emotion of FEAR.

Here you have the nine major approaches to all minds! The leader of a successful Master Mind alliance must depend upon one or more of these basic motives to induce each member of his group to give the harmonious cooperation required for success.

HILL: Mr. Carnegie, in your vast experience, what would you say were the emotions which draw the greatest response?

CARNEGIE: The two motives to which men respond most generously in business alliances, are the emotion of sex and the desire for financial gain. Most men want money more than any other thing; but they often want it *mainly to please the woman of their choice.* Here, then, the motivating force is three-fold: LOVE, SEX, AND FINANCIAL GAIN.

There is a type of man, however, who will work harder for recognition than he will for material and financial gains.

HILL: Mr. Carnegie, it appears that the man who successfully builds an organization of men into a Master Mind alliance must know men quite well. Will you explain how you managed to choose, so successfully, the men in your Master Mind group? Did you pick your men at sight, or did you select them by the trial and error method, replacing those that proved unsuited for the purpose for which they were chosen?

CARNEGIE: No man is smart enough to judge other men accurately by sight. There are certain surface indications which may be suggestive of a man's ability, but there is one quality which is more important than all others, as the deciding factor of a man's value as a member of a Master Mind alliance, and that is his "mental attitude" toward himself and his associates.

If his mental attitude happens to be negative, and he is inclined to be selfish, egotistical or adversely provocative in his relationship with others, he will not fit into a Master Mind alliance. Moreover, if such a man is allowed to remain as a member of a Master Mind group he may become so obstructive in his influence with the other members that he will destroy their usefulness as well as his own.

Some of the members of our Master Mind group came up from the rank and file of our workers, after having demonstrated their ability. Some of them were chosen from the outside, through the trial and error method. Some of the ablest men in our Master Mind group started at the very bottom and worked their way up through many different departments of our industry.

These men know the value of harmony and cooperative effort. That is one of the secrets of their ability to promote themselves into high positions.

The man who has ability in any line, plus the right mental attitude toward his associates, usually is found at the top of the ladder, no matter what his occupation may be. There is a great premium on efficiency plus the right mental attitude. I wish you would stress this fact in your presentation of the philosophy of individual achievement.

HILL: What about the man who organizes a group of men into a Master Mind alliance? Is it not necessary for him to be a master in the field of endeavor in which he is engaged, before he can successfully manage others in that field?

CARNEGIE: I know but little of technical requirements in the manufacturing and marketing of steel; nor is it essential that I have this knowledge. Here is where the Master Mind principle comes to one's aid.

I have surrounded myself with more than a score of men whose combined education, experience, and ability, give me the full benefit of all that is known, up to the present time, about the making and marketing of steel. My job is *to keep these men inspired with a desire to do the finest possible job.*

My method of inspiration can be easily traced right back to the nine basic motives, and especially to the motive of desire for financial gain. I have a system of compensation which permits every member of my Master Mind group to name his own financial reward, but the system is so arranged that beyond a certain maximum salary which each man is allowed, an individual must establish definite proof that he has earned more than this amount, before he receives it. This system encourages individual initiative, imagination, enthusiasm, and leads to continuous personal development and growth.

Remember, my major purpose in life is the development of men

—not merely the accumulation of money. The money I possess came as a natural reward for the efforts I have put into developing men.

HILL: You say that all success, of noteworthy proportions is the result of understanding and application of the Master Mind principle. Are there not some exceptions to this rule, Mr. Carnegie? Couldn't a man become a great artist, or a great preacher, or a successful salesman, without the use of the Master Mind principle?

CARNEGIE: The answer to your question, the way you have stated it, is NO! A man might become an artist, or a preacher, or a salesman without direct application of the Master Mind principle, but he could not become *great* in these fields of endeavor without the aid of this principle.

An all-wise Providence has so arranged the mechanism of the mind that no single mind is complete. Richness of the mind, in its fullest sense, comes from the harmonious alliance of two or more minds, working together toward the achievement of some definite purpose.

There are one-man industries, and one-man businesses, but they are not great; and there are individuals who go all the way through life without allying themselves, in a spirit of harmony, with other minds, but they are not great, and their achievements are meager.

You must include in the philosophy those factors which enable an individual to rise above mediocrity. The most important of these factors is an understanding of the power that is available to the person who blends his mind-power with that of other people, thereby giving himself the full benefit of an intangible force which no single mind can ever experience.

HILL: Mr. Carnegie, could you give me one or two examples of a Master Mind alliance in action, which I could pass on to my students in the years to come?

CARNEGIE: Our form of government is an excellent example of the principle of the Master Mind, combining, as it does, the harmonious cooperative effort of both the State and Federal units of government. Under this friendly alliance we have grown and prospered as no other nation known to civilization has done.

Come over to the window and I will show you, out there in the railroad yards, a fine example of the Master Mind in action in transportation. Out there you will see a freight train being made ready for its run. The train will be in charge of a crew of men who coordinate their efforts in a spirit of harmony.

The conductor is the leader of the crew. He can take the train to its destination only because all the other members of the crew recognize and respect his authority and carry out his instructions in a spirit of harmony. What do you suppose would happen to that train if the Engineer neglected or refused to obey the Conductor's signals?

HILL: Why, there might be a wreck that would cost lives.

CARNEGIE: Exactly so! Well, running a business successfully calls for the application of the same Master Mind principle that is so essential in the operation of a railroad train. When there is lack of harmony between those engaged in running a business the bankruptcy court is not far away. Are you following me in this description? I want you to understand it, because it deals with the very heart of all successful achievement, in every field of human endeavor.

HILL: I understand the Master Mind principle, Mr. Carnegie, although I never thought of it as being the sole source of your stupendous achievements in the steel industry, and the basis of your huge fortune.

CARNEGIE: Oh no! It is not the sole source of my achievements. Other principles which I shall describe to you later on have entered into the accumulation of my money, and the building of a great steel industry; but they have been of less importance than the Master Mind. The principle of second importance to the Master Mind is Definiteness of Purpose, which I have already described. These two principles combined have produced what the world calls a successful industry. Neither of these, by itself, could have brought success.

Look at those hoboes down there in that freight car, and you'll see a perfect example of a group of men without either Definiteness of Purpose or a Master Mind. There is also an example of lack of purpose and coordination of effort. If these men would put their heads together, choose a definite purpose, and adopt a definite plan for carrying out their purpose, they might well be the crew that runs that freight train, instead of an unfortunate, poverty-stricken group of homeless men.

HILL: How is it that these men were never taught the principles of achievement as you are describing them to me? Why have they not discovered the power of the Master Mind, as you have done?

CARNEGIE: I did not discover the Master Mind principle. I appropriated it; took it literally from the Bible.

HILL: From the Bible, Sir? Why I never knew the Bible taught the practical philosophy of achievement. In what portion of the Bible did you find the Master Mind principle?

CARNEGIE: I found it in the New Testament, in the story of Christ and His Twelve Disciples. You remember the story, of course. As far as I have been able to learn, Christ was the first person in history who made definite use of the Master Mind principle. You recall Christ's unusual power and the power of His Disciples after He was crucified. It is my theory that Christ's power grew out of His relationship with God and that the power of His Disciples grew out of their harmonious alliance with Him.

He stated a great truth when He said to His followers that they could perform even greater things, for He had discovered that the blending of two or more minds in a Spirit of Harmony with a definite end in view, gives one contact with the power of the Universal Mind.

I call your attention to what happened when Judas Iscariot broke faith with Christ. The breaking of the bond of harmony brought the Master the supreme catastrophe of His life, and for the sake of practical paraphrasing may I suggest that when the bond of harmony is broken, by any cause whatsoever, between the members of a Master Mind group that operates a business, or a home, *ruination is just around the corner!*

HILL: Can the Master Mind principle be of practical benefit in other than business relationships, Mr. Carnegie?

CARNEGIE: Oh yes! It can be of practical use in connection with any form of human relationship where cooperation is necessary. Take the home, for example, and observe what happens when a man and his wife and other members of the family put their hearts and heads together and work for the common good of the entire family. Here you will find happiness, contentment, and financial security.

You have heard it said that a man's wife can make or break him!

Well, it is true, and I'll tell you why. The alliance of a man and a woman in marriage creates the most perfect known form of Master Mind, providing the alliance is blended with love, sympathy of understanding, oneness of purpose, and complete harmony. Evidence of this may be found in the fact that one may find the influence of a woman as the major motivating force in the life of practically every distinguished man of achievement down through the ages.

Fortunate indeed is the man who is married to a woman who devotes her life to strengthening his own mind power by blending with it her own, in a spirit of sympathetic understanding and harmony. That type of wife will never "break" any man, but she will most likely help him to rise to greater heights of achievement than any he would have known without her help.

HILL: If I understand you correctly, Mr. Carnegie, a proper application and use of the Master Mind principle gives an individual the benefit of the education and experience of other people, but it goes much beyond this and aids the individual in contacting and using the spiritual forces available to him. Is that your understanding of the principle?

CARNEGIE: That is precisely my understanding of it. A great psychologist once said that no two minds ever come into contact without there being born, of that association, a third and intangible mind, of greater power than either of the two minds. Whether this third mind becomes a help or a hindrance to one or both of the two contacting minds, depends entirely upon the mental attitude of each. If the attitude of both minds is harmonious, sympathetic, cooperative, then the third mind born of the contact may be beneficial to both. If the attitude of one or both the contacting minds is antagonistic, controversial, unfriendly, the third mind born of the contact will be harmful to both.

The Master Mind principle is no man-made principle, you know. It is a part of the great system of natural law, and it is as immutable as the law of gravitation which holds the stars and planets in their places, and as definite in every phase of its operation. We may not be able to influence this law, but we can understand it and adapt ourselves to it in ways that will bring us great benefits, no matter who we are or what our calling may be.

HILL: From your analysis of the Master Mind principle, I gather the impression, Mr. Carnegie, that men who have been deprived of an early education need not limit their ambition on that account, since it is both possible and practical for them to use the education of others. I also get the impression, from what you have said, that no man ever acquires so much education that he can achieve noteworthy success without the aid of other minds. Is this a correct conclusion?

CARNEGIE: Both of your statements are correct. Lack of schooling is no valid excuse for failure; neither is an exhaustive schooling a guarantee of success. Some one once said that knowledge is power, but he told only a half truth, for knowledge is only potential power. *It may become a power only when it is organized and expressed in terms of definite action.*

There is a big difference between having an abundance of knowledge and being educated. The difference will become apparent if you look up the Latin root from which the word educate is derived. The word educate comes from the Latin word *educare,* which means to draw out, to develop from within, to grow through use. *It does not mean to acquire and store knowledge!*

As I explained in the first principle, success is the power to get whatever one desires in life, without violating the rights of others. Observe that I used the word *power!* Knowledge is not power *but the appropriation and use of other men's knowledge and experience, for the attainment of some definite purpose, is power;* moreover, it is power of the most beneficial order.

HILL: Admitting the truth and wisdom in all that you have

said, Mr. Carnegie, how does one begin to appropriate and apply this power you mention?

CARNEGIE: The man who applies the Master Mind principle for the purpose of availing himself of the minds of other men, *usually begins by taking complete charge of the power of his own mind!* I will tell you more of the process by which this is done when we reach the lessons on Initiative and Self-confidence, but right now I wish to emphasize the importance of an individual's removing self-imposed limitations which most people set up in their own minds.

In a country like America, where there is an abundance of every form of riches; where every man is free to choose his own occupation and live his own life in his own way, there is no reason why any man should set low limitations on his achievements, nor be satisfied with less than all the material possessions his personal desires demand.

In our country there is a high premium on individual initiative, imagination, and definiteness of purpose, and it consists of the easy accessibility of the material things each man requires to fulfill his idea of success.

Here a man may be born in poverty, but he does not have to go through life in poverty. He may be illiterate but he does not have to remain so. But here, as in every other part of the world, *no amount of opportunity will benefit the man who neglects or refuses to take possession of his own mind power* and use it for his own personal advancement.

For the sake of emphasis, I repeat that no man can take the fullest possession of his own mind power without combining it, through the Master Mind principle, with the minds of others, for the attainment of a definite purpose.

HILL: Mr. Carnegie, will you outline for me step by step, a complete plan which one should follow in the organization of a Master Mind group? This procedure is not quite clear to me; it may be even less so to the person who has had no experience in the use of the Master Mind principle.

CARNEGIE: The procedure in every individual case would be slightly different, depending on the education, experience, personality, and mental attitude of the person starting to organize a Master Mind group, and the purpose for which he is organizing it; but in every instance there are certain fundamentals to be observed.

HILL: Because of what you have said on previous occasions, Mr. Carnegie, I am going to hazard a guess as to what the very first fundamental is. It's Definiteness of Purpose.

CARNEGIE: Right you are. DEFINITENESS OF PURPOSE. The starting point of all achievement is definite knowledge of what one wants. We have discussed this principle in our last two interviews.

And the second fundamental is that of CHOOSING MEMBERS FOR A MASTER MIND GROUP. As I have already stated, every person with whom an individual allies himself, under the Master Mind principle, *should be in complete sympathy with the object of the alliance,* and must be able to contribute something definite toward the attainment of that object. The contribution may consist of the member's education, experience, or, as is often the case, it may consist of the use of the good-will he has established in his relationship with the public, commonly known as "contacts."

HILL: And what is the third important fundamental requirement in the organization of a Master Mind group, Mr. Carnegie?

CARNEGIE: It is MOTIVE. No one has the right, and seldom does anyone have the ability, to induce others to serve as members of a Master Mind group, without giving something in return for the service received. The motive may be financial reward, or it may consist of some form of return favors, but it must be something which is of equal value to or greater than the service expected.

I cannot over-emphasize the fact that the man who tries to build a Master Mind alliance without determining that every member of his alliance *profits in proportion to his value in the alliance* is doomed to certain failure.

HILL: Am I correct, Mr. Carnegie, in recalling that on previous occasions you have stressed the need for harmony in a Master Mind group?

CARNEGIE: You are indeed. Complete harmony must prevail among all members of a Master Mind alliance, if success is to be insured.

There can be no "behind the back" disloyalties on the part of any member of the group. Every member of the alliance must subordinate his own personal opinions, his own desires for personal advancement, for the fullest benefit of the group as a whole, *by thinking only in terms of the successful achievement of the object of the alliance.*

In the choice of individuals to serve as allies in a Master Mind group, first consideration should be given to the question as to whether or not the individual *can and will* work for the good of the group. Any member who is unable to do this must, upon discovery of his deficiency, be replaced by someone who can and will do so. *There can be no compromise on this point.*

HILL: Mr. Carnegie, I have the feeling that you are leading up to something. What happens after a definite objective has been decided upon and the proper persons selected to work in harmony for its attainment?

CARNEGIE: Then the time has arrived for action! Once formed, a Master Mind group must become and remain active to be effective. The group must move on a definite plan, at a definite time, toward a definite end.

Indecision, inaction, delay will destroy the usefulness of the entire group. Moreover, there is an old saying that the best way to keep a mule from kicking is to keep him so busy pulling he will have neither the time nor the inclination to kick.

The same may be said about men. Success in any undertaking calls for definite, well-organized, and continous WORK! Nothing has yet been invented to take the place of WORK! Not all the brains of the world are sufficient to enable a man to achieve outstanding success without WORK!

HILL: Mr. Carnegie, as you continue your discussion of the fundamental requirements for the organization of a successful Master Mind group, will you please explain the role of the group leader?

CARNEGIE: The leader who organizes the group must actually lead. As far as work is concerned he should be the first to arrive at the place of work, and the last to leave; moreover, he should set his associates a good example by doing as much or more work than they. The greatest of all "bosses" is the man who makes himself the most nearly indispensable, and not the man who happens to have the last word when decisions are to be made and plans are to be chosen. Every leader's motto should be "The Greatest Among You Shall Be the Servant of All!"

HILL: Well, Mr. Carnegie, there is one question I have been waiting to ask, hoping that perhaps you would volunteer the answer before I asked it. From your rich experience, Sir, what single factor, above all others, determines the success or failure of the Master Mind alliance?

CARNEGIE: *MENTAL ATTITUDE.* In a Master Mind alliance, as in all other human relationships, the factor which, more than all others, determines the extent and nature of the cooperation one gets from others is his own MENTAL ATTITUDE.

I can say truthfully that in my relationship with my own Master Mind group there never was a time when I did not hope that every man in the alliance would get from the alliance the fullest possible measure of personal benefit; and there never was a time when I did not try, with all the resources of what ability I possessed, to develop in every member of my alliance the fullest potentialities of his own ability.

One of the most beautiful sights on earth, and one of the most inspiring, is that of a group of men who work together in a spirit of perfect harmony, each man thinking only in terms of what he can do for the benefit of the group. It was this spirit that gave almost superhuman power to the ragged, underfed, underclothed armies of George Washington, in their fight against the overwhelming odds of better-equipped soldiers. Wherever one finds an employer and his employees working together in this spirit of mutual helpfulness, one finds a successful organization.

One of the major benefits of athletic training is that it tends to teach men to do team work in a spirit of harmony! What a pity that after leaving school men do not always carry with them into their jobs this same spirit of team work.

Life is less burdensome to the man who has the spirit of good sportsmanship in his make-up. Therefore, let the spirit of sportsmanship become an important factor in every undertaking based on the Master Mind principle, and *let it begin with the man who organizes the group.* The others will get the spirit from his example.

HILL: How much better things would be in the world today, if people everywhere could learn to observe just the one fundamental you called "teamwork," Mr. Carnegie. Tell me, are there still more rules for building a successful Master Mind alliance?

CARNEGIE: There is one more, that might be named the CONFIDENTIAL RELATIONSHIP. The relationship existing between men, under the Master Mind principle, should be a confidential one. The purpose of the alliance *should never be discussed outside the ranks of the members* unless the object of the alliance is that of performing some public service. The best of all possible ways of telling the world what one is going to do is by *showing the world what one has already done.*

I have heard it said that every great man—and there are a few such men during every generation—always has some aims and purposes in his mind which are *known to no one except himself and his God.* Perhaps you may not aspire to be great, but you may profit greatly if you bear this statement in mind and refrain from announcing your aims and plans prior to their fulfillment.

HILL: Mr. Carnegie, will you describe what you believe to be the most important Master Mind alliance in the United States?

CARNEGIE: The most important Master Mind alliance in America, or for that matter in the entire world, is the alliance between the States of our country. From this alliance comes the freedom and liberty of which we in America feel so proud. *The strength of the alliance lies in the fact that it is voluntary,* and that in a spirit of harmony it is supported by the people.

The alliance between the States has created a greater variety of opportunities for the exercise of individual initiative than exists anywhere else in the whole world. Our entire system was designed and is maintained as a favorable medium for the support of private enterprise and as an encouragement to personal initiative, based on the nine basic motives.

HILL: Would you care to refresh our minds as to how this wonderful alliance operates, Mr. Carnegie?

CARNEGIE: The operating principle of the Master Mind alliance under which our country is managed is simple. It consists of a triumvirate known as the executive, the judiciary, and the legislative bodies, all working in a spirit of harmony, in direct response to the will of the people.

This system is used in the management of the individual States, as well as in the management of the entire alliance of States known as the Federal Government. The system can be changed by the will of the people, and the public officials who administer the system can, with very few exceptions, be retired on short notice.

So far, no better system of human relationship has been found, and no better system is in the prospect of being found within the near future. Perhaps no better system than ours will ever be found, and none will be necessary *as long as our present system is managed as its founders intended it should be managed*—for the greatest possible benefits to all, with special privileges for none.

HILL: You made some brief reference to application of the Master Mind principle in the successful operation of the home, Mr. Carnegie. Will you now go further into this subject and explain just how this principle can be applied in the management of the home?

CARNEGIE: I am glad you thought of this, because my experience has taught me that a man's home relationships have an important bearing on his business and professional achievements.

The alliance between a man and a woman in marriage creates a relationship which reaches deeply into the spiritual nature of both parties. Marriage is therefore the most favorable of all human alliances for the effective use of the Master Mind principle.

HILL: I suppose, Mr. Carnegie, that in marriage, as in all other relationships, there are certain precautions one can take to insure the successful operation of the Master Mind principle. Will you name and discuss the more important of these safeguards for me, Sir?

CARNEGIE: Heading the list is THE CHOICE OF A MATE. A successful marriage begins with an intelligent choice of a partner. Let me explain what I mean by an intelligent choice. In the first place, a man should test his prospective partner in marriage through a series of frank and intimate talks with her. He should tell her how he intends to make a living and be very sure she is in full accord with him, both as to his chosen occupation and his methods of following it.

It will be of priceless help to a man if his wife becomes so thoroughly sold on his occupation, and his method of earning his living that her interest may be described as intensely enthusiastic; but her minimum interest in this very important fundamental of the marriage partnership should be an unreserved approval of his occupation. Failure to have an understanding on this subject has destroyed the possibility of applying the Master Mind principle in many marriages.

HILL: Mr. Carnegie, what do you think about the so-called "eternal triangles" we hear so much about, where married men become interested in other women, more than in their wives?

CARNEGIE: I think it is no exaggeration to say that most of them have their beginning in the discovery of lack of interest by their wives, in their chosen work. It is a part of a man's nature to seek close association with those who show a keen interest in his work. A man's ego needs food in the form of personal encouragement, and no one is in as favorable a relationship with him to supply this as his wife.

HILL: Well, Mr. Carnegie, what about instances where a man and his wife are engaged in the same occupation, or the same business and are working together for a common purpose?

CARNEGIE: In every instance I have observed such circumstances, I was impressed by the fact that their close association in occupation led also to a close relationship in their social affairs, which left very little surplus time for either of them to become interested in anyone else, or in anything that did not concern both.

HILL: Is there any other advantage to a man and his wife having a mutual interest in the source of the family income, Mr. Carnegie?

CARNEGIE: Yes, because this leads to a mutual understanding

regarding their household and personal expenses. If a man's wife knows precisely how he makes his money, and how much he makes, she will, if she is a faithful partner, adjust her household and personal expenditures to fit his income; moreover, she will do it cheerfully.

HILL: So far, Mr. Carnegie, you have spoken for the benefit of the man who has not yet chosen a life partner in marriage. What about the man who is already married? What can he do if he has chosen a wife who has no interest in his occupation, or perhaps no common interest with him on any subject?

CARNEGIE: In most cases of this sort, it calls for a reselling job on the husband's part, with the object of inducing the wife to begin all over again, under a plan that will insure close cooperation between them. There are but few marriages which do not need a new and improved plan of relationship at frequent intervals, to insure the fullest measure of benefits to both parties to the marriage and to their children, where there are children.

HILL: What is the plan for improving and maintaining relationships you speak of, Mr. Carnegie? Can you give me some specific instructions?

CARNEGIE: The time would be well spent if married people set aside a regular hour for a confidential Master Mind meeting at least once every week, during which they would come to an understanding concerning every vital factor of their relationship, both in and outside of the home associations. Continuous contact between a man and his wife is an essential for harmony and cooperative effort.

HILL: I take it, Mr. Carnegie, that you definitely do not approve of either party to a marriage taking things for granted. Is that correct?

CARNEGIE: It is. The Master Mind principle cannot be successfully applied in marriage without a deliberate, carefully planned program. An occasional discussion of the mutual affairs of marriage is not enough. There must be an established period set aside for the Master Mind meetings and this program should be respected and carried out with the same courtesy, the same definiteness of purpose and the same formality that is observed by business men who use the Master Mind principle for the management of their affairs.

Fortunate, indeed, will be the couples who heed this counsel and make the fullest possible use of it, for they are sure to discover in it an approach to perfection in marriage which can never be attained through mere physical attraction or sex emotion.

HILL: In your last statement, Mr. Carnegie, you mentioned sex emotion. Because of the lack of education on the subject of sex, I realize its discussion calls for delicate discrimination. However, it is a subject of such major importance that it cannot be ignored. I recall that you placed the emotion of sex as the second of the nine basic motives which spur men on to voluntary action. Undoubtedly you, who understand men so well, have some words of wisdom for us on this subject, Sir. Will you please discuss the subject as you see fit?

CARNEGIE: The emotion of sex is Nature's own source of inspiration, through which she gives both men and women the impelling desire to *create, build, lead* and *direct!* Every great artist, every great musician, and every great dramatist gives expression to the emotion of sex, transmuted into human endeavor. It is also true that men of vision, initiative, and enthusiasm who lead and excel in industry and business, owe their superiority to transmuted sex emotion.

HILL: It is obvious that the emotion of sex is the major source of attraction which brings men and women together in marriage. For this reason, it is well for us to inquire into the relationship between the emotion of sex and the Master Mind principle. What have you to say on this question, Mr. Carnegie?

CARNEGIE: The well-informed man will not be slow to recognize the possibilities available to him, by combining the emotion of sex with whatever plan he adopts for the object of his Master Mind alliance with his wife. The same suggestion offers stupendous benefits to the married woman who is interested both in aiding her husband in his occupation and in holding his interest in herself. Let it be remembered, however, that the relationship of sex, to be of enduring benefit as a medium of inspiration, must be kept on a high pedestal of romance.

HILL: Why do you stress the importance of romance, Mr. Carnegie?

CARNEGIE: Because wherever evidence of greatness in men is found, no matter in what age or calling, there one may also find evidence of the spirit of romance. The acorn yields an oak tree only in response to the stimulus of the sun's rays. The bird breaks the shell and takes to wing only in response to warmth outside itself. And the seed of achievement that reposes in the brain of every man responds most quickly to the warmth of a woman's love and affection.

Ignore the call of romance when it appeals to you from within, and you thereby hide your talents in the darkness of obscurity. On the contrary, listen for the call of this messenger of Infinite Intelligence, treat it with civility and understanding when it arrives, and it will hand you the Key to the Temple of Wisdom whose doors are locked within your heart and brain. All that is great and good in man and woman comes to be there only through God's gift of love.

Keep the fire of romance burning. Let it become a part—an important part—of the Master Mind ceremony and your marital relationship will yield priceless returns in both material and spiritual measures.

HILL: From what you have said about the spirit of romance, Mr. Carnegie, I get the impression that it is a great driving force which may be used in the pursuit of a man's calling, as well as in devotion to the object of his affection. Is that the impression you intend to convey?

CARNEGIE: That is precisely what I have been saying, and I have said it because the force that is born of a combination of love and sex is the very *elixir of life* through which nature expresses all creative effort. Understand this truth and you will know why a man's greatest use of the Master Mind principle is that which grows out of his alliance with the woman of his choice; and you will understand, also, why it is so essential for a man to keep his relationship with his wife on the plane of romance.

HILL: How does one go about kindling this emotional fire which is so powerful?

CARNEGIE: The spirit of romance is born of the combination of the emotions of LOVE and SEX. *Enthusiasm, driving force, keen interest* and *vision* are essential for success in any calling and these states of mind can be produced at will by the person who converts the motives of SEX and LOVE—two of the strongest of the nine basic motives—into an obsessional interest in his occupation.

Romance is a blend of the emotions of LOVE and SEX. It is a healthy, normal impulse, if it is not degraded by physical desire. It takes drudgery from toil. It raises the thoughts of the most humble worker to the status of genius. It drives away discouragement and replaces it with definiteness of purpose. It transforms poverty into a mighty and irresistible power for achievement. It fires the imagination and *forces it to become active and creative!* It has been the heart and soul of every outstanding man of achievement who has ever "left footprints on the sands of time."

HILL: Will you now analyze the Master Mind principle as it applies to the efforts of an individual in his daily efforts to appropriate his share of American opportunity?

CARNEGIE: I will now analyze some of the individual uses of this great universal principle, as it may be applied in the development of various human relationships *contributory to the attainment of one's Major Purpose in life.*

Every student of the Philosophy of American Achievement should recognize the fact that the attainment of his highest aim in life can be reached only by a series of steps; and that every thought he thinks, every transaction in which he engages in relationship with others, every plan he creates, and every mistake he makes, has a vital bearing on his ability to attain his chosen goal.

One's MAJOR PURPOSE must be backed up and followed through by continuous effort, the most important part of which consists of *the sort of effort that is applied in relationship with other people.* With this truth well fixed in the mind it is not difficult to understand how necessary it is for an individual to be careful in his choice of associates, *especially those with whom he comes into close daily contact.*

HILL: That being the case, Mr. Carnegie, will you name and discuss some of the sources of human relationship which the man with a Definite Major Purpose in life must cultivate in his progress toward his chosen goal? What, for instance, is the first of such sources?

CARNEGIE: The first important source of human relationships, outside of marriage, is that which exists between a man and those with whom he works, in the pursuit of his daily occupation. There is a tendency, common to all men, for an individual to take on the mannerisms, the mental attitude, the philosophy of life, the political viewpoint, the economic leaning, and the other general traits of the most outspoken of the men with whom he associates in his daily work. The tragedy of this tendency is the fact that not always is the most outspoken man among one's daily associates the soundest thinker; and very often he is a man with the *poorest character!*

However, one may find in almost every group of associates in his daily work, some persons whose influence and cooperation may be helpful. The discriminating man with a Definite Major Purpose in life will prove his wisdom if he forms close friendships only with those who can be, and are willing to be mutually beneficial to him. The others he will *tactfully avoid!*

The man with a Definite Purpose will take careful inventory of every person with whom he is associated in his daily work, and he will look upon every such person as a possible source of knowledge or influence that he can borrow and use in his own promotion. If he looks around him intelligently he will discover that his daily place of labor is literally a school room in which he can acquire the greatest of all educations, that which comes from *experience.* The man with a constructive purpose in life will never envy his superiors; he will study their methods and appropriate their knowledge instead.

HILL: Well, Mr. Carnegie, how can one make the greatest use of the sort of schooling you have just mentioned?

CARNEGIE: By remembering the nine basic motives, together with the suggestion that *no one ever does anything without a motive.* Men lend their experience, their knowledge, and their aid to other men because they have been given a sufficient motive for doing so.

Obviously, the man who relates himself to his daily associates in a friendly, cooperative mental attitude, stands a better chance of learning from them than the man who is belligerent, irritable, discourteous or neglectful in the little amenities of courtesy that exist between all cultured people.

The old saying that "a man can catch more flies with honey than he can with salt" might well be remembered by the man who wishes to go to school to his daily associates who know more than he does, and whose cooperation he needs and seeks.

HILL: Thank you, Mr. Carnegie, for a splendid summary of the advantages to be gained from what we might term an OCCU-PATIONAL Master Mind Alliance. What is another type of alliance which is necessary for the attainment of one's Major Purpose in life, Sir?

CARNEGIE: Next in importance is an EDUCATIONAL alliance. No man's education ever is finished. The man whose Definite Major Purpose in life is of noteworthy proportions must continue to be a student, and he must learn from every possible source —especially those sources from which he can gather specialized knowledge and experience related to his major purpose.

The public libraries are free. They offer a great array of organized knowledge on every subject known to civilization. They carry, in every language, the sum total of all man's knowledge. The successful man makes it his business to read books, and to learn important facts concerning his chosen work which have come from the experience of other men who have gone before him.

A man's reading program should be as carefully chosen as his daily diet, for it, too, is food without which he cannot grow mentally. The man who spends all his reading time on the funny papers and the sex magazines is not headed toward great achievement. A man should include in his daily reading program some material which definitely provides him with knowledge which he can use in the attainment of his major purpose. Random reading may be pleasing, but it seldom is helpful in connection with a man's occupation.

HILL: Mr. Carnegie, you have stressed reading. Is reading the only source of education available to a man with a Definite Purpose in life?

CARNEGIE: Not at all. By a careful choice among his daily associates, a man may ally himself with men from whom he can acquire a very liberal education, through ordinary conversation. Business and professional clubs offer an opportunity for one to form alliances of great educational benefit, provided a man chooses his clubs and his individual associations in them, with a definite objective in mind. In this way, many men have formed both business and social acquaintances of great value to them in carrying out the object of their major purpose.

No man can go through life successfully without the habit of cultivating friends. The word "contact," as it is used in connection with personal acquaintanceship, is an important word. If a man makes it a part of his duty to extend his line of personal "contacts," he will find the habit of use to him in ways that cannot be foreseen while he is cultivating his acquaintances, but the time will come when they will be ready and willing to aid him if he has done a good job of selling himself to them.

If you wish a job done promptly and well get a busy man to do it. The idle man knows too many substitutes and short cuts.

Chapter Three

Develop an Attractive Personality

HILL: Mr. Carnegie, we come now to the third of the seventeen principles of individual achievement, which you have named "Attractive Personality." I understand that you have separated the factors behind personality into distinct traits, all but one of which may be developed by any normal person. Now, Sir, will you describe these characteristics of personality, with special emphasis on those which you consider of greatest importance to an individual in selling his way through life successfully?

CARNEGIE: I will not only describe the traits of an attractive personality, but before I have finished, *I will also give you a simple formula with which all but one of these traits may be developed and maintained.* The mere naming of these personality traits will be of little value to anyone unless he appropriates and uses them. We will begin the outline of the factors with a description of the most important of these, which is POSITIVE MENTAL ATTITUDE. One may get a fair idea of the important part mental attitude plays in the affairs of an individual's life by considering the fact that it influences the tone of voice, the expression of the face, the posture of the body, and modifies every word that is spoken, as well as determining the nature of every emotion one feels. It does more than these; *it modifies every thought* one releases, thereby extending its influence to all within its range, through the principle of telepathy.

For the sake of contrast, let us list some of the disagreeable things that a bad mental attitude causes. It dampens a man's enthusiasm, curtails his initiative, overthrows his self-control, subdues his imagination, undermines his desire to be cooperative, makes him sullen and intolerant, and as if these were not enough damage to insure a man's failure, it puts on the finishing touch by throwing his reasoning power out of gear. These are but a few of the ways in which a negative mental attitude *may damage the individual himself,* quite apart from the damage he does to others, through his negative influences.

HILL: How does a negative mental attitude affect a salesman, starting out in the morning, Mr. Carnegie?

CARNEGIE: He would be better off, far and away, if he remained at home. He not only will not make the sales he would make if his mental attitude were pleasant, but he will make enemies and lose customers as well.

HILL: Would a negative mental attitude affect a professional man, such as for instance, a lawyer, or a doctor, Mr. Carnegie?

CARNEGIE: The lawyer who goes into court with a bad mental attitude will find the court and the jury opposing him, although he may have a perfectly just case; and the doctor who comes into the presence of his patients with a negative mental attitude will do them more harm than good, although he may be skilled in the knowledge of his profession.

A man may have all the culture modern civilization can provide, and he may have a string of degrees after his name a yard long, and he may be the most skilled man in his field, but he will be a failure, as surely as two and two make four, *if he carries a bad mental attitude around with him!* The one thing people simply will not tolerate is a negative mental attitude.

HILL: Mr. Carnegie, you have given us some examples of the results of a negative mental attitude. Now will you name an outstanding example of a man with a positive mental attitude, and how it affected his life?

CARNEGIE: Take Charlie Schwab, for example, whom I have paid as high as a million dollars in extra bonus in a single year. Analyze his personality in minute detail, and you will come close to discovering why many of my associates have accumulated fortunes of their own. Charlie came to me as an ordinary laborer. He had but little schooling, and very few special talents for anything; but he had one important asset that gives you the clue to his success. *He had a perfect mental attitude toward himself and all others with whom he came into contact!* Where and how did he come by that attitude? Well, he probably was born with a favorable background for the cultivation of such an attitude, but he acquired the habit of expressing it because he was associated with a group of men who made it a part of their daily duty to develop and maintain a positive mental attitude.

Before we pass on to the next factor of attractive personality, let me say that this subject of mental attitude will show up for consideration in connection with every one of the other qualities of personality we are to analyze. It is definitely related to all of them, a fact that is very significant.

HILL: Mr. Carnegie, since I am to present the philosophy of achievement to many realistic thinkers, I am keenly interested in the "why" and "how" of every principle you mention. Will you, therefore, give me an idea of how one may go about the development of such an attitude?

CARNEGIE: The simplest way to answer your question is to say that a positive mental attitude can be developed by *understanding and applying* all of the factors of attractive personality. You will see, therefore, when I finish my analysis of these qualities of personality, that I will have given the complete answer to your question.

HILL: Very well, Mr. Carnegie. I shall listen carefully to what you say, so as to gather clues which may be helpful in the development of these desirable traits. What is the second factor of personality, Sir?

CARNEGIE: *FLEXIBILITY.* By this term I have reference to the ability to adapt one's self to quickly changing circumstances, and emergencies, without losing one's sense of balance. A man with a flexible disposition must be something like a chameleon, the little member of the reptile family that quickly changes its color to harmonize with its environment. Without this ability an attractive personality is hardly possible, as the everchanging conditions of life and of human relationships require individual adaptability.

Some men are uncharitable enough to blame their misfortunes on others, but the truth is that every man is where he is and what he is *because of his own mental attitude as it is expressed through his personality.*

HILL: Why, Mr. Carnegie, that is a tremendous statement! It rules out almost completely the elements of "luck" and "pull" which most people bemoan the lack of when evaluating their status in life.

CARNEGIE: Yes, indeed. When you present the philosophy of achievement, get the idea over in terms that will cause people to take honest inventory of themselves so they may find and correct their faults of personality. I have often thought that it would be a blessing of the first magnitude if all public schools made the study of attractive personality a "must" requirement of their curricula. Young people should be taught, very early in life, that no amount of schooling will insure their success unless they learn to negotiate with others pleasantly.

And observe how definitely the quality of flexibility is related to one's *mental attitude!*

HILL: And that, Mr. Carnegie, brings us down to number three of the important factors of a pleasing personality, which is:

CARNEGIE: *SINCERITY OF PURPOSE.* This is one trait of character for which there has never been found a satisfactory substitute. I say it is a trait of character because it is something that *reaches deeper into a human being than any mere quality of personality.*

Sincerity of purpose, or the lack of it, writes itself so indelibly into the words and deeds of men that even the novice at character analysis can recognize its presence or its absence. The insincere person announces his weakness in every word he speaks, in the expression of his face, in the trend of his conversation, in his choice of intimate associates, in the sort of service he renders in connection with his occupation, and in other ways that are less noticeable, and this despite the fact that he may be a skilled actor with great ability to camouflage his real nature.

The proverbial type of "yes man" is an object of derision the world over, mainly because everyone recognizes his insincerity. I shall never forget the first definite opposition I experienced from Charlie Schwab. He had been with me only a short time when I called him in and gave him a definite order to make certain changes in his work which I believed should be made. He listened until I finished; then he looked me squarely in the eyes, with a broad good-natured smile on his face, and said, "All right, Chief, you are the boss; but I'm going to tell you that your request is going to cost you money because you haven't investigated this matter as closely as I have."

There was something about the manner in which he spoke which left me no room to construe his remarks as insubordination, but I held up the order and investigated, only to find that he was right and I was wrong. From that day on I began to watch Charlie very closely, only to discover in him qualities of both personality and character which made him of priceless value to me. You may say, therefore, that Charlie got his real start with me by his sincerity of purpose, for that is no exaggeration of the facts.

Verily it pays to include sincerity of purpose as one of the factors of personality!

HILL: With that sound truth still ringing in our ears—the ring of sincerity, if you please, Mr. Carnegie—we pass on to the fourth factor comprising a pleasing personality. Will you name it, Sir?

CARNEGIE: It is *PROMPTNESS OF DECISION.* Observe men wherever you will, and you will notice that those who dilly-dally around, trying to make up their minds, are neither popular nor successful. This is a fast moving world in which we live and those who do not move quickly cannot keep up with the parade.

Successful men reach decisions definitely and quickly, and they become annoyed and inconvenienced by others who do not act promptly. I call your attention to the fact that promptness of decision is a habit, and therefore it is definitely related to and a part of one's mental attitude. Try as you may, but you cannot separate any of these traits of attractive personality from their relationship to mental attitude.

I call your attention, also, to the close relationship between promptness of decision and definiteness of purpose; thus you will observe that these traits of personality have a very direct connection with the entire seventeen principles of the philosophy of achievement.

We live in a country where individual achievement is possible on a grand scale, because of the abundance of opportunity on every hand; but opportunity waits for no man! The man with the vision to recognize opportunity, and the promptness of decision to embrace it, will get ahead; but no others will.

This is the way of the world! It always makes a place for the man who knows exactly what he wants, and is determined to get it!

HILL: Mr. Carnegie, someone has said that courtesy is the cheapest, yet the most profitable thing in the world. Where do you place this trait of personality, Sir?

CARNEGIE: *COURTESY* is the very next factor to be discussed. It is an essential part of an attractive personality. As to its cheapness, I will go a step further and say it is absolutely *free.* All it costs is the time required to express it, in one's daily contact with others. Perhaps its very cheapness accounts for its scarcity, as it is a quality of personality so rare that when one comes upon it one is quick to take note of the person expressing it.

HILL: Well, Mr. Carnegie, just what is your definition of courtesy?

CARNEGIE: My idea of courtesy is this: It is the *habit* of respecting other people's feelings under all circumstances; the *habit* of going out of one's way to help any less fortunate person whenever and wherever possible; and last, but by no means least, the *habit* of controlling selfishness in all its forms. Again take notice of the definite relationship between courtesy and one's mental attitude! Courtesy is a medium with which one may project his influence to sources of opportunity he could not reach without it.

HILL: And after *COURTESY,* Mr. Carnegie, what comes next on the list of the essential elements of a pleasing personality?

CARNEGIE: Next, I shall mention a pair of twin brothers. The first one is *TONE OF VOICE.* The spoken word is, by great odds, the medium through which one expresses his personality most often; therefore the tone of one's voice should be so thoroughly under control that it can be colored and modified so as to make it carry a meaning quite in addition to the mere words expressed, for it does carry a separate meaning, whether one is conscious of this fact or not. The idea, therefore, is to so cultivate the voice that it can be used to convey the particular meaning desired.

The man who has developed a one hundred percent attractive personality knows how to convey, through the tone of his voice, every emotion he feels. He can express anger, fear, curiosity, contempt, doubt, affection, courage, sincerity, derision, anxiety, and a wide range of other feelings.

Moreover, he makes it a *habit* to control his voice every time he speaks, for it is only through habit that one reaches perfection in the dramatization of speech. The price of perfection here, as is true in so many other things, is eternal practice. *Every person who develops an attractive personality must study his own voice and place it under control so he can make it convey any feeling he desires.* If no teacher of voice is at hand, one can become his own teacher by practicing before a mirror until he gains perfection.

HILL: Did you say, Mr. Carnegie, that TONE OF VOICE was only one of a pair of twin brothers? What is the nature of the other brother, Sir?

CARNEGIE: Oh, the other brother is *THE HABIT OF SMIL-ING*. Now, don't make the mistake of feeling that the simple habit of smiling is not an important part of one's personality, and don't forget that it is a habit that is directly associated with mental attitude. If you aren't sure about this, *just try smiling when you are angry!* I suggest that one should stand before a mirror when practicing voice control, because there are certain expressions of speech which cannot be dramatized properly unless they are accompanied by a smile.

HILL: Is it possible, Mr. Carnegie, that these twin brothers have some other close relatives? What is the next trait of a desirable personality, Sir?

CARNEGIE: It is *EXPRESSION OF THE FACE*. You may have heard it said that character analysts can tell, by a glance at the expression on one's face, much about the nature of one's character. Well, it is true; but character analysts are not alone in this ability to judge people by their facial expression. We all do it constantly, whether we do so consciously or not.

You can tell a great deal of what is going on in one's mind by the expression on his face. Master salesmen can tell, by careful observation of a prospective buyer's facial expression, much about what his real thoughts are. If they cannot do this, they are not master salesmen. Moreover, the clever salesmen learn to judge what is going on in the other fellow's mind by the tone of his voice.

Thus the smile, the tone of voice, the expression of the face constitute an open window through which all who will may see and feel what takes place in the minds of people. This naturally suggests to the smart person, the use of caution in connection with this open window. The smart person will know when to keep the window closed! He will also know when to open it!

HILL: Mr. Carnegie, I haven't been keeping too accurate a count of the different traits of an attractive personality which you have mentioned, because of my intense interest in your remarks. Which trait is next, Sir?

CARNEGIE: We are up to number nine, which is *TACTFUL-NESS*. There is always a right time and a wrong time for everything. Tactfulness consists of the habit of doing and saying the right thing at the right time, and I'm going to enumerate for you a list of the more common ways in which people show their lack of tactfulness. I suggest that this list may be of immeasurable benefit as a check-up on one's personality. Here is the list:

1. Carelessness in the tone of the voice, often speaking in gruff, antagonistic tones that offend.
2. Speaking out of turn, when silence would be more appropriate.
3. Interrupting others who are speaking.
4. Overworking the personal pronoun.
5. Asking impertinent questions, generally to impress others with the questioner's own importance.
6. Injecting intimately personal subjects into the conversation where such action is embarrassing to others.
7. Going where one has not been invited.
8. Boastfulness.
9. Flaunting the rules of society in matters of personal adornment.
10. Making personal calls at inconvenient hours.

11. Holding people on the telephone with needless conversation.
12. Writing letters to people whom one has no reasonable excuse for addressing.
13. Volunteering opinions when not requested, especially on subjects with which they are not familiar.
14. Openly questioning the soundness of the opinions of others.
15. Declining requests from others in an arrogant manner.
16. Speaking disparagingly of people in front of their friends.
17. Rebuking people who disagree with one on any subject.
18. Speaking of people's physical afflictions in their presence.
19. Correcting subordinates and associates in the presence of others.
20. Complaining when requests for favors are refused.
21. Presuming upon friendship in asking favors.
22. Using profane or offensive language.
23. Expressing dislikes too freely.
24. Speaking of ills and misfortunes.
25. Criticising our form of Government or some other person's religion.
26. Over-familiarity on all occasions with people.

HILL: The person who checks his personality against that list and finds himself not to be a violator in any of those ways, is indeed fortunate and he is a rare individual. I can see that tactfulness is another trait of personality which is related to mental attitude. Now, Mr. Carnegie, what is coming up as number ten?

CARNEGIE: Tenth place goes to *TOLERANCE*. Let us define tolerance simply as open-mindedness. The tolerant person is one who holds his mind open for new facts and new knowledge and new viewpoints on all subjects. *I hazard the guess that this definition classifies most of us as being intolerant.*

Observe, too, before we get too far into the analysis of this subject, how closely related are tolerance and tactfulness, and also how definitely both are related to mental attitude. Try as you may, there is no escape from consideration of the subject of mental attitude. *It crops up everywhere, in every human relationship!*

Before leaving this subject, I wish to enumerate a few of the specific handicaps which men set up for themselves through their intolerance:

1. It makes enemies of those who would like to be friends.
2. It stops the growth of the mind, *by limiting the search for knowledge.*
3. It discourages imagination.
4. It prohibits self-discipline.
5. It prevents accuracy in thinking and reasoning.

Added to all these, it also damages the character through unseen and unknown ways that limit one's use of the spiritual forces which are available to open minds.

HILL: Mr. Carnegie, you surely gave intolerance the stinging indictment it deserves. This rounds out the first ten essential elements of a desirable personality. I suppose we might call them the "Big Ten" of a positive personality. And now for the next round, Mr. Carnegie. What is number eleven?

CARNEGIE: The eleventh trait of attractive personality is *FRANKNESS OF MANNER AND SPEECH.* Everyone mistrusts the man who resorts to subterfuge instead of dealing frankly with his daily associates. I have known men who were so slippery that you could not pin them down to a direct, clear-cut statement on any subjects, and I have never yet seen a man of this type who could be depended upon.

This sort of man doesn't come right out and lie, but he does what amounts to exactly the same thing, by deliberately withholding important facts from those who have a right to know the facts. This habit is a form of dishonesty which, if indulged in very long, will undermine the soundest character. Men of sound character always have the courage to speak and deal directly with people, and they follow this habit, even though it may, at times, be to their personal disadvantage. Men who resort to subterfuge to deceive others seldom have very much confidence in themselves.

HILL: I'm sure, Mr. Carnegie, that everyone prefers dealing with a man who is frank and honest. In the long run, people who think they are deceiving others are only deceiving themselves. But, Mr. Carnegie, what is number twelve in this series of desirable personality traits?

CARNEGIE: Number twelve is *A KEEN SENSE OF HUMOR.* A well-developed sense of humor aids a man in becoming flexible and adjustable to the varying circumstances of life. It also enables him to relax and become human instead of remaining cool and distant. Moreover, a keen sense of humor *keeps a man from taking himself and life too seriously*—a tendency toward which altogether too many people are inclined.

I always feel sorry for the man who cannot or will not relax and laugh when it is proper for him to do so, for laughter is the finest of mental tonics. I am not so sure but what it is also a good physical tonic. A keen sense of humor, no matter how it is indulged, provides relaxation. The people of America spend millions of dollars annually for the circus and the stage and screen plays, to provide such an escape.

A sense of humor even serves to give one a better physical appearance, too, as it helps to keep the lines of the face softened. It also leads to the *habit of smiling,* which is one of the important traits of attractive personality. And there is a definite relationship between a sense of humor and mental attitude. A keen sense of humor encourages a *positive mental attitude.*

HILL: Mr. Carnegie, you make it very clear that an attractive personality is an asset of the greatest worth to anyone. The factors you are presenting will make it possible for people to take inventory of their personality assets, as well as any possible liabilities. Your suggestions and instructions will enable them to strengthen any weak spots and thus increase their ability to negotiate with life on more favorable terms. What is the next trait necessary to the development of an attractive personality?

CARNEGIE: Now we come to the most profound and far-reaching of all the elements comprising an attractive personality—*FAITH IN INFINITE INTELLIGENCE.* Faith is woven into every principle of the philosophy of achievement, since the intangible power of faith is the essence of every great achievement, no matter what may be its nature or purpose. My analysis of this subject, therefore, is a responsibility I dare not neglect. *To do so would be something like trying to teach astronomy without reference to the stars!*

Understand, however, that any reference I make to the subject of Faith has nothing whatsoever to do with the supernatural, nor has it any theological connotations. I shall speak of the power of Faith only as it is an inescapable necessity to the man who wishes to make the fullest use of his mind, for the attainment of material ends.

No philosophy dealing with the subject of personal achievement would be complete without a definite and direct recognition of the power of Faith. The reason for this is that the state of mind known as Faith provides the greatest outlet for the expression of *initiative, imagination, enthusiasm, self-reliance,* and *definiteness of purpose.* Without it no one could rise above mediocrity! To neglect the subject of faith would, therefore, be something like providing a man with an intricate piece of machinery without giving him any power with which to operate it.

HILL: Are you saying, Mr. Carnegie, that a man's brain is actually a piece of very fine machinery, intricately and accurately constructed to perform a definite function in the business of living?

CARNEGIE: That I am, and the power that operates this machine is a form of energy which comes from the outside; and Faith is the master gate through which an individual may give his brain full and free access to the great universal power which operates it.

The hand that opens the gate and permits the free entry of the power which operates the brain is desire, or *motive!* No one has ever yet discovered any other method of opening the gate. There are various degrees to which it can be opened, all depending upon *motive* and *desire.* Only those desires which take on the proportion of an obsession—*burning desires*—serve to open wide the valve.

A *burning desire,* in the sense that I am using this term, is one that is accompanied by a deep emotional feeling. Mere head desires, growing out of pure reason, do not open the gate to the brain as widely as heart desires that are mixed with emotion. I wish to make this point very clear, and to emphasize it in every way possible, *for it is the very warp and woof of the subject of Faith.*

HILL: Mr. Carnegie, can you give us a few illustrations of the practical benefits to be derived by those who learn to use the power of Faith?

CARNEGIE: I would start out by saying that the state of mind known as Faith automatically wipes out intolerance by freeing the mind of the man-made limitations. After all, *what is intolerance but a partially closed mind?* Just as darkness is dispelled by the simple process of turning on the light, so is intolerance eliminated by opening the mind for the influx of the power that gives the brain the vision to encompass all of life's realities instead of only a few of them.

Next, I'd say that opening the mind, through Faith, provides one with a greater perspective of the world about him and the people that live in it. This same receptiveness paves the way for a better understanding *in all human relationships;* therefore it serves to support *all the traits* of attractive personality.

The third benefit to those who use the power of Faith is that an open mind allows the influx of power that removes all the imaginary obstacles in the way of individual achievement, and aids in surmounting the real obstacle. As one man so aptly stated this truth, "Where Faith is the guide, the individual cannot lose his way."

HILL: Mr. Carnegie, will you name in order the facts you consider to be most significant in connection with this subject of Faith?

CARNEGIE: One fact of deep significance is that the power available through Faith is inexhaustible, and there are no penalties, *of any nature whatsoever, for the free use of this power!* This fact connotes the intention of the Creator for full and complete use of this universal power, by all who desire to use it, and for every purpose essential for man's welfare.

It is also significant that the method of contacting and using this power is simple, and *within the reach of every person.* It consists of voluntary appropriation of the power, through the medium of *desire,* or *motive.*

Still another profound fact is that the power of thought is the only thing over which any human being has complete control, and the individual's prerogative in this respect has been cleverly protected by a system which makes it impossible for one individual to know what use another makes of the power of thought.

HILL: It would appear, then, Mr. Carnegie, that the only real privacy a man has is that which he enjoys within himself and his own thoughts, in the chambers of his own mind. This, in itself, is a profound and awe-inspiring truth!

CARNEGIE: Aye, and the man who fails to grasp the significance of the facts we have mentioned can never have an attractive personality in the fullest meaning of that term. The man who does understand and apply them thereby removes all limitations from his own mind. *The promise of reward is worthy of all the effort one may put into understanding.*

HILL: Now, Mr. Carnegie, what is the next trait of attractive personality?

CARNEGIE: It's a *KEEN SENSE OF JUSTICE.* It seems trite to remind people that an individual cannot hope to become popular and attractive unless he deals justly with others, but man's well known deficiency in this respect makes it necessary to discuss this subject.

HILL: Perhaps, Mr. Carnegie, it would be well for you to define what you mean by justice.

CARNEGIE: Justice, as I use the term here, has reference to *intentional honesty!* Many people are honest for the sake of expediency, but their brand of honesty is so flexible that they can stretch it to fit any circumstance where their immediate interests can be best extended. It is not that brand of honesty we are analyzing. We are talking about deliberate honesty that is so rigidly adhered to that the individual is motivated by it under circumstances that may not be to his immediate benefit, the same as to those that promise the greatest possible reward.

HILL: Mr. Carnegie, would you care to name some of the more obvious practical benefits of a keen sense of justice?

CARNEGIE: It establishes the basis of confidence, without which no one can have an attractive personality.

It builds a fundamentally sincere and sound character which, of itself, is one of the greatest of all attracting forces.

It not only attracts people, but it offers opportunities for personal gain in one's occupation.

It gives one a feeling of self-reliance and self-respect.

It places one in a better and more understanding relationship with one's own conscience.

It attracts friends and discourages enemies.

It clears the way for that state of mind known as Faith.

It protects one from the destructiveness of controversies with other people.

It helps one to move with more initiative in connection with one's major purpose in life.

It never damages one nor does it subject one to any form of embarrassment.

A keen sense of justice not only aids in the development of attractive personality, but it is an asset of priceless value in almost every human relationship. It discourages avarice, greed, and selfishness, and gives an individual a much better understanding of his rights, privileges, and responsibilities. *A keen sense of justice has a very definite and very great contributory influence in the development of the other traits of attractive personality.*

HILL: Mr. Carnegie, that brings us down to number fifteen of the traits of a pleasing personality, which is—

CARNEGIE: *APPROPRIATENESS OF WORDS.* Among cultured people there is perhaps no greater source of annoyance than the careless use of words. Colloquialisms and slang may be passable at times, but the less these are used, the better. The English language is replete with a stock of words possessing every possible shade of meaning. Hence there can be no valid excuse for the common habit of using words which offend. And of course the use of profane words, at any time, is inexcusable.

HILL: Mr. Carnegie, could you suggest a method whereby a person may assure himself of an adequate and appropriate vocabulary?

CARNEGIE: A man of my acquaintance whose accomplishment in the use of words is the most outstanding of any person I have ever known, devotes thirty minutes daily to *reading the dictionary!* Yes, literally *reading* it. He has an astonishingly large vocabulary, and I have never heard him use an inappropriate word in my life. Moreover, his choice of words shows that he uses only those which convey the precise meaning intended.

HILL: Now that you mention it, Mr. Carnegie, it is true that the words a man uses are the gauge by which he is first judged by others, and they therefore assume tremendous importance, as a factor of personality.

CARNEGIE: The words are the media through which a man most often expresses his thoughts, so the nature of the words he uses gives an accurate clue to the type of mind he possesses. This fact leads me to the conclusion that two things should be on the "must" list of daily habits of every person who has an attractive personality: *Care in the choice of words and care in the tone of voice in which words are expressed!*

HILL: As a result of your analysis, Mr. Carnegie, the thought has just struck me; what a wonderful thing a word is. I wish you would continue developing the importance of words for a moment.

CARNEGIE: The ability to express thoughts through the use of words is one of the definite distinctions which separate man from all other living things. Words are the Creator's ingenious means by which man has been given an unlimited outlet for the expression of his thoughts. Words are God's special gift to man.

With this gift the combined knowledge and experience of mankind may become the common property of the humblest individual. If we had no words with which to convey thoughts, the use of the Master Mind principle would be exceedingly limited, and every man would be practically compelled to go through life without benefiting by the knowledge gained by men before him.

HILL: Now, Mr. Carnegie, what is the sixteenth trait of an attractive personality?

CARNEGIE: I have termed it *EMOTIONAL CONTROL.* It has been said by men who have studied the subject, that man's emotions control his conduct! The claim seems reasonable. Most of us are directed, not so much by our reason as by our emotions.

We do things or we refrain from doing them, because of the way we feel. Emotion, therefore, may be defined with one word, "FEELING." This is a mighty important word, since it defines the motivating force which controls most of our actions throughout life. We certainly owe it to ourselves to learn as much as possible about the force which *lifts us to great achievements, or hurls us downward to defeat*. That is precisely what the power of emotion does. In view of this significant fact, we should get control over this power, not only to add to the attractiveness of our personality, *but to insure us against a life of failure and misery.*

HILL: What do you suggest as the first step toward gaining such control over our emotions, Mr. Carnegie?

CARNEGIE: The first step is to identify the emotions so we will recognize them, and to aid us in this task a noted psychologist has prepared a list of the most common emotions expressed in our daily lives. There are seven positive emotions and seven negative emotions. I shall give you the negative emotions first.

The seven negative emotions are:
1. FEAR (There are seven different forms of fear, which we shall discuss later.)
2. JEALOUSY
3. HATRED AND ENVY
4. REVENGE AND MALICE
5. GREED
6. SUPERSTITION AND DISTRUST
7. ANGER

Now for the seven positive emotions, which are:
1. LOVE
2. SEX
3. HOPE
4. FAITH
5. DESIRE
6. OPTIMISM
7. LOYALTY

In these fourteen emotions one may find the letters of the alphabet of a language that spells either SUCCESS or FAILURE!

These fourteen words literally represent the keyboard of the musical instrument of Life, on which an individual plays the chords of harmony that lead to happiness in its fullest meaning, or the discords of unhappiness that lead to misery and obscurity.

Each of the fourteen emotions is related to "mental attitude." This is why I have stressed the importance of mental attitude. These fourteen emotions represent nothing *except* mental attitude. They are nothing but feelings, or states of mind. More important still, they are subject to organization, guidance and complete control by any normal person. Here is the keyboard of Life, on which an individual may compose the tune that his soul will sing all through life.

HILL: In what way has the Creator given man control over this grand score for the symphony of life, Mr. Carnegie?

CARNEGIE: By giving man control over his powers of thought. *The only thing the individual has to do is to take charge of his own mind and exercise this control.* That is something he cannot neglect or avoid, *without condemning his entire life to the stray winds of chance!*

Remember, before we leave this subject, that the point at which an individual begins to take control of his own mind—and this includes emotions, of course—is when he adopts a Definite Major Purpose.

Definiteness of Purpose is the starting point of all achievement. You see, therefore, how definitely success and failure are related to the fourteen emotions. One-half of the fourteen are harbingers of failure. The other half are success builders.

HILL: I dare say, Mr. Carnegie, that anyone who secures a copy of this list of the fourteen emotions and who carefully examines himself in connection with each of them on the basis of a definite schedule, will make tremendous strides toward gaining control of his emotions.

CARNEGIE: That is correct. A person should construct a check chart and make a habit of rating himself on each one of the emotions daily. The experiment will surprise anyone who attempts it. It may also lead to changes in one's personality which will agreeably surprise all of his associates. This is a positive approach to self-mastery, the end which must be *sought* and *attained* by all who wish to be sure of making Life pay.

HILL: Mr. Carnegie, you have covered the first sixteen of the traits of an attractive personality. What is coming up now, Sir?

CARNEGIE: Let us call it *ALERTNESS OF INTEREST* in persons, places and things. Without the ability to fix one's interest at will on any subject or person and hold it there for whatever time the occasion requires, no person will have an attractive personality. You can pay another person no greater compliment, generally speaking, than that of concentrating your attention upon him when he desires your attention. It has been said that it is a greater accomplishment to be able to listen well, than it is to be able to talk well.

This is one way in which a person may please others and at the same time acquire usable knowledge. The habit of looking in some other direction, of fidgeting with some pocket gadget when others are talking, is among the worst forms of effrontery. The habit of interrupting when others are speaking is an *unpardonable insult!* Strong language, perhaps, but accurately descriptive of an important fact.

HILL: Are you implying, Mr. Carnegie, that lack of observation of what is going on around one, and failure to notice details, is an all too common weakness?

CARNEGIE: Precisely that. It is a common weakness that costs people a tremendous price. If one will make a careful study of one's self, when conversing with others, he may discover that he can add substantially to his own personality by taking a keener interest in the other fellow's personality.

I have often suggested to some of the young men who worked with us, that if they would become as alertly interested in the associates with whom they work, and in their jobs, as they do when talking to their sweethearts, the results would show a healthy change in their pay envelopes.

Alertness of interest in other people not only serves to please them, but it also provides one with an excellent opportunity to know people by observing their mannerisms. One may learn valuable lessons by observing the faults as well as the virtues of other people, as this habit causes one to take more accurate inventory of himself, to make sure he does not display the same faults.

HILL: It would seem to me, Mr. Carnegie, that the memory would be associated with this matter of alertness of interest and observation. Am I correct in this assumption, Sir?

CARNEGIE: Everyone knows that a good memory is an asset of great value, but not everyone seems to know that one of the greatest functions of a good memory is that of taking accurate inventory of, and remembering, the characteristics of individual personalities. Such retentiveness always requires keen observation and intensity of interest in ordinary conversation with people.

Few circumstances annoy a person more than to be introduced to someone a second time without that person showing any sign of recognition. Such situations occur every day. It is no compliment to a man, and especially if he be a man of considerable reputation in his field, to be made to feel that he is so unimpressive and unimportant that someone to whom he had been introduced a second time does not remember him. Conversely stated, nothing pleases a man more than to have people show that they remember him, and favorably.

One of New York's largest hotels employs a desk man who has a system by which he remembers practically every person who registers at that hotel a second time, and he never misses if the person is fairly well known to the public. He calls people by their names and lets them know that he recognizes them. The manager of that hotel told me that this man is one of the greatest assets of the hotel, and what is still more interesting, he receives almost three times as much salary as the job he holds usually pays.

It is part of a man's duty—to himself at least—to see everyone he knows, and to recognize his acquaintances in some manner, every time he comes within speaking distance of them. Lack of alertness of interest in other people is usually a sign of egotism. One who falls in love with himself will find few rivals!

HILL: Everyone readily agrees that an attractive personality is greatly to be desired and sought after. The elements comprising a pleasing personality which you have presented thus far will make a wonderful list by which people may compare their own personalities, counting up their assets and their liabilities, if any. You have previously covered the first seventeen desirable personality traits. What have you in store for me today.

CARNEGIE: The eighteenth trait of an attractive personality is —*EFFECTIVE SPEECH*. The person who cannot stand on his feet and speak with force and conviction, on any subject within the range of his knowledge, is under a great handicap as far as the attraction of people is concerned. The same applies to the man who cannot express himself forcefully in ordinary conversation and in small group gatherings, such as business conferences.

There is a general acceptance of the belief that the ability to dramatize words and express them forcefully at all times, under all conditions, is among the greatest of human achievements. In fact, some people place this power at the head of the list of all personal achievements.

Times without number, as we can see by examining the history of mankind, the entire trend of civilization has been influenced by men who could dramatize an idea with the spoken word. We have only to look around us to find men who have risen to great heights of personal achievement because of their ability to sell themselves to other people, through dramatized speech. Let it be remembered that in my use of the term *speech,* I have reference to man's spoken words as a means of influencing others, whether he is speaking to one person or to many.

HILL: It might be helpful, Mr. Carnegie, if you were to mention some of the steps one must take to prepare to give an effective speech.

CARNEGIE: By far the most important factor of effective speech is a thorough knowledge of the subject on which one speaks. *No amount of dramatic technique will ever take the place of the self-assurance a speaker feels when he knows his subject!*

Someone whose hobby was terseness of speech, once said that a whole course on public speaking could be taught in one sentence: "Know what you wish to say and say it with all the feeling you can command, and then sit down!" *The last two words are important.* The time to stop speaking is the exact moment at which you have conveyed the thought you wish to get over, and not one second beyond that time. Long-winded speakers generally are boresome; but the short speech will be no less so if it does not say something that people wish to hear, and say it effectively.

HILL: Several times, Mr. Carnegie, you have used the word "dramatize" in connection with effective speech. Just how is the ability to dramatize acquired?

CARNEGIE: The ability to dramatize speech comes through habit; therefore one should begin this habit *by speaking forcefully in ordinary conversation!* There is the place where great speakers learn the art of effective speech. They practice on every person with whom they converse. They never utter a word *without placing back of it the necessary feeling* to make it penetrate and affect the mind of the listener. This simple procedure will make an effective speaker of anyone who follows it as a matter of daily habit, and *nothing else will!*

HILL: Mr. Carnegie, in our last discussion you stressed the importance of the proper choice of words. Will you tell me now, Sir, where the proper use of words fits into this business of effective speech?

CARNEGIE: Words will not produce effective speech unless they are grouped so as to convey ideas through illustrations and similes that are well within the experience of all! Remember this, because it is of the utmost importance to all who aspire to become effective speakers.

I have heard some well educated men make speeches which were masterpieces of English, but they failed to influence anyone because they were not properly attuned to the minds of the listeners, through the right sort of illustrations.

People wish to hear about subjects that help to solve their daily problems, subjects that aid them in their struggle for the necessities and the luxuries of life. People will listen to the discussion of other subjects, *but they will be more greatly influenced when discussions are made interesting by dramatization and illustration.*

All people resent the use of words which they do not understand, no matter how correctly they may be used. Remember, then, that the effective speaker must not only use illustrations within the range of his listeners, but he must describe them in words which anyone of ordinary educational advantages may understand.

HILL: Mr. Carnegie, what about gestures? I've listened to some speakers who wildly beat the air and pounded the lectern in driving home their points. What is your opinion in this matter, Sir?

CARNEGIE: Gestures can do only one of two things to a speech; either add to, or detract from, its effectiveness. If they do not add, they detract. Gestures should therefore be harmonized appropriately with the content of the speech. One should avoid distracting personal gestures, such as running the fingers through the hair, shoving the hands down in the pockets, and fumbling with watch chains, or rattling coins. Also, one should avoid slouchy posture of the body. Such mannerisms may imply familiarity and take the mind of the listeners off the speech.

HILL: It seems to me, Mr. Carnegie, that a good many of the traits of a pleasing personality may be incorporated right into an effective speech. I'm thinking, for instance, of tone of voice.

CARNEGIE: The tone of the voice is important. It should, therefore, be controlled. High, harsh tones always offend the listener. The low, rich tones are much preferable. A voice that is off tone is as offensive as a musical instrument that is out of tune, and for the same reason; it destroys the harmony of the tone.

Here, again, remember that one should begin training the tone of the voice in ordinary conversation. A well disciplined voice can convey feeling—not by the mere meaning of words alone, but by the tone of the voice—which produces either laughter or tears! The effective speaker must learn to distinguish between words that are spoken without feeling and those which depend almost, if not entirely, upon feeling for their influence on the listener. *The tone of the voice is the instrument* by which feeling is conveyed.

HILL: You'll agree with me, Mr. Carnegie, that another one of the traits of personality which obviously enters into effective speech, is facial expression?

CARNEGIE: The effective speaker must remember to make the expression of his face fit the feeling he wishes to convey. Both the smile and the frown have their appropriate places in speech, but it is important that each should be used only at the right places. The governing rule is that the expression of the face should harmonize with the nature of the thought to be conveyed by speech.

HILL: Mr. Carnegie, what ingredient of a speech transmits the all important "feeling" or mood of the speaker to the members of his audience and inspires them to react in the way the speaker desires them to respond?

CARNEGIE: Enthusiasm is the essential element of effective speech which gives words the necessary "feeling" to enable a speaker to project his thoughts into the minds of listeners.

It is difficult for anyone to close his mind against the enthusiastic speaker, or to keep his mind from being penetrated by the thoughts of one who speaks with the fire of enthusiasm back of every word. *Enthusiasm is very contagious!* It is a form of feeling that gives power to words as nothing else will.

HILL: If that's the case, Mr. Carnegie, please tell us how one generates this magic power of enthusiasm.

CARNEGIE: The starting point in the development of enthusiasm is *sincerity of purpose* and a *complete belief* of the speaker in the thought he is endeavoring to convey to others.

Any attempt to feign enthusiasm where it is not actually felt by the speaker, will be more than apt to be recognized and resented by the listeners. Here, again, *the tone of the voice speaks so loudly that mere words get in the way* and serve only to expose the insincerity of the speaker who does not actually believe in what he is saying.

HILL: Could you tell us, Mr. Carnegie, what is considered to be the most effective speech of all time?

CARNEGIE: The speech which has been delivered more than any other is one of the shortest, one of the most dramatic, one of the most romantic, and sometimes one of the most tragic of all human speeches. It consists of only three words: "I love you!"

Yet I have heard it said that the three short words are only incidental to the conveyance of the thought back of them.

The thing that counts most, so *experts* on the subject tell me, is the tone of the voice, the look in the eyes, and the feeling of enthusiasm the speaker sometimes puts back of this speech. When you can explain how one clothes that speech with the necessary feeling to make it effective, you will also know a great deal about how one dramatizes any speech with depth of feeling and enthusiasm. It all goes back to sincerity of purpose and desire. *We have no trouble in giving feeling to speech when we believe what we are saying!* Moreover, if we believe what we say, and give our words the right amount of feeling, the world is apt to recognize us as having attractive personalities!

HILL: And what is the nineteenth trait of a pleasing personality, Mr. Carnegie?

CARNEGIE: *VERSATILITY.* It is hardly necessary to mention the obvious fact that people who lack a general understanding of the world in which they live, including at least a surface knowledge of human nature, are seldom interesting or attractive.

A general interest in things and people is one of the essentials of flexibility of personality, without which one is seldom attractive except to a very small percentage of those with whom one associates.

With books and educational advantages as plentiful as they are in our country, there is little excuse for any person neglecting to inform himself on a great variety of subjects. Every man should have at least a surface acquaintanceship with the vital topics of the day—especially those which are associated with the political and economic fortunes of his own country.

A man should have at least a shade more than a surface knowledge of himself, for it is true that the man who understands himself knows a great deal about other people, and he is thereby qualified to make himself attractive to them. The man who really knows himself has little difficulty in knowing others, *because he is so much like the "others."*

HILL: According to my count, Mr. Carnegie, you are now about to discuss the twentieth trait of a pleasing personality, which is—

CARNEGIE: *A GENUINE FONDNESS FOR PEOPLE.* Everyone who understands dogs knows that a dog instantly recognizes people who do or do not like dogs. Moreover, dogs express their recognition in no uncertain terms. People also recognize, with the slightest association, individuals who like people; and they resent those who have a natural dislike for others, just as definitely as they are attracted to the person who likes people.

The law of retribution always operates so that people are judged and dealt with, not alone by their deeds, but by their dominating *mental attitudes,* through which they express their likes and their dislikes with unerring definiteness. It is inevitable, therefore, that the person who dislikes people will be disliked, *although he may never openly express his feelings.* Through telepathy every mind communicates with other minds. Therefore, the person who wishes to have an attractive personality is under the constant necessity of watching not only his deeds, *but also his thoughts.*

HILL: What you have just said, Mr. Carnegie, seems to be closely related to what we commonly call a man's "temper." Do you wish to explain your idea of "temper"?

CARNEGIE: I wouldn't expect very much in the way of achievement of a man who has no "temper," because the thing we call "temper" is nothing but uncontrolled emotion, and emotion under control is one of the most essential of all the powers of the mind.

Perhaps the greatest injury an uncontrolled temper does is that which results from an uncontrolled tongue. The person with an uncontrolled temper generally has a tongue that is mounted on ball-bearings in the middle, so to speak, and swings loosely at both ends, with an edge as sharp as a razor blade, and with no regard for whom it cuts. We have all known of such tongues, *but we have never been greatly attracted to the owner of any of them!*

Most people talk too much and say too little under the most favorable circumstances; but the man with a bad temper and a ball-bearing tongue often talks when he does not intend to do so, and says things that he lives to regret. Such a person, obviously, does not have an attractive personality.

HILL: What have you to say about those who express defeatism and accept failure as their lot in life?

CARNEGIE: Nobody cares very much for the person who has abandoned the hope of personal achievement, or lacks the ambition to achieve some worthy objective in life. The world will forgive a man for most of his mistakes if he has high aims and definite hopes for their attainment, but it will not forgive him for failures due to indifference or hopelessness.

HILL: Mr. Carnegie, is it possible for a man to allow his personal habits to control him, through lack of self-discipline, and still remain attractive to other people?

CARNEGIE: Excess in the habits of eating, drinking, or sexual relationships destroys personal magnetism and makes the offender an object of derision among all who know him. I shall not preach on morals; but simply say that the man who hasn't enough pride in himself to control these intimately personal habits will more than likely be a failure in everything he undertakes, for these habits generally have associated with them other objectionable habits which make the development and maintenance of an attractive personality impossible.

HILL: One of the most common causes of an unattractive personality, I should say, Mr. Carnegie, is the tendency to be grouchy, irritable, nervous and impatient. Do you care to express yourself on this subject, Sir?

CARNEGIE: Impatience is nothing but a visible expression of selfishness or lack of self-discipline. Consequently, it never inspires sympathy from anyone. It is a negative mental attitude that is caused usually by intemperate habits in connection with eating, drinking, and sex which I mentioned before, or is due to poor health brought about by these forms of intemperance.

Toxic poisoning, due to improper eating habits, is one of the major causes of impatience and irritability. A doctor once told me that if people would keep their sewer systems as clean as they keep the outside of their bodies, there would be fewer of them calling for a physician.

HILL: What trait of personality is next on the list, Mr. Carnegie?

CARNEGIE: It is *HUMILITY OF THE HEART*. Arrogance, greed, vanity and egotism are never found in the man who has a pleasing personality.

HILL: But isn't humility usually associated somewhat with timidity?

CARNEGIE: Not in the sense in which I'm using the term. It means a humble spirit based on the recognition that even the greatest of men are, by comparison with the scheme and plan of life generally, but fragments of the whole.

Humility of the heart is the result of a true understanding of man's relationship to his Creator, plus recognition that the material blessings of life are a gift of the Creator for the common good of all mankind. The man who is on good terms with his own conscience and in harmony with his Creator always is humble of heart; and he generally has an attractive personality.

HILL: I believe we are down to the twenty-second trait which comprises an attractive personality. Mr. Carnegie, will you name and discuss it, please?

CARNEGIE: I call it *GOOD SHOWMANSHIP*. Showmanship, as one of the traits of attractive personality, is a combination of several of the other traits, properly blended and used.

It is the ability to combine facial expression, tone of voice, appropriate personal adornment, choice of words, control of the emotions, courtesy, effective speech, versatility, mental attitude, sense of humor, emphasis, and tactfulness, in such a manner as to dramatize any circumstance or occasion, so as to attract *favorable attention*.

As the term "showmanship" is used here, it has no reference to the common habit of wise-cracking, clowning or gossiping, which is used too often as a means of attracting attention.

And the next trait of an attractive personality is somewhat related to this one. It is called:

CLEAN SPORTSMANSHIP. The man who can win without boasting and lose without squealing, generally has the admiration of other people.

The colleges advocate clean sportsmanship in athletics because educators know that *this habit becomes a part of one's character,* and as such it becomes of great benefit in human relationships outside of athletics. Clean sportsmanship is an important trait of attractive personality because it inspires people to cooperate in a friendly manner.

HILL: Speaking of a friendly manner, Mr. Carnegie, I have always felt that a man with a good personality reveals it when you first meet him, by the way in which he shakes hands.

CARNEGIE: The *ABILITY TO SHAKE HANDS PROPERLY* has a great deal to do with this subject of an attractive personality. The person who understands how to shake hands effectively can convey very definite impressions of many different types, by this means. The man who is skilled in the art of hand-shaking has a big advantage over the man who lacks this *studied accomplishment.*

HILL: Well, Mr. Carnegie, we have come down to the last of the traits of a pleasing personality. What is it, Sir?

CARNEGIE: It is *PERSONAL MAGNETISM.* Let us be frank, at the outset, and say that personal magnetism is a polite way of describing sex energy, for that is precisely what it means. Now we need not evade the admission that sex energy is something with which an individual is born, and it therefore cannot be developed by personal effort.

Sex energy is nature's own device with which she creates and perpetuates every living thing, from God's smallest creature to his greatest handiwork, man. I see no reason, therefore, for subterfuge in connection with the analysis of sex emotion as one of the most important traits of personality, but I do see a reason for making it plain that this universal power adds attractive qualities to the personality only when it is *controlled and used properly.*

HILL: What is the method of control you refer to?

CARNEGIE: I have reference to transmutation, which means the diversion of sex emotion from physical sex expression into whatever constructive purpose one wishes to carry out.

It is a well-known fact that when a man who is highly sexed organizes this irresistible creative force and places it back of his occupational endeavors, he has but little difficulty in persuading people to cooperate with him.

The emotion of sex must be considered as one of the most important factors of an attractive personality; therefore, I have given here a clue from which anyone smart enough to recognize it, may add greatly to his ability to influence people through his personality.

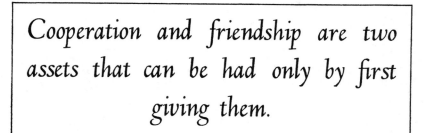

Cooperation and friendship are two assets that can be had only by first giving them.

Employ Applied Faith *Chapter Four*

HILL: Can I develop the faith necessary to carry me over the obstacles with which I shall likely meet during my research?

CARNEGIE: My answer will describe perhaps the most important of the seventeen principles of achievement. It is "Applied Faith," and it is one factor of human achievement which gives power to all who apply it. It is the great equalizing force which *truly makes all men equal.*

HILL: Am I to understand you to say, Mr. Carnegie, that all men are born equal? Do you mean that men who have great self-reliance are born with that trait?

CARNEGIE: Now let me get you straightened out on this vital point before you make the same mistake that so many others have made, of assuming that individuals who achieve outstanding success are born with some peculiar quality of genius not possessed by others. Self-confidence is a state of mind that is under the control of the individual, and it is not an inborn trait possessed by some and lacking in others.

There are varying degrees of self-confidence, the reason for which I will explain later. Supreme self-confidence is based upon Faith in Infinite Intelligence, and you may be certain that no one ever attains this state of mind without having a definite belief in Infinite Intelligence and establishing contact with it.

The starting point in the development of self-confidence is Definiteness of Purpose. That is why this principle was given first place in the Philosophy of Individual Achievement.

It is a well-known fact that the man who knows exactly what he wants, has a definite plan for getting it, and is actually engaged in carrying out that plan, has no difficulty in believing in his own ability to succeed. It is equally well-known that the man of indecision, the fellow who flounders around and procrastinates, soon loses confidence in his own ability and winds up by doing nothing. There is nothing difficult to understand about this.

HILL: But what happens when one knows what he wants, has a plan for getting it, puts his plan into operation and meets with failure? Doesn't failure destroy self-confidence?

CARNEGIE: That is the very question I hoped you would ask. It gives me an opportunity to set you right on a common mistake that many people make. Failure has one peculiar benefit that is deserving of emphasis, and it is the fact that every failure carries with it, in the circumstance of the failure itself, the seed of an equivalent advantage. Examine the records of the truly great leaders in all walks of life and you will discover that their success is in exact proportion to their mastery of failures.

Life has a way of developing strength and wisdom in individuals through temporary defeat and failure, and do not overlook the fact that there is no such reality as a permanent failure until an experience has been accepted as such.

The power of the mind is so great that it has no limitations other than those which individuals set up in their own minds. The power that removes all limitations from the mind is Faith; and I have emphasized the fact that the source of all Faith is belief in Infinite Intelligence. Once you have reached an understanding of this truth you will not need to worry about self-confidence, for you will possess it in abundance.

HILL: Most people are not experienced philosophers, and they are not going to believe that every failure carries with it the seed of an equivalent advantage when failure overtakes them. What I want to know is this: What is one going to do when he meets with failure and the experience destroys his confidence in himself? To whom does such a person turn for aid in the restoration of confidence in himself?

CARNEGIE: Your question, at first, appears to be one that is very difficult to answer, but the appearance is deceiving as I shall explain. Let me answer you briefly in this way. The best way to guard against being overcome by failure is to discipline the mind to meet failure before it arrives. This can best be accomplished by forming habits that enable one to take full possession of his mind and use it for the attainment of definite ends, on all occasions, from the smallest to the greatest daily task.

HILL: Mr. Carnegie, how does one go about taking possession of his own mind, as you suggest?

CARNEGIE: The answer to that question is the burden of this entire philosophy, as no one may take complete possession of his mind until he assimilates and puts into action the entire seventeen principles of the philosophy. The starting point, as I have stated, is the adoption of a Definite Major Purpose.

The second step consists of the formation of a Master Mind alliance.

The third step is the development of an attractive personality, with which one may properly relate himself to the members of his Master Mind group, and with others who are essential in the achievement of his Major purpose.

The fourth step consists of a form of mental discipline which we have designated as Applied Faith, the details of which we are now analyzing. Faith is the power that gives effectiveness to the other three principles, and it is a state of mind that anyone can develop and use.

HILL: Is there a law or a formula behind the principle of Faith, which a person may lay hold of and follow through to a definite end?

CARNEGIE: Before beginning the analysis of the formula through which Faith is acquired, let me remind you that there is a law known as the law of harmonious attraction, through the operation of which like attracts like. With the aid of this law the successful man either deliberately or unknowingly makes his own mind "success conscious" *by vitalizing it with a keen desire* for the achievement of his major purpose. It is a known fact that men of great achievement form the habit of making an obsession of their Definite Major Purpose. In extreme cases this obsession becomes intensified until it reaches the proportion of *self-hypnosis.*

HILL: How does one go about the development of that state of mind which you mention as an obsession?

CARNEGIE: It is accomplished by adopting a definite purpose or plan and backing it with a burning desire for its realization.

Here the habit of repetition of thought comes into action. The habit may be developed by making the object of one's plan or purpose the dominating thought of the mind.

If the desire back of the plan or purpose is strong enough it will have the effect of calling into the mind a picture of the object of the purpose, and of dwelling upon that picture at all times when the mind is not occupied with less important subjects.

This is the way that all obsessions are developed. The more one thinks and talks of an idea or plan the nearer it comes to being an obsession. Here the Master Mind round-table discussions become powerful factors in vitalizing one's mind with the necessary obsessional quality.

HILL: I have heard it said that a man comes finally to believe anything he repeats often, even though it is a falsehood, and some of the political demagogues seem to capitalize on this principle.

CARNEGIE: That's quite true. The principle of repetition is the medium through which one may fan his desires into a burning flame of intensity.

Any thought that is expressed orally, and continuously repeated from day to day, through Master Mind discussions and otherwise, will be taken over by the subconscious mind eventually and carried out to its logical conclusion.

All great leaders who make life pay on their own terms, through what the world commonly calls success, do so by giving orders to their own minds in the manner I have suggested.

The mind can take and carry out orders, just as if it were a person, and it will act first upon one's dominating thoughts, whether or not they are given as direct orders. Thoughts of limitation and poverty will be carried out to their logical conclusion, which is poverty. The subconscious mind acts on one's thoughts without trying to modify or change their nature in the least. Moreover, it acts automatically, whether or not one is conscious of this action.

HILL: If I understand you clearly, Mr. Carnegie, one can develop self-confidence by thinking in terms of what one desires to do and can do, and by excluding thoughts of the difficulties one may encounter in carrying out one's plans.

CARNEGIE: You have the idea precisely. While I was working as a laborer I heard a fellow worker say, "I hate poverty and I'll not endure it." He is still doing day labor, and lucky to have a job. You see, he fixed his mind on poverty and that is what his subconscious mind gave him.

It would have been different if he had said, "I enjoy riches and I shall earn and receive them." It would have helped, too, if he had gone still one step further and described what sort of service he intended to give in return for the riches he desired.

HILL: Then the mind brings the physical equivalent of that which it dwells upon.

CARNEGIE: Make no mistake about the fact that it does so. And brings it by the shortest, most economical and practical means available, by using every opportunity to achieve the object of one's desires.

HILL: What is the effect of two or more people joining the forces of their minds and working harmoniously for the attainment of their definite purpose?

CARNEGIE: They attain the object of that purpose much more quickly than they could if they worked independently.

When the leaders in a business organization begin to think, talk and act together in a spirit of harmony they generally get that which they seek. It is true that people can talk and think themselves into anything they desire.

Thoughts are things, and powerful things at that. They are more powerful when expressed in the words of an individual who knows exactly what he wants, and more powerful still when they are expressed in the words of a group of people who think, speak and act together.

HILL: From what you have said, Mr. Carnegie, I understand that when the people of a community or a nation begin to think and act in connection with any definite objective, they soon find ways and means of attaining it.

CARNEGIE: That is not only my belief, but it is a fact. If the newspapers begin to publish stories about wars, and the people begin to think and talk of war in their daily conversations, they soon find themselves at war. People get that which their minds dwell upon; and this applies to a group or a community or a nation of people, the same as to an individual.

One reason why we Americans are the richest and the freest people in the world—and perhaps this is the only reason—is the fact that we think and talk and act in terms of freedom and riches. Our nation was literally born of our desire for liberty. Our history books are filled with the spirit of liberty. We have talked of liberty so much that we have it in abundance. We shall cease to have it if we stop talking and thinking about it.

HILL: Mr. Carnegie, can you give me an illustration of how people get that about which they *think* and *talk*?

CARNEGIE: Why just go back to the history of this country and study the events that led up to the signing of the Declaration of Independence. Here you will discover something that most students of history overlook entirely—namely, the real source of the power that enabled George Washington's armies to win over vastly superior and better equipped armies.

The power of which I speak is the power that began in the form of a Definite Purpose in the minds of a few men. It extended itself, through the Master Mind relationships of these men, until it gave this country the liberty and freedom we now enjoy.

HILL: Well, Mr. Carnegie, this is certainly a new story for me. Tell me how it came about, if you please?

CARNEGIE: It started definitely with three men; John Hancock, Samuel Adams, and Richard Henry Lee, who communicated freely, mostly by correspondence, expressing their views and hopes regarding the freedom of the Colonies.

From this practice Samuel Adams conceived the idea that a mutual exchange of letters between the prominent people of the thirteen Colonies might help to bring about the coordination of effort so badly needed to solve their common problems.

Accordingly, a Committee of Correspondence was organized. This move increased the power of the Master Mind alliance of the three men by adding to it men from all the Colonies. These three men did not content themselves by merely *writing letters,* but they kept up the agitation by correspondence until it led, finally, to the historic meeting in Independence Hall, in Philadelphia, at which fifty-six men signed their names to the document that was destined to give birth to a new nation—the Declaration of Independence. *They were motivated by an active Faith.*

HILL: This is a thrilling chapter of our history indeed, Mr. Carnegie. Was it actually that simple?

CARNEGIE: It was far from simple; but the principles at work are simple. While the letter writing program was going on, Samuel Adams and John Hancock called a secret meeting of their close friends for the purpose of outlining the steps necessary to translate their Definite Purpose into action.

When the meeting had been called to order, Samuel Adams locked the door, placed the key in his pocket, and calmly told those present that it was imperative a Congress of the Colonists be organized; and informed them that no man would be permitted to leave the room until the decision for such a Congress had been reached. Here is more evidence of *active Faith.*

Through the influence of Hancock and Adams the others present were induced to agree that, through the Correspondence Committee, arrangements would be made for a meeting of the First Continental Congress, to be held in Philadelphia, September 5, 1774, almost two years before the actual signing of the Declaration of Independence.

Remember this date, and remember the two determined men who brought it about, for if there had been no decision to hold a Continental Congress, there could have been no signing of the Declaration of Independence. PASSIVE FAITH never would have led to this daring move.

HILL: I must say that we need some of that brand of faith in our nation today.

CARNEGIE: Agitation was kept up, by correspondence and by secret meetings between the members of the Master Mind alliance organized by Hancock, Adams, and Lee, for almost two years; resulting in the famous meeting at Philadelphia in 1776. By this time the Master Mind had grown to fifty-six men. The meeting lasted for several days, during which those men engaged in the most stupendous round-table conversations known to modern civilization.

On June 7th, 1776, Richard Henry Lee recognized that the time for mere conversations had come to an end and the time for action had arrived. He arose, addressed the Chair, and to the startled Assembly made this motion:

"Gentlemen, I make the motion that the United Colonies are, and of right ought to be, free and independent states; that they be absolved from all allegiance to the British Crown; and that all political connection between them and the State of Great Britain is, and ought to be totally dissolved."

Out of that motion, based on *active Faith,* was born the world's greatest nation! Out of that motion was born the spirit that gave Washington's soldiers the power to win over seemingly insurmountable difficulties. Study carefully what happened and you will see that these men devoted nearly two years of highly concentrated effort to the preparation of their minds for the performance, through *active Faith,* of a difficult and dangerous task.

HILL: Describing it as a "difficult and dangerous task" is putting it mildly. Each of those men was literally "sticking his neck out" as the slang saying goes, for a hangman's noose as a traitor to the Crown.

CARNEGIE: I have told you this bit of history because it is in a similar manner that all great leaders condition their minds for unusual tasks. This is how men acquire self-confidence! This is an example of the method by which Faith is developed through deeds.

Remember the fact that *action* must follow the adoption of a definite purpose. *Without action, plans and aims are fruitless.* The three men who started America on the road to liberty and freedom made use of the self-same principles of achievement that must be used by the successful leader in business or in any other calling.

In the development of self-confidence, as in all other worthy undertakings, one must begin with a motive based upon a definite purpose.

HILL: I believe I now understand the procedure by which self-confidence may be acquired. Now, Mr. Carnegie, will you, for the purpose of emphasis, explain how you applied these principles in the crowning achievement of your career, when you converted all your holdings into the United States Steel Corporation?

CARNEGIE: First, I applied the principle of Definiteness of Purpose by reaching a decision to consolidate all my steel industrial interests into one company and to sell the company.

Second, having decided to sell, I called certain members of my Master Mind group together and we spent several weeks in analysis of the values of my properties in order that I might set a fair price for my interests. We also had to work out a plan by which to find buyers for the properties, and arrange ways and means of approaching prospective buyers without placing ourselves at a great disadvantage, since the buyers would know in advance that we were desirous of selling.

The complete plan represented the combined efforts of the members of my Master Mind group who sat in on the discussions, and myself, and it was so devised that instead of our being in the position of offering our properties for sale, we *would be approached by the buyers with an offer* to purchase the properties.

This we accomplished with very little maneuvering, by arranging a dinner in New York City at which my chief Master Mind aid, Charlie Schwab, and a group of Wall Street bankers, whom we had chosen as prospective buyers, would be guests. Mr. Schwab was to deliver a speech painting a vivid picture of the great possibilities of such a consolidation of my steel interests into one company, as we had planned. The speech had all the earmarks of being spontaneous, as Schwab made it clear that the plan he outlined could be carried out only by gaining my consent, and gave no indication that he already had that.

The speech made such an impression that the meeting lasted into the late hours of the night, and before Schwab left, the bankers present at the meeting, including J. P. Morgan, gained from him a promise to place the proposed plan before me and to do what he could to gain my consent to it.

Not until long after the deal had been closed and I had been paid off did the bankers learn that the speech was carefully planned months in advance.

HILL: From that story I gather the fact that your confidence in your ability to sell your properties was so great that you planned every move well in advance of your knowledge as to who the actual buyers would be.

CARNEGIE: Every move was planned in advance, but we had a pretty good idea who our buyers would be. However, we planned this particular transaction no more carefully than we planned every business move we made in the operation of our steel industry.

Faith has sounder legs to stand upon when it is backed by definite plans.

Applied Faith is never based on blind moves. Blind Faith is something of which I know nothing. The only sort of Faith I know anything about is that which is supported by some combination of facts or reasonable assumption of facts. One of the major purposes of a Master Mind alliance is that of providing one with reliable knowledge upon which to build plans. With such knowledge in hand you can readily see how easy it is to develop that state of mind known as Faith.

HILL: That statement appears to contradict your earlier statement that "supreme self-confidence is based on belief in Infinite Intelligence." If you do not recognize blind Faith, and have Faith only in provable facts or knowledge, how do you justify your Faith in Infinite Intelligence, since definite knowledge on this subject is elusive?

CARNEGIE: You have made the mistake of assuming that there is no source of definite knowledge about Infinite Intelligence. As a matter of fact, the existence and the working principles of Infinite Intelligence are more easily proved than any other fact.

HILL: Will you please give me a few reasons why you hold this belief?

CARNEGIE: In the first place, the orderliness of all natural law and all that we know of the universe is indisputable evidence that there is back of all this a universal plan, a form of intelligence far superior to that which we human beings understand.

I can see it in the predictable movements and positions of the stars and planets, which can be calculated and foretold hundreds of years in advance.

I can see it in the mystery that brings together two small cells, each no larger than the fine point of a pin, and converts them into the marvelous machine we call man, carrying in those two small particles of *energy, matter* and *intelligence* a portion of the ancestral qualities of man for generations back.

There are many theories which are not provable, but Infinite Intelligence is not one of them, and I may as well tell you here that I believe the power with which we think and reason is nothing other than a minute portion of Infinite Intelligence functioning through man's brain. It is fairly obvious that Infinite Intelligence works through the minds of men and uses the most practical natural media available for carrying out the plans of the Creator. Once you acquire this viewpoint you will be better prepared to depend upon Faith in carrying out the task I have assigned you.

You mentioned the fact that the task I have given you calls for more self-confidence than you possess. Here, then, I am offering you a viewpoint which, if you will accept it and act upon it, will provide you with a form of inspiration vastly greater than self-reliance. It will give you access to an abundance of Faith with which your success is assured even before you begin your task. I sincerely hope that you will open your mind to the guidance of this Faith.

HILL: At the close of our last discussion, Mr. Carnegie, you made the statement that Infinite Intelligence works through the minds of men, and uses the most practical natural media available for carrying out the plans of the Creator. While you were speaking, the thought was running through my mind that the human brain, with its intricate system for receiving and sending thoughts, is the greatest of all the evidence of your theory that Infinite Intelligence is the real source of the power of thought. If this is correct, and I believe it to be, it is equally true that the greatest of all sources of power for the solution of our problems of life is that which is available through our own minds. Have I caught your viewpoint on this subject, Sir?

CARNEGIE: You have, and now I wish to take you for a little trip into the inner workshop of my own mind, where you will be permitted to take inventory of the vast resources of the mind as I see them.

Once you have a complete perspective of the actual service the mind performs, I believe you will never again lack the self-reliance to draw upon the forces available to you through your mind, for every need of life; and I believe, too, that you will have no difficulty in opening your mind, at will, for the guidance of Infinite Intelligence when you are faced with problems you cannot solve through reliance on your own reason.

HILL: I shall consider it a rare privilege, Mr. Carnegie, to have your comments on the mind's vast store of riches. What peculiarity of the mind do you consider to be most significant?

CARNEGIE: The most significant fact is that the mind is the only thing over which an individual has complete control. Surely the Creator did not provide man with this astounding prerogative without thereby conveying the definite idea that it is man's greatest asset. It also involves a responsibility to use and develop this asset.

And second only to this right to control the mind, is the important and equally significant fact that the mind has been wisely provided with a *conscience* to guide it in the use of the vast power it carries.

It is also highly significant that the mind has been carefully screened against all outside intruders, through a system that makes possible the opening and the closing of the mind at will.

HILL: You speak of "opening and closing" the mind, as though it were equipped with a door, or a gate, or some type of shutters. Will you please clarify your meaning on this point, Mr. Carnegie?

CARNEGIE: The mind has been cleverly provided with a gateway of approach to Infinite Intelligence, through what is known as the subconscious mind; and this gateway has been so arranged that it cannot be opened for voluntary use except by the mind that has been first prepared by Faith.

However, the gateway can be opened voluntarily, from the "other side" as it were, by Infinite Intelligence, when communication with man is necessary, and without his consent. Man's control over his own mind relates only to his conscious mind.

HILL: Someone has said that "The imagination is the workshop of the soul." Would you like to comment on that statement?

CARNEGIE: Well, of this I'm quite sure; the mind has been provided with a faculty of imagination, wherein may be fashioned ways and means of translating hope and purpose into physical reality. This is evidence to me that imagination is indeed the workshop of the conscious mind.

Also the mind has been provided with the stimulative capacity of desire and enthusiasm, with which man's plans and purposes may be given action through the imagination.

It has been provided with the power of will, through which both plan and purpose may be sustained indefinitely, thereby giving man adequate power to master fear and discouragement and opposition.

It has been given the capacity for Faith, through which the will and the reasoning faculty can be subdued while the entire machinery of the brain is turned over to the *guiding force* of Infinite Intelligence. Get the full significance of this fact and you will be near to the method by which one may develop Faith.

HILL: I have often heard you refer to the "sixth sense" of the mind. Just what do you mean by that term?

CARNEGIE: The sixth sense prepares the mind for direct connection with other minds, thus making possible the operation of the Master Mind principle, by which it may add to its own power the stimulative forces of other minds that serve so effectively, at times, to stimulate the imagination.

The mind has been given the power to project itself into other minds, through what is known as telepathy, and it may do so freely under two circumstances: First, where other minds have been left open, either voluntarily or neglectfully, and second, where a relationship of harmony and oneness of purpose has been arranged between two or more minds, as in the case of the Master Mind alliance.

HILL: So far, you have not mentioned the two rather obvious functions of the mind, the faculty of reason and the power of deduction. Where do these fit into your conception of the mind?

CARNEGIE: The mind, through its capacity to reason may

combine facts and theories into hypotheses, ideas and plans. By the power of deduction, the philosopher analyzes the past in order to predict the future.

The mind has the power to select, modify and control the nature of its thoughts, thus giving man the privilege of building his own character, and of determining what sort of thoughts shall dominate his mind.

HILL: And what a power that is! I recall how you have repeatedly said that the dominating thoughts a person holds in his mind determine the "set of his sails."

CARNEGIE: Yes, and the mind has an unlimited capacity to receive, organize and store knowledge. It has been provided with a marvelous filing system for recording and recalling every thought it has expressed, through what is called memory. This astonishing system automatically classifies and files related thoughts in such a manner that the recall of one particular thought leads to the remembrance of its associated thoughts. And the mind functions secretly, and in absolute silence, thereby assuring privacy under all circumstances!

HILL: What might one say about the power of the mind over the functions of the physical body?

CARNEGIE: It has the power to aid in the maintenance of the health of the physical body, and apparently is the sole source of cure of physical ills; all other sources being merely contributory. It also keeps the physical body in repair.

It controls and directs, automatically, a marvelous system of chemistry through which it converts all food taken into the body into suitable combinations for the sustenance of the body.

It automatically operates the heart, with which the blood stream is circulated to distribute food to the places where it is needed, and to carry off the waste materials and the worn out cells of the body.

HILL: Would you say that the mind has a spiritual function, in addition to the physical functions you have just enumerated?

CARNEGIE: The mind is the common meeting ground wherein man may commune with the Creator, through prayer, by the simple process of setting aside the power of the will and opening the gateway of the subconscious mind, through Faith.

It has been given the power of emotion, or feeling, through which it can stimulate the body for any desired action, at will.

It is the source of all happiness and all misery, of both poverty and riches of every nature whatsoever, and it devotes its energies to whichever of these is dominated by the power of thought.

It is the source of all human relationships, the builder of friendships, the creator of enemies, according to the manner in which it is used.

It has no limitations, within reason, save only those which the individual accepts through his lack of Faith! Truly, "Whatever the mind can believe, the mind can achieve!"

HILL: To what extent do people generally avail themselves of the wonderful faculties of the mind which you have mentioned?

CARNEGIE: Regrettably, with all this miraculous power the majority of the people of the world permit themselves to be cowed by fears of difficulties which do not exist save in their own imaginations. *The archenemy of mankind is fear!*

HILL: Perhaps it would be a good idea to name some of the most common fears which we permit to enter our minds and thereby become literally "self-imposed" limitations.

CARNEGIE: We fear poverty in the midst of an over-abundance of riches.

We fear ill health in spite of the ingenious system nature has provided, by which the physical body is automatically maintained in working order.

We fear criticism when there are no critics save those which we set up through our own imaginations.

We fear the loss of love of friends and relatives although we know well enough that our own conduct is sufficient to maintain love through all ordinary circumstances of human relationships.

We fear old age whereas we should accept it as a medium of greater wisdom and understanding.

We fear the loss of liberty although we know that liberty is a matter of harmonious relationships with others.

We fear death when we know it is inevitable, therefore beyond our control.

We fear failure, not recognizing that every failure carries with it the seed of an equivalent benefit.

Instead of opening our minds for the guidance of Infinite Intelligence, through Faith, we close our minds tightly with every conceivable shade and degree of limitation, based upon our unnecessary fears.

HILL: But, Mr. Carnegie, how may one develop Faith? I'm sure that any help you can give along this line will be greatly appreciated. I repeat the question, Sir, "How may one develop Faith?"

CARNEGIE: I'll tell you how. Faith may be developed by clearing the mind of its enemies. Clear the mind of negative thoughts and fears and self-imposed limitations and lo! Faith has filled the place without effort. If you cannot take my word for this, try it for yourself and be forever convinced.

There is no great mystery about the state of mind known as Faith. Give it a place to dwell and it will move in without ceremony or invitation. *Stop talking about Faith and start practicing it.* What could be more simple?

We preach sermons and offer up prayers in the name of Christ, yet we rarely make more than a gesture at following His admonition for us to liquidate our problems through the simple state of mind known as Faith.

We build great edifices of worship in the name of Christ, yet we profane them with minds that are steeped in fear and self-imposed limitations which *He clearly promised us we need not endure.*

HILL: You are surely speaking plainly on this subject and I hope people will profit by it.

CARNEGIE: If I seem to speak plainly, be assured it is because I feel that mankind needs the quickening influence of plain speech to shock people into recognizing that everything they need or want is already within their grasp. All they need to do is to take possession of their own minds and use them! *To do this, man has no one to consult except himself.* The approach to liberty, freedom and abundance of the material necessities and luxuries of life is through the individual's mind. This mind is the only thing over which he has complete control, *yet it is the one thing he so seldom uses intelligently.*

HILL: Mr. Carnegie, would you care to name some examples of men who have taken possession of their own minds, and with what results?

CARNEGIE: Once in a great while the world is blessed by the presence of one who takes control of his mind and uses it for the good of mankind. Then it has found a genius; an Edison, an Aristotle, a Plato, or a great leader in thought and in action in some field of useful endeavor.

Columbus took possession of his mind and gave us a new world which now serves as the last frontier of human liberty and freedom.

Orville and Wilbur Wright took possession of their minds and gave man wings and mastery of the air.

Johannes Gutenberg took possession of his mind and gave us movable type, and thereby made possible every book we possess, and gave us the means of preserving the accumulated experience of mankind for the benefit of generations yet unborn.

The list could go on and on. Let us learn from these outstanding examples of achievement one great lesson we all need to know, and that is the obvious fact that self-reliance and Faith are based on definiteness of purpose, *backed by definite plans of action! Procrastination and Faith have nothing in common.*

HILL: From what you have said, Mr. Carnegie, the best way to start developing Faith is by choosing an objective and beginning at once to attain it, through whatever media available. Have I understood you correctly?

CARNEGIE: Quite correctly, lad. The development of Faith is largely a matter of understanding the astounding power of the mind. The only real mystery about Faith is man's failure to make use of it! I speak from personal experience when I say that Faith is a state of mind which can be acquired and used as effectively and easily as any other state of mind. It is all a matter of *understanding and application.* Truly, "Faith without works is dead."

My early days of youth were cursed by poverty and limitation of opportunity; a fact with which all who know me are acquainted.

I am no longer cursed by poverty because *I took possession of my mind,* and that mind has yielded to me every material thing I want, and much more than I need. Faith is no patented right of mine! It is a universal power as available to the humblest person as it is to the greatest.

HILL: Your description of the possibilities of the human mind is both interesting and revealing, Mr. Carnegie. In all the reading I have done on the subject of psychology and the working principles of the mind, I have found nothing that approaches, even approximately, your description of the powers of the mind. Where did you acquire all this knowledge?

CARNEGIE: What knowledge I have of the powers of the mind, I acquired from the greatest of all schools, the University of Life! It has been a habit of mine, extending backward over many years, to devote a certain amount of time daily to silent meditation and thought in connection with the plan and purpose and working principles of the mind.

Some might call this habit, "Getting in tune with the Infinite." At any rate it is a habit I shall continue as long as I live, and I heartily recommend it to all who wish to become better acquainted with the powers of their own minds.

I have one other suggestion to offer that may be helpful in the development of Faith, and that is the fact that all who master and apply the other sixteen principles of the Philosophy of American Achievement will thus have placed themselves within easy reach of Faith. This entire philosophy is one of action. It *inspires effort based on definiteness of purpose,* and this is exactly what is required in the development of Faith.

Go the Extra Mile

Chapter Five

Early one frosty morning, the private railroad car of Charles M. Schwab was shifted to the side-track at his steel plant, in Pennsylvania.

As he left the car he was met by a young man who explained that he was a stenographer in the office of the steel company, and he had met the car with the hope that he might be of some service to Mr. Schwab.

"Who requested you to meet me here?" Schwab asked.

"It was my own idea, sir," the young man replied, "and I knew you were coming on the early morning train because I handled a telegram that stated you were coming. I brought my notebook with me, sir; and I'll be glad to take any letters or telegrams you may wish to send."

Mr. Schwab thanked the young man for his thoughtfulness, but said he needed no service at the moment, although he might send for the lad later in the day. And he did! When the private car returned to New York that night it carried that young man back to the city, where he had been assigned, at Mr. Schwab's request, for duty in the steel magnate's private office.

The young man's name was Williams. We do not recall his first name, but that is unimportant. What we do recall is the fact that Mr. Williams *promoted himself* from one job to another in the steel organization until he earned and saved enough money to enable him to go into business for himself, and he later founded a drug company of which he became the president and majority stockholder.

Nothing very dramatic or interesting about this brief story, is there? Well, the answer depends altogether upon what one calls drama. To every man who is trying to find his place in the world, this story, if analyzed carefully, carries the deepest sort of drama, for it describes the practical application of one of the more important of the 17 principles of individual achievement; the habit of *Going the Extra Mile!*

We said that this young man Williams *promoted himself* from one job to another in the steel company. Let us find out how he managed this self-promotion in order that we may learn how others can profit by his technique. Let us learn, if we can, what young Williams had in the way of ability which other stenographers in the general plant operation office of the steel company did not have, that caused him to be singled out by Mr. Schwab and assigned to his personal service.

We have Mr. Schwab's own word that young Williams did not possess a single quality that entitled him to rate above the average as a stenographer, but he did have one quality; a quality that he developed on his own initiative and practiced as an inviolable habit; which but few people possess, and that was the habit of rendering more service and better service than he was paid for.

It was this habit that enabled him to *promote himself!* It was this habit that attracted the attention of Mr. Schwab. It was this habit that helped him to become the head of a corporation where he became also his own boss.

And it was this habit, as we shall soon see from Andrew Carnegie's analysis of the subject in this chapter, which, many years previous to the incident here related, brought Mr. Schwab himself to the attention of Mr. Carnegie and gained for him his opportunity to *promote himself* into a position in which he became his own boss.

It was also this same habit that enabled the irrepressible Carnegie to rise from the position of day laborer to that of the owner of America's largest industry, where he accumulated a vast fortune in money and a *still greater fortune in useful knowledge,* which is now available to the people of America who have the vision and the ambition to appropriate and use it.

Mr. Carnegie's views on the subject of *Going the Extra Mile* provide the students of this philosophy with a practical working technique with which they may use this principle effectively for their own self-promotion. His analysis of the subject is here presented in his own words:

HILL: Mr. Carnegie, I have heard some men express the belief that success often is the result of luck. Many people seem to believe that successful men achieve their success because they get the favorable "breaks" of life, and that others fail because they get the unfavorable "breaks."

Croesus, the wealthy Persian philosopher, made some such reference to chance when he said:

> "There is a Wheel on which the affairs of men revolve, and its mechanism is such that it prevents any man from being always fortunate."

Have you, in the richness of your business experience, seen any evidence of such a wheel? Do you attribute any portion of your success to luck, or favorable "breaks"?

CARNEGIE: Your questions give me a suitable starting point for an appropriate description of the fifth of the 17 principles of achievement. Let us call it the habit of *Going the Extra Mile,* by which I mean the habit of rendering more service and better service than one is paid for.

First, I will answer your questions by saying yes, indeed, there is a wheel of life that controls human destinies, and I am happy to be able to tell you that this wheel can be definitely influenced to operate in one's favor. If this were not true there would be no object in organizing the rules of personal achievement.

HILL: Will you tell me, in the simplest words possible, just how one may control this wheel of fortune? I would like a description of this important success factor which the young man or young woman just beginning a business career may understand.

CARNEGIE: First of all, to control the wheel of fortune one must understand, master and apply the 17 principles of achievement. I have already named five of these principles, and I might here suggest that these five, if properly applied, will carry one a long way on the road toward success in any calling.

HILL: Am I to understand that the five principles of *Definiteness of Purpose, The Master Mind, Attractive Personality, Applied Faith,* and *Going the Extra Mile,* are sufficient to insure one's success?

CARNEGIE: No, one cannot depend upon these five principles alone. There are twelve other principles of achievement which I have not yet mentioned, and you will observe, when I explain them, that they provide contributory knowledge needed in the attainment of success that one may not acquire from the five principles I have already named.

The five principles are sufficient to enable a man to establish a definite goal in life and determine approximately the amount of wealth he intends to accumulate, what he intends to give in return for that wealth, and so relate himself to other people that they will not place unnecessary obstacles in his way; but one has a considerable distance to travel beyond this point before he attains enduring success by writing his own price tag, as the master of the entire 17 principles may do.

HILL: Do you mean to say that there are definite rules of procedure through which a person may literally write his own price tag and be sure of getting it? Surely I must have misunderstood you, because it seems to me that if such rules do exist there would not be so many poverty-stricken people in the world; especially in view of the fact, that we, in America, are surrounded with an abundance of every form of wealth, and gifted with the freedom of initiative to choose our own occupation and live our own lives as we choose.

CARNEGIE: Yes, you understand me correctly, and I will describe the particular rule of success which will, if properly applied, enable a person literally to write his own price tag, with more than an average chance of getting that which he desires.

Moreover, this rule is so potent that it practically insures one against serious opposition from those who purchase his services. As I have already stated, this rule is known as the habit of *Going the Extra Mile,* which means the habit of doing more than one is paid to do. You will observe that I have injected an important word into the description of this rule; the word *habit!*

Before the application of the rule begins to bring back appreciable results it must become a habit, and it must be applied at all times, in all possible ways. It means that one must render the greatest amount of service of which he is capable, and he must render it in a friendly, harmonious mental manner. Moreover, he must do this regardless of the amount of the immediate compensation he receives; *even if he receives no immediate compensation whatsoever.*

HILL: But, Mr. Carnegie, most of the people I know, those who work for wages or a salary, claim that they are already doing more work than that for which they are paid. If this is true, why aren't they doing a better job of influencing the wheel of fortune in their behalf than they appear to be doing? Why aren't they rich, as you are?

CARNEGIE: The answer to your question is simple enough, but it has many angles I shall have to explain before you'll understand it. In the first place, if you will accurately analyze those who work for wages you will learn that 98 out of every hundred have no Definite Major Purpose greater than that of working for a daily wage. Therefore no matter how much work they do, or how well they do it, the wheel of fortune will turn on past them without providing more than a bare living, *because they neither expect nor demand more!* Ponder over this truth for a moment and you will be better prepared to follow the logic I will present in the remainder of this lesson.

The major difference between those who accept limitation of daily wages sufficient only for a bare living, and myself, is this: *I demand riches in definite terms; I have a definite plan for acquiring riches; I am engaged in carrying out my plan, and I am giving an equivalent, in useful service, of the value of those riches I demand, while the others have no such plan or purpose.*

Life is paying me off on my own terms. It is doing precisely the same thing for the man who asks no more than daily wages. You see, the wheel of fortune follows the mental blueprint that a man sets up in his own mind, and it brings back to him, in physical or financial measure, an exact equivalent of that blueprint.

Unless you grasp the full meaning of this statement of truth you will miss the important portion of this lesson. There is a law of Compensation through the operation of which a man may establish his own relationship with life, including the material possessions he accumulates. There is no escape from the acceptance of the reality of this law, *for it is not a man-made law.*

HILL: I can understand your viewpoint, Mr. Carnegie. Stating the matter in another way, may we not say that every man is where he is and what he is because of the use he makes of his own mind?

CARNEGIE: You have stated the idea correctly. The major difficulty of most men who go through life poverty-stricken is that they neither recognize the power of their own minds nor make any attempt to take possession of their minds. That which a man can accomplish with his hands seldom brings more than a mere living. That which a man can accomplish through the use of his mind may give him whatever he asks of life.

Now let us get on with our analysis of the principle of *Going the Extra Mile.* I am going to explain some of the more practical advantages of this principle. I call them *practical* because they are benefits of which anyone may avail himself, without the consent of others.

Let us consider, first, the fact that the habit of doing more than one is paid for brings one to the *favorable attention* of those who have opportunities to offer. I have never yet known of any man *promoting himself* to a higher and more profitable position without adopting and following this habit.

The habit aids one in developing and maintaining the right "mental attitude" toward others, thereby serving as an effective means of gaining friendly cooperation.

It helps one to profit by the law of contrast, since obviously a majority of the people follow the exact opposite of this principle, by doing just as little work as they can get by with; and that is about all they are getting; *just getting by!*

It creates a continuous market for one's services. Moreover, it insures one a choice of jobs and working conditions, at the top of the scale of wages or other forms of compensation.

It attracts opportunities which are not available to those who render as little service as possible, and thereby serves as an effective medium for self-promotion from wage earning to business owner-ship.

Under some circumstances it enables one to become indispensable in his job, thereby paving the way for him to name his own compensation.

It aids one in the development of self-reliance.

Most important of all its benefits, it gives one the advantage of the law of increasing returns through which he will eventually receive compensation far beyond the actual market value of the service he renders. Therefore, the habit of doing more than one is paid for is a sound business principle, even if it is used purely as a measure of expediency, to promote one's personal interests advantageously.

The habit of doing more than one is paid for is one that an individual may practice without asking the permission of others; therefore, it is under one's own control. Many other beneficial habits can be practiced only through the consent and cooperation of other people.

HILL: Mr. Carnegie, do all the men who work for you have your permission to render more service and better service than that for which they are paid, and if so, how many are taking advantage of this privilege in a manner that is beneficial to themselves?

CARNEGIE: I'm glad you asked that question, because it gives me an opportunity to drive home an important viewpoint on this subject. First, let me say that every person working for me (and this applies with equal truth to all who have worked for me in the past) not only has the privilege of doing more than he is being paid for, but I encourage all who work for me to do this very thing, *for their benefit* as well as my own.

It may surprise you to hear that of the many thousands of men who work for me, but a very small number have taken the trouble to place me under obligations to them by rendering more service and better service than that for which they are paid. Among the few exceptions are the members of my Master Mind group, every man of whom practices the habit as definitely as he eats his meals.

There are others among our supervisory and managerial groups who practice the habit of doing more than they are paid for, and every one of them is receiving compensation far greater than that received by the majority of our workers, although every man in my employ has the privilege of rendering this sort of service without asking the consent of anyone.

As I have told you previously, some of the members of my Master Mind group, such men as Charlie Schwab, have made themselves so definitely indispensable to our business that they have earned as much as a million dollars in one year, over and above their fixed salaries. Not a few of the men who have thus promoted themselves into the higher brackets of income, in our organization, have attracted opportunities to go into business for themselves.

HILL: Couldn't you have driven a better bargain with those to whom you paid as much as a million dollars a year in extra compensation?

CARNEGIE: Oh, to be sure I could have had their services for much less money, but you must remember that this principle of doing more than one is paid for operates in favor of an employer just the same as it operates for the benefit of the employee. Therefore, it is just as much an act of wisdom for an employer to pay a man *all he earns* as it is for an employee to endeavor to earn more than he receives. By paying Charlie Schwab all he earned I thereby insured myself against the loss of his services.

HILL: You speak of paying your men who render more service than they are paid for, *all they earn*. If you do that, how can they render more service than they are paid for? It seems that there is an inconsistency in your statement.

CARNEGIE: That which you mistake for inconsistency is only the mistake of many others on this subject, and is due to a lack of understanding of the habit of *Going the Extra Mile*. The apparent inconsistency is, therefore, an illusion, but I will set you right on this subject.

It is a fact that I pay my men all they earn, even though I sometimes have to pay them huge sums, but there is one important point you have overlooked. It is the fact that before I begin paying them all they earn they must establish their indispensability by doing more than they are paid for.

Now, here is the fine point that most people overlook. Until a man begins to render more service than that for which he is paid he is not entitled to more pay than he receives for that service, since obviously he is already receiving full pay for what he does.

I think I can make the point clear by calling attention to the simple illustration of the farmer. Before he collects pay for his services, he carefully and intelligently prepares the soil, plows and harrows it, fertilizes it if need be, then plants it with seed.

Up to this point he has gained nothing whatsover for his labor, but, understanding the law of growth as he does, he rests after his labor while nature germinates the seed and yields him a crop.

Here the element of time enters into the farmer's labor. In due time nature gives him back the seed he planted in the ground, together with an abundant overplus to compensate him for his labor and his knowledge. If he sows a bushel of wheat in properly prepared soil he gets back the bushel of seed, together with perhaps as many as ten additional bushels as his compensation.

Here the law of increasing returns has stepped in and compensated the farmer for his labor and his intelligence. If there were no such law man could not exist on this earth, since obviously there would be no object in planting a bushel of wheat in the ground if nature yielded back only a bushel of grain. It is this overplus which nature yields, through the law of increasing returns, that makes it possible for man to produce from the ground the food needed for both man and beast.

But little imagination is needed to see that the man who renders more service and better service than that for which he is paid thereby places himself in a position to benefit by this same law. If a man rendered only as much service as he is paid to render, then he would have no logical reason to expect or demand more than the fair value of that service.

One of the evils of today is the attempt, on the part of some, to reverse this rule and collect more pay than the value of the service they render. Some men endeavor to force down the hours of labor and boost up the rate of pay. This practice cannot be pursued indefinitely. When men continue to collect more for their labor than the value of their services, they ultimately exhaust the source of their own wages, and the sheriff makes the next move.

I want you to understand this point clearly, because lack of knowledge on this subject is destined to bring ruin to the American system of industry if the practice of endeavoring to secure more for labor than one puts into it is not corrected. The man to do the correcting is the man who depends upon his labor for a living, *for he is the only man who has the privilege of initiative* in the correction of this unsound practice.

Please do not misunderstand me to be speaking disparagingly of the man who earns his living from daily labor, for the truth is that I am endeavoring to aid the laboring man by giving him a sounder philosophy of relationship in connection with the marketing of his services.

HILL: Then you believe it would be just as unwise for an employer to withhold from an employee any portion of the wages he had justly earned, as it would be for an employee to set up a handicap for himself by doing less than he is paid to do. And I reach the conclusion, from what you have said, that your reasoning on this entire subject is based on your understanding of sound economics and the principle of increasing returns.

CARNEGIE: You have grasped the idea perfectly, and allow me to congratulate you, because most people never seem to understand the great potential benefits available to those who follow the habit of rendering more service than that for which they are paid.

Often I have heard working men say, "I'm not paid to do that;" or, "This is not my responsibility;" and "I'll be blankety-blankety-blank if I'll do anything I'm not paid for." You've heard statements like that. Everyone has.

Well, when you hear a man talking like this you may mark him down as one who will never get more than a bare living from his work. Moreover, that sort of "mental attitude" makes one disliked by his associates, and it therefore discourages favorable opportunities for self-promotion.

When I go in search of a man to fill a responsible position, the very first quality I look for is that of a positive, agreeable mental attitude. You may wonder why I do not look first for ability to do the work I want done. I'll tell you why! The man with a negative mental attitude will disturb the harmony of relationship of all with whom he works; therefore he is a disintegrating influence which no efficient manager wants to deal with. I look first for the right mental attitude, because where this is found one generally finds along with it a willingness to learn. Then the ability necessary to do a certain job can be developed.

When Charlie Schwab first went to work for me he had no ability as far as surface appearances went, other than that possessed by any other day laborer. But Charlie had an unbeatable mental attitude and a disarming personality that enabled him to win friends among all classes of men.

He also had a natural willingness to do more than he was paid for. This quality was so pronounced in him that he actually *went out of his way to get into the way of work*. He not only went the extra mile, but he added two or three extra miles, and went with a smile upon his face and the right attitude in his heart.

He also went in a hurry and *came back for more* when he had finished any task assigned to him. He took hold on a hard job as eagerly as a hungry man takes on food when it is set before him.

Now, what can one do with a man like that, except to give him plenty of rein and let him go as fast as he pleases? That sort of mental attitude inspires confidence. It also attracts opportunities that would run away from the man who carries a frown on his face and a grouch in his heart.

I tell you frankly that there is no way to hold back a man with that sort of mental attitude. He writes his own price tag *and gets it willingly*. If one employer is shortsighted enough to withhold recognition of such a man, through adequate compensation, some wiser employer will soon discover him and give him a better job. The law of supply and demand, therefore, steps in and forces the proper reward for such a man. The employer has very little to do about such circumstances. *The initiative is entirely in the hands of the employee.*

Nor is this example of the wisdom of rendering more service than one is paid for applicable only to the relationship of employer and employee. The same rules apply with equal definiteness to professional men; in fact to all who make their living by serving others. The grocer who tilts the scales in favor of the customer when he is weighing a pound of sugar is wiser, by far, than the grocer who waters his sugar to make it weigh more.

The merchant who gives the customer the odd half cent in making change, instead of taking it himself, is wiser by far than the merchant who refuses to do this. I have known merchants to lose the business of customers worth hundreds of dollars a year, by this pinch-penny habit that some merchants have, of taking the odd half cent in making change.

I once knew a little merchant who went up and down the Monongahela Valley, near Pittsburgh, peddling his merchandise from a pack that he carried on his back. I have heard it said that the pack weighed more than the man who carried it.

When this merchant made a sale he usually threw in some extra article that had not been paid for, as an expression of his gratitude for the patronage given him. Oh, the gift did not amount to much as far as its monetary value was concerned, but he made it with such a pleasant mental attitude that the customer always spoke of the courtesy to all the neighbors, thereby giving the merchant free publicity he could not have purchased with money alone.

In a little while this merchant disappeared from his established route. His customers began to make inquiries as to what had happened to him. The inquiries were prompted by a genuine affection for "the little man with the big pack," as they called him.

Within a few months the little man showed up again. This time he came without his big pack. He came to tell all his customers that he had opened a store of his own in Pittsburgh.

That store is now one of the largest and most prosperous in the city. It is known as the Horn Department Store, founded and owned by "the little man with the big pack" and, one might add, "the little man with the big heart and the wise brain."

We look at men who have "arrived" and say "how fortunate" or "how lucky." All too often we fail to inquire into the source of their "luck," for if we did we might learn that their luck consisted of their habit of rendering more service and better service than they were paid for, as in the case of "the little man with the big pack."

Word has reached my ears, many times, that Charlie Schwab got a favorable "break" because old man Carnegie took a fancy to him and pushed him up front ahead of all the others.

The truth is that Charlie pushed himself up front. All I had to do in the matter was to *keep out of his way and let him go.* Any favorable "break" that he received he created for himself, through his own initiative.

When you describe this principle in the philosophy of individual achievement be sure to emphasize what I have told you about it, because it is the one safe and sure rule through which anyone may influence the wheel of life so it will yield benefits that will more than offset any misfortunes it may bring.

When you take the philosophy to the world be sure to tell the people how to use this principle of doing more than they are paid for, as a definite means of *making themselves indispensable* to those whom they serve. Be sure, also, to explain that this is the success rule through which the law of Compensation *can be deliberately* put into operation in one's behalf.

I have always thought it was a great tragedy that Emerson did not explain more clearly, in his essay on Compensation, that the habit of rendering more service and better service than one is paid for has the effect of placing the law of Compensation back of one's efforts.

HILL: Do you know of other men, besides yourself, who deliberately and with purpose aforethought, follow the habit of doing more than they are paid for, who have not found the habit beneficial?

CARNEGIE: I know of no successful man, in any calling or business, who does not follow this habit either consciously or unconsciously. Study any successful man, regardless of his vocation, and you will learn quickly enough that *he does not work by the clock!*

If you study carefully those who let their picks hang in the air the moment the whistle blows for quitting time, you will learn that they are making nothing but a bare living.

Find me one person who is an exception to this rule and I'll give you a check for a thousand dollars, on the spot, provided that this man will permit me to have a photograph of himself.

If any such man exists he is a rare specimen and *I wish to preserve his picture for the museum,* so all may see the man who successfully defied nature's laws.

Successful men are not looking for short hours and easy jobs, for if they are truly successful they know that no such circumstance exists. Successful men are always looking for ways to lengthen instead of shortening the working days.

HILL: Have you always followed the habit of doing more than you were paid for, Mr. Carnegie?

CARNEGIE: If I had not done so, you would not be here seeking to learn the rules of successful achievement, for I would still be working as a day laborer, right where I began. If you asked me which of the 17 principles of achievement has aided me most, I think I would be.compelled to say it was *Going the Extra Mile.* However, you must not reach the conclusion that this principle, alone, can be depended upon for success. There are sixteen other success principles, some combination of which must be used by all who achieve outstanding and enduring success.

Now is an appropriate time to call your attention to the importance of combining *Definiteness of Purpose* with the habit of *Going the Extra Mile.* In going that *extra mile* one should have a definite, final destination in view, and I see no reason why one should not render more service than he is paid for as a deliberate means of influencing the wheel of life in the attainment of a definite goal.

What if one does follow this habit as a matter of expediency? It is every man's privilege to promote himself in every legitimate way possible, and especially is it his privilege to advance himself through methods which satisfy and benefit others.

As I have stated before, the habit of rendering more service than one is paid for is one habit against which no opposition can be legitimately offered. It is a habit which anyone may exercise on his own initiative, without the necessity of asking permission to do so. *No purchaser of services will object if the seller delivers more than he promises.* And surely no purchaser of services will object if the seller delivers the services with a friendly, pleasing mental attitude. These are privileges within the rights of the seller.

Fortunately we live in a country whose founders wisely preserved for every man the right to exercise his own initiative through all forms of useful service. This privilege, together with the abundance of wealth and opportunity with which we are surrounded in this country, makes it difficult for any man to complain of his not having had a chance.

Here we may create opportunities for ourselves. This still is a comparatively new country. Its future development offers every man an opportunity to exercise both his initiative and his imagination in rendering needed service.

HILL: What about the man whose lack of education forces him to accept only such opportunities as are available to common laborers who work with their hands? Would you say that this man has an equal opportunity with those who have educated themselves?

CARNEGIE: I'm very glad you asked that question, because I wish to set you right on a common mistake that people make in connection with this question of education.

First, let me explain that the word "educate" means something entirely different from that which many believe it to mean. An educated man is one who has taken possession of his own mind and has so developed it, through organized thought, that it aids him efficiently in the solution of his daily problems in the business of living.

Some people believe that education consists of the acquisition of knowledge, but in a truer sense it means *that one has learned how to use knowledge.*

I know many men who are walking encyclopedias of knowledge but make such poor use of it that they cannot earn a living.

Another mistake that many people make is that of believing

that schooling and education are synonymous terms. Schooling may enable a man to acquire much knowledge and assemble many useful facts, but schooling alone does not necessarily make a man educated. Education is self-acquired, and it comes through development and use of the mind, and in no other way.

Take Thomas A. Edison, for example. His entire schooling was a little more than three months, and it was not the most efficient of schooling at that. His real "schooling" came from the great School of Experience, from which he learned how to take possession of his own mind and to use it. Through this use he became one of the best educated men of our times.

Such technical knowledge as he needed in the business of inventing he acquired from other men, through application of the Master Mind principle. In his work he requires knowledge of chemistry, physics, mathematics, and a great variety of other scientific subjects, none of which he personally understands. But since he is *educated,* he knows how and where to procure knowledge on these and all other subjects which is essential in his work.

So, disabuse your mind of the belief that knowledge, of itself, is education! The man who knows where and how to procure the knowledge he needs, when he needs it, is much more a man of education than *the man who has the knowledge but does not know what to do with it.*

Now, there is another angle in connection with this old, time worn alibi through which men explain away their failure by claiming they have had no opportunity to acquire education. It is the fact that schooling is free in this country, and it is so abundantly provided that any man can go to school at night if he really wishes to do so. We also have correspondence schools through which men may acquire knowledge on almost any subject, and for a very small price.

I have but little patience with those who claim that they have not succeeded because they lacked schooling, because I know that any man who really wants schooling can acquire it. The fallacy of this "no schooling" alibi, in most instances, is that it is used *as an apology for plain laziness or lack of ambition.*

I had but little schooling, and I began my career on exactly the same basis that any other working man begins. I had no "pull," no extra favors, no "rich uncle" to help me along, and no one to inspire me to promote myself into a more favorable economic status in life. *The idea of doing so was entirely my own.* Moreover, I found the task to be comparatively easy. It consisted, mainly, of my taking possession of my own mind and using it with *Definiteness of Purpose.*

I did not like poverty, therefore I refused to remain under it. My own mental attitude on this subject was the determining factor that helped me to force poverty to give place to riches. I can truthfully tell you that of all the thousands of working men who have been employed by me, I do not know of one person who could not have equalled, if not excelled, me if he had wanted to do so.

HILL: Your analysis of the subject of education is both interesting and revealing, Mr. Carnegie, and you may rest assured I will include it in the philosophy of achievement, because I feel sure there are many others who have the wrong conception of the relationship between "schooling" and "education." If I understand you correctly, you believe the better part of one's education comes from *doing* and not merely from the acquisition of knowledge.

CARNEGIE: That is exactly correct! I have men working for me who have college degrees, but many of them find their college training only incidental to their success. Those who combine college training with practical experience soon become educated in a practical sense, provided they do not lean too heavily upon their academic degrees as a means of minimizing the importance of practical experience.

Right here is an appropriate place to tell you that the college graduates whom I have employed, who develop the habit of rendering more service than they are paid for, usually advance themselves to more responsible and better-paying positions very quickly, while those who neglect or refuse to adopt this principle make no more progress than the average man without college training.

HILL: Do you mean that college training is worth relatively less than the habit of doing more than one is paid for?

CARNEGIE: Yes, you might put it that way; but I have observed that men with college training who follow the habit of doing more than they are paid for, combining their college training with the advantages they gain from this habit, get ahead much more rapidly than men who do more than they are paid for but have no college training. From this I have reached the conclusion that there is a certain amount of thought discipline that a man gets from college training which men without this training do not generally possess.

HILL: Are a majority of the members of your Master Mind group men with college training, Mr. Carnegie?

CARNEGIE: About two-thirds of them are without college training, and I might add that the one who has been of greatest service to me, weighing everything they have all done, did not finish his common school training. It may be interesting, also, to know that his voluntary habit of rendering more service than he was paid for was the quality which made him of greatest value to me.

I say this because his example seemed to set the pace for other members of my Master Mind group. Moreover, his attitude on this subject spread to the rank and file of our workers, many of whom caught his spirit, practiced it, and thereby promoted themselves into better-paying and more responsible positions with the company.

HILL: Have you any definite method by which you endeavor to inform all your men of the advantages they may gain by rendering more service than they are paid for?

CARNEGIE: We have no direct method of doing this, although the news has been passed along, by the "grape-vine" route, that the men who promote themselves to better positions follow the habit of doing more than they are paid for. I have often thought we should have gone much further by some form of more direct approach by which our men would have been taught the benefits of rendering this sort of service, and we would have done so had we not feared our efforts would have been misconstrued as an attempt on our part to get more work from our men without paying for it.

You see, most working men are skeptical and suspicious of all efforts on the part of an employer to influence them to improve themselves. Perhaps some smarter man than I will find a way through which employers may gain the confidence of their employees and convince them of the benefits, to employer and employee alike, of the habit of rendering more service than the wage scale calls for.

Of course the rule must work both ways, and it will where an employee understands this principle and applies it deliberately. The matter is in the hands of the employee entirely. This is something he can do on his own initiative, without consulting the employer. *The wiser employees discover and apply this principle voluntarily!*

There is not a man in my Master Mind group who did not voluntarily promote himself to that position through the habit of doing more than was expected of him. I tell you frankly that the man who follows this habit voluntarily soon makes himself indispensable and thereby *sets his own wages and chooses his own job.* There is nothing an employer can do but cooperate with a man who has the sound judgment to do more than he is paid for.

HILL: But, aren't there some employers who selfishly refuse to recognize and reward an employee for the habit of doing more than he is paid for?

CARNEGIE: Undoubtedly there are some employers who are shortsighted enough to withhold reward from a man of this type, but you must remember that the man who habitually does more than he is paid for is so rare, that there is keen competition among employers for his services.

If a man has the sound judgment to understand the advantages of doing more than he is paid for, he generally has sense enough, also, to know that all employers are seeking this sort of help; and even those who do not know this will, sooner or later, come to the attention of an employer who is looking for that sort of service, even though they do not deliberately endeavor to promote themselves.

Every man gravitates to where he belongs in life, just as surely as water seeks and finds its level!

Charlie Schwab, for example, did not seek me out (as far as I know) and say, "See here, I am doing more than I am paid for." I made the discovery in my own way because I was searching for that sort of mental attitude.

No employer can successfully conduct an industry of the size of ours without the aid of a large number of men who put heart, soul and all the ability they have into their jobs. Therefore I keep a close lookout at all times for this type of men, and when I find one I single him out for close observation, *to make sure that he follows the habit consistently.* The truth is that all successful employers do the same thing. That is one reason why they are successful.

Whether a man occupies the position of employer or employee, the space he occupies in the world is measured precisely by the quality and the quantity of the service he renders, plus the mental attitude in which he relates himself to other people.

Emerson said, "Do the thing and you shall have the power." He never expressed a more truthful thought than this. Moreover, it applies to every calling, and to every human relationship. Men who gain and hold power do so by making themselves useful to others. All this talk about men holding fat jobs through "pull," is nonsense. A man may procure a good job through pull, but take my word for it when I tell you that if he remains in the job he will do so through "push," and the more of it he puts into the job, the higher he will rise.

I have known of a few young men who were placed in positions beyond their earned merits and ability, through the influence of relatives or others, but seldom have I known of one of them making the fullest use of this unearned advantage; and such exceptions as I have known were due to their having acquired the habit of putting into their jobs more than they tried to take out.

HILL: What about the man who does not work for wages? The small merchant, or the doctor or lawyer? How can they promote themselves by rendering more service than they are paid for?

CARNEGIE: The rule applies to them the same as to the man who works for wages. As a matter of fact those who fail to render such service remain small, and often they fail completely. There is a factor in a successful man's life known as "good will," without which no man can achieve noteworthy success in any calling.

The finest of all methods of building good will is that of rendering more service and better service than that which is expected. The man who does this, in the right sort of mental attitude, is sure to make friends who will continue to patronize him out of choice. Moreover, his patrons will tell their friends about him, thereby putting the law of increasing returns into operation in his behalf.

The merchant may not be always in a position to put more merchandise in a package than the customer pays for, but he can wrap courteous service in the package and thereby build friendships that insure him continuous patronage.

The doctor, lawyer or other type of professional man may have no more ability in connection with his profession than his competitors possess, but he can master and apply the qualities of *attractive personality* and thereby build good will that binds his patrons to him.

I have heard that this quality of personality is the determining factor which influences a majority of the people who seek the services of either a lawyer or a doctor. Most people who employ either a doctor or a lawyer do so on the recommendation of an acquaintance, and the first thing they ask is not, "How much professional ability has he?" but, "What sort of a man is he?"

I have heard it said, too, that nine-tenths of those who buy life insurance policies never take the trouble to read their contracts. *What they really buy is the personality of the agent who sells the policy.* And I heard a very prosperous life insurance agent say that most of his sales were made through friendly introductions made by policy-holders to whom he had sold himself.

You see, good will and confidence are essentials of success in all walks of life. Without these one is forever confined to mediocrity. There is no better way of building these relationships than that of rendering more service and better service than that which is customary. This is one method of self-advancement which one may exercise on his own initiative, and generally speaking it is a form of service that can be rendered *during odd time which would be otherwise wasted.*

HILL: Mr. Carnegie, is your analysis of the habit of doing more than one is paid for based entirely upon your personal experience and your observation of the experience of others?

CARNEGIE: Not entirely. I have found supporting evidence of the soundness of this principle in nature. In fact, it appears that nature herself applies this principle.

Let me give you a few illustrations of what I mean:

First, we can see nature *Going the Extra Mile* by creating an over-abundance of blooms on the fruit trees. Here nature makes allowance for the emergencies of wind and storm through which many of the blooms will be destroyed.

Observe with what careful planning she provides for the fertilization of the blooms by painting them with attractive colors and filling them with sweet perfumes and nectar which attract the attention of the bees, whose services are needed to carry the fertilizing pollen from flower to flower. All this preparatory work is done by nature in advance of the benefits which result in the form of the fruit that the flowers are to produce.

Notice, in this elaborate set-up which nature has prepared to attract the bees, how cleverly she has arranged her plan so that the bees must render useful service before they can collect their pay.

Without this exchange of values between the flowers and the bees neither could exist. Thus we see here the perfect illustration of the soundness of the principle of doing more than one is paid for as a means of producing fruit and perpetuating the life of the bees.

HILL: I had never thought of nature as a teacher of the principle of doing more than is paid for, but I can see a perfect working example of this principle in the illustration you have given. Does nature use the same principle in other ways, Mr. Carnegie?

CARNEGIE: Indeed she does! Nature goes the extra mile in everything she does. When she creates frogs in the pond she does not stop by producing the minimum number needed to perpetuate the species, but she arranges for an over-production sufficient to provide for all emergencies.

She does the same with the fish in the sea, and the birds of the air, and with every form of vegetation that grows from the soil. Everywhere one looks one may see nature going the extra mile, through a system of production that provides for every circumstance essential for the perpetuation of her species.

In her clever scheme for the perpetuation of life she makes use of two natural laws with which every person should be familiar: the law of Compensation and the law of Increasing Returns.

Let us take farming as an example of how cleverly nature uses these two laws. You were reared on a farm. Therefore you will readily grasp and understand the illustration I have in mind. In order to produce the food he needs the farmer must adapt himself to the working principle of both the law of Compensation and the law of Increasing Returns. He must also apply the principle of *Going the Extra Mile,* whether he recognizes the full significance of what he does or not.

First, the farmer must clear the soil of trees and shrubs. Next, he must plow the soil and give it extra fertilization if needed. Then he must plant the soil with seed. He must mix intelligence with this labor by planting the seed at the right season of the year.

After these steps have been taken the farmer has gone as far as *he* can go in connection with the production of food from the soil. Here he must stop and wait for nature and time to do their work through germination and growth of the seed that produces the crop. Up to this point the farmer receives nothing for his labor, *having literally done more than he was paid for!*

If the farmer has performed his part of the labor intelligently nature will reward him, through the law of Compensation and the law of Increasing Returns, by giving back to him the seed he planted in the ground, plus a margin of many times the amount of seed he planted, as his reward for having done more than he was (temporarily) paid for.

HILL: What a clever alliance between the farmer and nature! Without this exchange of favors man, under our present form of civilization could not perpetuate himself, could he?

CARNEGIE: Now you have the idea. Nature provides for the perpetuation of all her living creatures of lower intelligence, through a system of food production which we call "wild growth," but study her system carefully, as in the example of the bee, and observe how inexorably she forces every living thing to labor in order to live, and notice particularly, that the labor must be delivered before the benefits are received.

Notice, too, that nature provides food for man, the same as she does for living things of a lower intelligence, through her system of "wild growth," as long as man remains a child of the jungle. But, she changes her system the moment man leaves the jungle life and becomes a part of civilization, and forces him to earn his right to the privileges of higher intelligence by producing his own food from the soil.

HILL: How perfectly simple are nature's plans, once we follow through, as you have done, and observe with what regularity nature applies principles you have described. I see, now, exactly what you mean by your reference to the law of Compensation. It appears that nature neither permits any living thing to get something for nothing nor allows any form of labor to be done without adequate reward. Moreover, nature tends to protect her creatures against destructive forces. Note how she heals man's wounds and restores the skin that is cut or torn away. Observe also how the injured tree heals over and seals the scar against further destruction.

CARNEGIE: You are beginning to discover where I get my authority for the strong emphasis I have placed on the habit of *Going the Extra Mile*. I get it from a source which cannot be questioned; no less an authority, in fact, than that which unfolds to us the plan by which all life on earth is perpetuated.

You see, therefore, why I said that the laws which make the principle of doing more than one is paid for operative, and essential to all who achieve outstanding success, *are not man-made laws*. I concede the truth of your statement that nature's plans which we are here discussing are simple, as far as the *effects* of these plans are concerned, but I would hardly apply the word "simple" as an explanation of the *cause* back of the plans.

That *cause* is as profound and imponderable as are all other natural laws through which this little world, and the universe of which it is an infinitesimal part, are harmoniously related and maintained with orderliness throughout time and space. Here we must be content to observe and comply with effects even though we do not understand the *cause* of those effects.

Of one thing we can, however, be very sure, and it is the fact that nature has provided definite laws to which man can adapt himself profitably in connection with the business of living, without the necessity of inquiring into the broader purpose of those laws. Two of these are the law of Compensation and the law of Increasing Returns, both of which provide a sound reason why we should render more service than we are paid for. We may observe this reason in the effects of these laws as nature herself applies them for the perpetuation of the species of living things.

HILL: From your description of the law of Compensation, I reach the conclusion that the term "Doing more than is paid for" is somewhat a misnomer in that it is impossible, in the broader meaning of this term, for one to do more than he is paid for. Is that your understanding, Mr. Carnegie?

CARNEGIE: I was waiting to see if you would grasp this point without my calling it to your attention! You are correct. All forms of constructive labor are rewarded, in one way or another, and in the broader sense there really is no such possibility as that of "Doing more than one is paid for."

Moreover, I wish to call attention to the great variety of ways in which man is compensated for *Going the Extra Mile*. Living creatures of a lower order than man (and even man himself, where he lives in the jungle, as one of nature's responsibilities) receive nothing from their labor except food and clothing necessary for existence. But man has been elevated to a position of power from which he commands and receives the bounties of the earth, in whatever forms and quantities he desires, for he has learned *the art of translating thought* into material things!

Let us state the case this way: Man is the Creator's greatest handiwork and has been given the privilege of self-determination. The very fact that man has control over his own thought-power is a profoundly significant fact. It connotes the power of thought to be man's greatest asset. The fact that thought is a man's gateway of voluntary approach to the source of Infinite Intelligence is definite evidence of its importance.

Now let us see what specific benefits are available to man (through his exalted powers of thought and speech) which compensate him for *Going the Extra Mile*. The more useful of these compensating advantages are these:

SOME ADVANTAGES OF DOING MORE THAN ONE IS PAID FOR

1. The *habit* of *Going the Extra Mile* gives one the benefit of the law of Increasing Returns, in a variety of ways too numerous to be described here.

2. This habit places one in a position to benefit by the law of Compensation, through which no act or deed will or can be expressed without an equivalent response (after its own nature).

3. It gives one the benefit of growth through resistance and use, thereby leading to mental development and increased skill in the use of the body. (It is a well-known fact that both body and mind attain efficiency and skill through systematic discipline

and use which call for the rendering of service that temporarily is not paid for.)

4. The habit develops the important factor of initiative, without which no individual ever rises above mediocrity in any calling.

5. It develops self-reliance, which is likewise an essential in all forms of personal achievement.

6. It enables an individual to profit by the law of contrast, since obviously a majority of the people do not follow the habit of doing more than they are paid for. On the contrary, they endeavor to "get by" with a minimum amount of service.

7. It helps one to master the habit of drifting aimlessly, thereby checking the habit which stands at the head of the major causes of failure.

8. It definitely aids in development of the habit of Definiteness of Purpose, which is the first principle of individual achievement.

9. It tends strongly to aid in the development of Attractiveness of Personality, thereby leading to the means by which one may relate himself to others so as to gain their friendly cooperation.

10. It often gives an individual a preferred position of relationship with others through which he may become indispensable, thereby fixing his own price on his services.

11. It insures continuous employment, thereby serving as insurance against want in connection with the necessities of life.

12. It is the greatest of all the known methods by which the man who works for wages may promote himself to higher positions and better wages, and serves as a practical means by which a man may attain the position of ownership of a business or industry.

13. It develops alertness of the imagination, the faculty through which one may create practical plans for the attainment of one's aims and purposes in any calling.

14. It develops a positive "mental attitude," which is one of

the more important qualities that are essential in all human relationships.

15. It serves to build the confidence of others in one's integrity and general ability, which is an indispensable essential for noteworthy achievement in every calling.

16. Finally, it is a habit which one may adopt and follow on his own initiative, without being under the necessity of asking the permission of anyone to do so.

Compare these sixteen definite advantages that are available to man, in return for doing more than he is paid for, with the one sole benefit (that of acquiring food necessary for existence) that is available to the other creatures of the earth through the same habit, and you will be forced to the conclusion that overwhelmingly the greater number of benefits enjoyed by man serve as adequate compensation for his development and use of this habit. This comparison substantiates your statement that it is an impossibility for one to do more than one is paid for, and for the very obvious reason that *in the mere act of doing* that which is constructive *one acquires power* that can be converted into whatever one desires.

This analysis gives greater meaning to Emerson's statement, "Do the thing and you shall have the power."

This is the idea you should emphasize throughout the philosophy of individual achievement. No one who follows this analysis carefully can help discovering the truth that it is impossible for one to do more than one is paid for. The pay consists in the self-discipline and self-development one attains through the rendering of service, as well as in the material effects of the service, in the form of economic compensation.

HILL: Your analysis of the habit of doing more than one is paid for suggests that this habit is one of the "musts" of the philosophy of individual achievement.

Will you describe some of the definite circumstances in your own business experience through which you have profited by the habit, Mr. Carnegie?

CARNEGIE: You have given me a big order. First, let me give you a blanket answer by saying that all the material riches

I possess, and every business advantage I enjoy, might be attributable to my having followed this habit. But I will give you one specific example of an experience which gave me one of the greatest opportunities to promote myself that I ever enjoyed. I mention this particular experience because it was one of the most dramatic of my life, and I might add that it carried with it one of the *greatest risks* that I ever assumed in order to *Go the Extra Mile*. The risk was of that type which one should never assume unless he knows he is making the right move, and even then it is the sort of risk which might be fatal to one's opportunities for self-promotion under most circumstances.

When I was a very young lad I studied telegraphy at night and learned to operate a telegraph key efficiently. (I was not paid to do this, nor did anyone tell me to do it.) I was rewarded for my labor, however, by attracting the attention of Thomas Scott, division superintendent of the Pennsylvania Railroad, in Pittsburgh, who gave me the position as his private operator and clerk.

One morning I arrived at the office ahead of everyone else, and discovered that a bad train wreck had tied up the line and the whole division was in a jam.

The dispatcher was frantically calling Mr. Scott's office when I walked in, so I took the key and found out quickly what had happened. I tried to reach Mr. Scott by telephone, but his wife reported that he had left home. So, there I was, sitting on top of a veritable volcano that was sure to explode and ruin my chances with the Pennsylvania Railroad forever if I made the wrong move, and it might do the same thing *if I made no move at all.*

I knew precisely what my chief would have done had he been there, and also knew well enough what he might do to me if I assumed the risk of acting for him in such an important emergency. But time was important, so I took the plunge and sent out the train orders in his name that re-routed traffic and untied the traffic snarl.

When my chief arrived at the office he found a written report of what I had done, with my resignation attached to it, on his desk. I had violated one of the strictest rules of the railroad, so I made it easy for my chief to save face with his superiors by placing my own head on the block.

About two hours later I received the verdict. My resignation came back to me with the words, "Resignation refused," boldly written across it in the chief's handwriting. He made no further reference to the circumstance until several days later, and even then he brought the subject up, discussed it in his own way, and dismissed it without either reprimanding me or giving me a clean bill of health for my violation of the rules.

He simply said: "There are two types of men who never get far in life. One is the type that cannot do what he is told, and the other is the type that can do nothing else." Here the subject was dismissed with an air of finality which enabled me to determine to which of these types he believed I belonged.

It should be the aim of every young man to go beyond the sphere of his immediate instructions and render service that is not required of him, but one should be extremely cautious in assuming such risks beyond the letter of his instructions as I did on this occasion. Above all, he must know that he is making the right move, but even then he may at times run into difficulty.

A young man who worked as confidential secretary to a New York broker lost his job by mixing bad judgment with his well-meant exercise of the habit of going beyond the letter of his instructions. His chief went away for a vacation and left him in charge of certain funds which he was to invest in the stock market, at a definite time and in a definite manner. Instead of following his instructions, he invested the funds in an entirely different manner. The transaction yielded a much greater profit than would have been received had the employer's instructions been carried out, but the employer took the view that the young man's violation of specific instructions clearly marked him as one who lacked sound judgment, and reasoned that he might violate his instructions again some time, under circumstances that would be disastrous. The result was a discharge.

So, I repeat, with emphasis, be sure you are right before breaking rules in order to do more than you are paid for, and be sure of your relationship with the man who may swing the axe above your neck for doing so. There is no quality that can take the place of sound, *well-balanced judgment.* Be active, be persistent, be definite, but also *be cautious in your judgment.*

If I had to deal with the same emergency again I would handle it exactly as I did. The man who cannot deal with emergencies with sound judgment never can become indispensable in any business, as business cannot be operated successfully on unbreakable rules. The rub comes in knowing *when to break them.*

Make yourself indispensable in your job and see how quickly you are pushed out of it into a better one.

Chapter Six

Use Organized Individual Endeavor

This chapter begins the analysis of one of the distinguishing features of all successful leaders. This quality is also a distinguishing feature of Americanism, so important that it has been guaranteed to every American citizen, in the Constitution of the United States.

It is the privilege of individual initiative, a quality that is no less essential in the achievement of personal success than that of Definiteness of Purpose.

Without doubt the *privilege of exercising one's own initiative* is the very last that any ambitious American would wish to give up, for it is obvious that without this privilege noteworthy achievement is an impossibility in any calling.

We, the people of the United States, have set the whole world a worthy example in the exercise of our personal initiative in the field of industry and commerce and in the professions. To this one quality, more perhaps than to any other, we owe our right to claim this to be "the richest and the freest" country of the world.

The subject of *Organized Individual Endeavor,* as presented in this chapter, describes the methods by which an individual may make purposeful and profitable use of his right to and responsibility for the exercise of personal initiative. No privilege is of benefit if one sleeps upon it. No privilege can be of great benefit to anyone unless it is organized into a definite plan and put into action.

Andrew Carnegie describes the methods through which personal initiative can be *organized* and used for the attainment of definite ends.

HILL: You have stated, Mr. Carnegie, that *Organized Individual Endeavor* is the sixth of the 17 principles of individual achievement. Will you analyze this principle in its relationship to personal achievement?

CARNEGIE: Very well, let us begin by saying that personal initiative may be likened to the steam in the boiler in this respect: It is the power through which one's plans, aims and purposes are put into action! It is the antithesis of one of the worst of all human traits, *procrastination.*

Successful men are known, always, as men of action! There can be no action without the exercise of one's initiative. There are two forms of action, namely (1) that which one indulges in from the force of necessity and (2) that which one exercises out of choice, on his own free will. Leadership grows out of the latter. It comes as the result of action in which one engages in response to his own motives and desires.

HILL: Would you say that the right of individual initiative is among the greatest of the privileges we enjoy as citizens of the United States?

CARNEGIE: It is not merely among the greatest; it is the greatest! This privilege was considered of such great importance that it was specifically guaranteed in the Constitution to every citizen of the United States. The privilege of exercising one's personal initiative is of such great importance that every well-managed business recognizes and properly rewards individuals who show aptitude in the use of their own initiative for the betterment of the business.

It is through the exercise of personal initiative that the most humble worker may become an indispensable factor in any business. It is through the exercise of this privilege that the humblest day laborer may become the owner of the business in which he works, or raise himself to the ownership of a business of his own.

HILL: From what you say I take it that you believe the privilege of acting on one's own initiative is the stepping stone of major importance in all individual achievement.

CARNEGIE: I have never known of anyone achieving outstanding success without acting on his own initiative. Under our form of government and our industrial system every man is rewarded according to the service he renders through his own initiative. No one is forced to do anything against his will. But the American way of life is such that it encourages everyone to promote himself through his own efforts into whatever station in life he wishes. Those who organize their efforts naturally get ahead faster than those who drift, without definite aim or purpose.

HILL: There must be certain definite characteristics of leadership which the more successful leaders develop and apply. Will you give me a catalogue of such traits as you believe to be essential for leadership?

CARNEGIE: From my own experience with men I have observed that successful leaders in all walks of life exemplify one or more of thirty or more traits of leadership, and in some instances they possess all of these traits:

1. The adoption of a Definite Major Purpose and a definite plan for attaining it.

2. The choice of a motive adequate to inspire continuous action in pursuit of the object of one's major purpose. Nothing great is ever achieved without a definite motive.

3. A Master Mind alliance through which to acquire the necessary power for noteworthy achievement. That which one man can accomplish by his own efforts is negligible, confined in the main to the acquisition of the bare necessities of life. Great achievement always is the result of coordination of minds working toward a definite end.

4. Self-reliance in proportion to the nature and scope of one's major purpose. No one can go very far without relying largely upon his own efforts, his own initiative, his own judgment.

5. Self-discipline sufficient to give one mastery over both the head and the heart. The man who cannot or will not control himself never can control others. *There are no exceptions to this rule.* This is so important that it should probably have headed the entire list of the essentials of leadership.

6. Persistence, based on a will to win. Most men are

good starters but poor finishers. The man who gives up at the first signs of opposition never goes very far in any undertaking.

7. A well-developed faculty of imagination. Able leaders must be eternally seeking new and better ways of doing things. They must be on the lookout for new ideas and new opportunities to attain the object of their labors. The man who trails along in the old path, doing things merely because others have done them, without looking for methods of improvements, never becomes a great leader.

8. The habit of making definite and prompt decisions at all times. The man who cannot or will not make up his own mind has little opportunity to induce others to follow him.

9. The habit of basing opinions on known facts instead of relying upon guesswork or hearsay evidence. Able leaders take nothing for granted without a sound reason. They make it their business to get at the facts before forming judgments, but they move promptly and definitely.

10. The capacity to generate enthusiasm at will and direct it to a definite end. Uncontrolled enthusiasm may be as detrimental as no enthusiasm. Moreover, enthusiasm is contagious, as is also lack of enthusiasm. Followers and subordinates take on the enthusiasm of their leader.

11. A keen sense of fairness and justice under all circumstances. The habit of "playing favorites" is destructive to leadership. Men respond best to those who deal with them justly, and especially where they are dealt with fairly by men in higher positions of authority.

12. Tolerance (an open mind) on all subjects at all times. The man with a closed mind does not inspire the confidence of his associates. Without confidence great leadership is an impossibility.

13. The habit of *Going the Extra Mile*—(doing more than one is paid for and doing it with a positive, agreeable "mental attitude.") This habit on the part of a leader inspires unselfishness on the part of his followers or subordinates. I have never known an able leader in business or industry who did not endeavor

at all times to render more service than any man under his authority.

14. Tactfulness and a keen sense of diplomacy, both in spirit and in deed. In a free democracy such as ours, men do not take kindly to brusqueness in their relationships with others.

15. The habit of *listening much* and *talking little*. Most people talk too much and say too little. The leader who knows his business knows the value of hearing other men's views. Perhaps we are equipped with two ears, two eyes and only one tongue that we may hear and see twice as much as we speak.

16. An observing nature. The habit of noting small details. All business is a composite of details. The man who does not become familiar with all the details of the work for which he and his subordinates are responsible will not be a successful leader. Moreover, a knowledge of small details is essential for promotion.

17. Determination. Recognition of the fact that temporary defeat need not be accepted as permanent failure. All men occasionally meet with defeat, in one form or another. The successful leader learns from defeat, but he never uses it as an excuse for not trying again. *The ability to accept and carry responsibilities* is among the more profitable of accomplishments. It is the major need of all industry and business. It pays higher dividends when one assumes responsibility without being required to do so.

18. The capacity to stand criticism without resentment. The man who "flares" up with resentment when his work is criticized will never become a successful leader. Real leaders can "take it" and they make it their business to do so. Bigness overlooks the smallness of criticism and carries on.

19. Temperance in eating, drinking, and all social habits. The man who has no control over his appetites will have very little control over other people.

20. Loyalty to all to whom loyalty is due. Loyalty begins with loyalty to one's self. It extends to one's associates in business. Dis-

loyalty breeds contempt. No one can succeed who *"bites the hand that feeds him."*

21. Frankness with those who have a right to it. Subterfuge which misleads is a poor crutch to lean upon, and it is one that able leaders do not use.

22. Familiarity with the nine basic motives which actuate men. (Already discussed in Lesson Two, these motives are re-listed here for review: Emotion of love, emotion of sex, desire for financial gain, desire for self-preservation, desire for freedom of body and mind, desire for self-expression, desire for perpetuation of life after death, emotion of anger, and emotion of fear.) The man who does not understand the natural motives to which men respond will not be a successful leader.

23. Sufficient attractiveness of personality to induce voluntary cooperation from others. (See the list of the factors of Attractive Personality in Lesson Three.) Sound leadership is based upon effective salesmanship, the ability to be sympathetic and to make one's self pleasing to others.

24. The capacity to concentrate full attention on one subject at a time. The jack of all trades is seldom good at any. Concentrated effort gives one power that can be attained in no other way.

25. The habit of learning from mistakes—one's own and the mistakes of others.

26. Willingness to accept the full responsibility of the mistakes of one's subordinates without trying to "pass the buck." Nothing destroys one's capacity of leadership quicker than the habit of shifting responsibilities to others.

27. The habit of *adequately* recognizing the merits of others, especially when they have done exceptionally good work. Men will often work harder for friendly recognition of their merits than they will for money alone. The successful leader goes out of his way to give credit to his subordinates. A pat on the back denotes confidence.

28. The habit of applying the Golden Rule principle in all human relationships. The Sermon On the Mount remains a classic

for all time, as a sound rule of human relationship. It inspires cooperation that can be had in no other way.

29. A positive "mental attitude" at all times. No one likes a "grouchy," skeptical person who seems to be at outs with the world in general. Such a man will never become an able leader.

30. The habit of assuming full responsibility for each and every task one undertakes, regardless of who actually does the work. Perhaps this quality of leadership should have headed the entire list, and it would have if the qualities of successful leadership had been listed in the order of their importance.

31. A keen sense of values. The ability to evaluate in the light of sound judgment without being guided by emotional factors. The habit of putting first things first.

All these qualities of leadership are capable of development and application by any person of average intelligence.

HILL: From your analysis of the qualities of leadership, it appears that successful leadership is largely a state of mind or mental attitude.

CARNEGIE: Leadership is not entirely a question of the proper mental attitude, although that is an important factor. The successful leader must possess definite knowledge of his life's purpose and work. Men do not like to follow a leader who obviously knows less about his job than they do.

HILL: Are all men capable of becoming successful leaders?

CARNEGIE: Not by any means! You would be surprised to know how few men there are who aspire to become leaders. Most men do not wish to assume the responsibilities of leadership. Others lack the ambition to put forth the extra effort that must go into successful leadership.

HILL: What is the best method for inspiring men to become leaders in their chosen occupations?

CARNEGIE: As I have already stated, men do things because of a motive. Leadership can best be inspired by planting in a man's mind a definite motive that forces him to acquire the qualities of leadership. The profit motive is one of the most popular. When men make up their minds to acquire wealth or attain success, they usually begin to exercise their privileges of personal initiative along lines that develop leadership.

HILL: Then you believe it would be inadvisable to discourage the desire for personal wealth?

CARNEGIE: Let me answer you in this way: This country is recognized the world over as having more leaders in industry and business than any other nation. These leaders developed their qualities of leadership in response to their desire for wealth. Obviously anything which kills off this desire would strike at the very roots of our national resources, *a major portion of which consists of the creative ability of the men who manage industry.*

HILL: Would you say that the desire for private riches is the only motive that has inspired so many Americans to develop the qualities of leadership?

CARNEGIE: Not at all. We have many able leaders in America whose major motive is that of building and creating. The pride of personal achievement is a strong factor in the American way of life. Beyond the point at which a man acquires economic security, he begins to become motivated largely by his pride of achievement.

One man can eat only one meal at a time, wear one suit of clothes at a time, and sleep in one bed. After he acquires security in connection with these necessities, he begins to think in terms of desire for public acclaim. He wishes to become recognized as a successful person.

There may be a few men with the hoarding instinct of the miser; but a majority of the successful men of America think in terms of the use they can give money instead of endeavoring to accumulate money for the sake of having it. It has been this desire for self-expression, through the use of money, that has made America the great industrial nation that it is.

HILL: I take it then that the possession of great riches by one individual may be either a blessing or a curse, according to the use he makes of his riches.

CARNEGIE: That is my belief, precisely. Take John D.

Rockefeller as an example. He has accumulated a vast fortune, but every dollar of it is at work, developing, extending, expanding some form of useful industrial, business, or philanthropic service. Through the use of his money, he provides employment to many thousands of men. But it serves a still higher purpose.

Through the Rockefeller Foundation the Rockefeller fortune is serving mankind in scores of ways that have nothing whatsoever to do with further profits for Mr. Rockefeller. His fortune is fighting disease and helping to suppress the enemies of mankind in other ways. It is helping to uncover useful knowledge through scientific research, the benefits of which will extend to generations yet unborn.

HILL: Then you would say that the people of America are better off because of the manner in which Mr. Rockefeller has exercised his personal initiative in the accumulation of riches?

CARNEGIE: Not only the people of the United States, but the people of the entire world are benefiting by his initiative and his acquisitive spirit. What this country needs is not fewer men like Mr. Rockefeller, but more of his type.

Take James J. Hill as another example. Through his personal initiative, he built the great transcontinental railroad system that opened up millions of acres of unused lands and brought the Atlantic and the Pacific Oceans within easily accessible proximity to each other.

It would be difficult to estimate the wealth which—by the exercise of his personal initiative—this one man has added to the riches of America. It probably amounts to billions of dollars. The private fortune he accumulated for his services is as nothing compared to the wealth his activities added to the nation as a whole.

HILL: You might include yourself in that category also, Mr. Carnegie. Would you mind estimating the wealth your own personal initiative has added to the country?

CARNEGIE: I much prefer to speak of the achievements of others who have done more than I. But if you insist on an answer, let me call your attention to the impetus that has been given to the building of skyscrapers since my associates uncovered more economical and better methods of producing steel.

You know, of course, that the modern skyscraper would be an impossibility without the use of the steel frame. The skyscraper would also be an economic impossibility if steel were as expensive as it was when I entered the business of manufacturing steel. We have given the country a better product than any it knew before we entered the business of making steel, and we have brought prices down to where steel can be substituted for the less satisfactory products of wood and other metals of less durability.

When I first entered the steel business, steel—such as it was —sold for around $130.00 per ton. We brought it down to around $20.00 per ton. Moreover, we so improved the quality that steel now serves scores of uses for which it was not suited until we improved it.

HILL: Was your major motive that of making money, Mr. Carnegie?

CARNEGIE: *No, my major motive always has been that of making men more useful to themselves and to others!*

As you may have heard, I have had the privilege of making millionaires of more than forty men, most of them men who began working with me as ordinary laborers. But the money these men accumulated is not the important thing I wish to stress. In helping them to accumulate money, I helped them to become a great asset to this nation. By inspiring them to exercise their own initiative, I started them to rendering useful service that has contributed richly to the development of the great industrial system of America.

You see, therefore, that these men became more than owners of riches; they became intelligent users of riches, and as such they provided employment for many thousands of men.

As I have already mentioned, wealth consists in material things and human experience properly mixed. The more important part of the mixture is brains, experience, personal initiative, the desire to build and create. Without these qualities money would be useless. Understand this truth and you will have a better knowledge of the nature of our American riches. We are a rich nation because we have a great number of pioneers whose pride of personal achievement has enticed them to exercise their right of individual initiative in all forms of business and industrial activity.

These men may think they were motivated by the desire for personal riches, but the truth is that they were influenced by the much greater desire for personal achievement. Regardless of the motives by which they were actuated, they have helped to convert a vast wilderness known formerly as the "land of the Indians" into the world's richest and most progressive nation. This could not have been accomplished without the free, voluntary exercise of the personal initiative of the men who did the job.

HILL: What part has the American form of government served in the development of American industry, Mr. Carnegie?

CARNEGIE: A very necessary part, indeed. If you will read the Declaration of Independence and the Constitution of the United States, you will see clearly that the men who wrote those profound documents clearly intended to surround the people of America with every conceivable right and opportunity for the free exercise of personal initiative. Under no other form of government do men receive such definite encouragement to exercise their personal initiative.

HILL: Then you see no reason for changing our form of government?

CARNEGIE: Not unless we find still better ways of influencing men to take possession of their own minds and use their abilities on their own initiative. Our form of government is not perfect, but it is the best the world has yet discovered. It provides far greater liberties and privileges of the use of personal initiative than the majority of men are using intelligently.

Why change it until the people of America catch up with it by using the opportunities it provides? Tinkering with things that serve satisfactorily is one trait that gets men into difficulty. This is one form of personal initiative that should be discouraged. It comes under the heading of "meddlesome curiosity." If a man has good health he should go about his business and not interfere with nature by experimenting with cures of diseases with which he does not suffer.

However, there are some who do not follow this rule. They are known as hypochondriacs, and they are always suffering with imaginary illness. We are in a healthy economic condition in this country. We have vastly greater undeveloped resources than any we are using. Let us not experiment with our economic system, but rather let us make more intelligent use of our present system, to the end that we may make better uses of our great resources.

Nations that are always experimenting with their systems of government and their economic systems are engaged in revolutions and counter-revolutions most of their time. No small part of our success here in America is due to the spirit of harmonious relationship existing between the States of the Union. That harmony is the direct result of our form of government which wisely provides an incentive for harmony among the people. In union there is strength. This is true of business and industrial groups the same as it is in the relationship between the States.

HILL: What do you believe to be the greatest possible evil that might curtail the success of the American people as a whole?

CARNEGIE: Anything, that would weaken the spirit of harmony between the people. *Our unity of purpose is our greatest national asset.* It is vastly more important than all our natural resources, for without this we would become the victims of any greedy nation that might wish to take our natural resources away from us.

We fought a tragic war among our own people to maintain our national unity. While memories of this war linger in the minds of some, now we all recognize that a separation of the States would have meant the beginning of our disintegration. And I might well add that the greatest evil that can overtake an industry or a business is that which disturbs the harmonious working relationship between those engaged in it. Business succeeds through the friendly cooperation of those engaged in it. Personal initiative is a power for good only when men combine their experience and ability and work toward a common end in a spirit of harmony and understanding.

HILL: Then you do not look with favor on those who make it their business to stir up strife, hatred, and envy among men who are engaged in the operation of the American industrial system?

CARNEGIE: No, this is a form of personal initiative which may help some; but it destroys the rights of many. In our own industry I have never had any misunderstanding with those who work for me except that which was inspired by professional agitators who profit by disturbing human relationships. That is the worst of all forms of personal initiative.

How could I have had any misunderstanding with men who, down to the humblest worker, knew that the door of opportunity was wide open day and night to those who wished to earn more by making themselves worth more? The man who helps wage earners to rise from day labor to become millionaires, as I have done whenever I had the opportunity, is not likely to have any misunderstanding with his men if he is left alone to deal with them on the basis of free enterprise.

HILL: But, Mr. Carnegie, are there not some employers who do not take such a constructive attitude regarding their relationship with their employees? Are there not some employers who greedily clamor for more than their share of what their business produces?

CARNEGIE: Yes, there are some such. There always have been. There will always be men of greed. But they do not last. Competition soon eliminates them. That is one of the benefits of the system of free enterprise under which we operate in America. Here an employer must make good or make room, and he cannot make good at the expense of his employees. His competitors see to that!

HILL: When and under what circumstances should one begin to exercise personal initiative? Is there not such a thing as favorable circumstances under which one may exercise initiative profitably, exactly right, while other circumstances make it advisable for one to remain inactive?

CARNEGIE: The time to begin using personal initiative is immediately following one's definite decision as to what one wishes to accomplish. The time to begin is right then.

If the plan chosen turns out to be weak, it can be changed for a better one; but any sort of plan is better than procrastination. The universal evil of the world is procrastination—the terrible habit people have of waiting for the time to begin something to be "just right." It causes more failures than all the weak plans of the world.

HILL: But, shouldn't one consult others and get their opinions before beginning important plans?

CARNEGIE: "Opinions" are like the sands of the desert, and most of them are about as slippery. Everyone has an opinion about practically everything, but most of them are unworthy of trust. The man who hesitates because he wants the opinion of others before he begins to exercise his personal initiative usually winds up by doing nothing.

Of course there are exceptions to this rule. There are times when the counsel and advice of others are absolutely essential for success; but if you refer to idle opinions of bystanders, let them alone. Avoid them as you would an epidemic of disease, for that is exactly what idle opinions are—a disease! Everyone has a flock of them, and most people hand them out freely, without being asked.

If you want an opinion on which you can rely, consult the man who is known to be an authority on the subject in connection with which you seek an opinion. Pay him for his counsel, but avoid "free opinions" because they are generally worth exactly what one pays for them.

I recall, quite clearly, what some acquaintances of mine said when they heard I was planning to cut the price of steel to twenty dollars a ton. "He'll go broke," they shouted! They gave me free advice without my seeking it. I passed it by, and went ahead with my plans. Steel came down to twenty dollars a ton.

When Henry Ford announced he would give the people a dependable automobile for less than a thousand dollars, they shouted, "He'll go broke;" but Ford went ahead with his plans, and one day he will be the dominating factor in one of America's greatest industries. *And he'll not go broke!*

When Columbus announced that he would sail his little boats across an uncharted ocean and discover a new route to India, the Doubting Thomases cried out, "He's crazy! He'll never come back." But he did come back.

When Copernicus announced he had invented an instrument with which he had revealed hidden worlds never before seen by the human eye, these same "free opinion" fellows hooted "heretic; put him to the torch!" They actually wanted to burn him for daring to use his own initiative.

When Alexander Graham Bell announced he had invented a telephone with which people could talk to one another at long distance, by the use of wires, the unbelievers yelled, "Poor Alex has gone crazy!" But Bell went ahead with his idea and perfected it, although the time did not appear to be "just right."

And you'll have your turn with these "free opinion" boys who spend their time trying to discourage men from using their own initiative. You'll hear them cry out, "He can't do it! He can't give the world a philosophy of individual achievement because no one has ever done it before." But, if you take my advice, you will go right ahead and back your judgment on your own initiative.

When you succeed, as succeed you will, the world will crown you with glory and lay its treasures at your feet; but not until you have taken the risk and have proved your ideas sound. Don't become discouraged because other people may tell you "the time is not right." The time is always right for the man who knows what he wants and goes to work to get it.

The world needs a philosophy of individual achievement. It has always needed such a philosophy. Go ahead and supply that need, no matter how long it takes, or what sacrifices you may have to make to do the job.

Do the job the best you can and you'll learn, from first-hand experience, that these calamity howlers are nothing but a bunch of disappointed human beings who are suffering with an inferiority complex because they have neglected to use their own initiative.

HILL: That was quite a speech, Mr. Carnegie, and I take it for granted that you meant it mostly for me.

CARNEGIE: Yes, I meant it for you, and through your efforts I hope it will serve the yet unborn generations, long after I shall have passed on. The world needs men who have the courage to act on their own initiative. Moreover, men of this type write their own price tag and the world willingly pays it. The world willingly rewards men of initiative.

The privilege of personal initiative is an important part of the American way of life, but the privilege is worth nothing if it is not exercised. What we need most here in the United States is a continuous sales campaign for the sole purpose of keeping the American people inspired with a desire to take advantage of the opportunities available for the accumulation of riches. The government should conduct a continuous campaign designed entirely to bring to the attention of the people the nature and scope of the opportunities available to them.

HILL: Then you believe there are still enough opportunities for individual success, in the United States, to go around to all the people?

CARNEGIE: Yes, there is an opportunity to match the *ambition* and the *ability* of every person in the United States. But opportunity will not hunt the man. The order must be reversed through *Organized Individual Endeavor*. The greatest opportunities will be available to those who are the most capable of organizing and directing their own efforts.

HILL: Some may not understand what is meant by the term *"Organized Individual Endeavor."* Would you define your understanding of this principle?

CARNEGIE: The principle of *Organized Individual Endeavor* consists of very definite procedure through which an individual may promote himself into whatever station he desires, or acquire whatever material things he wishes. The steps to be taken are these:

(a) Choice of a definite purpose or objective.
(b) Creation of a plan for the attainment of the objective.
(c) Continuous action in carrying out the plan.
(d) Alliance with those who will cooperate in carrying out the plan.
(e) Moving, at all times, on one's own initiative.

Organized Individual Endeavor might be briefly described as *"planned action."* Any action based on a definite plan has a better chance of success than effort of an unorganized, haphazard nature, such as that in which the majority of people engage. Able leadership, without *Organized Individual Endeavor,* is an impossibility. The two major points of difference between a leader and a follower are these: (1) the leader carefully plans his efforts, and (2) he moves on his own initiative, without being told to do so.

If you wish to find a potential leader, look around until you find a man who makes his own decisions, plans his own work, and carries out his plans on his own initiative. In such a man you will see the major requirements for leadership. This is the type of man who pioneered in American industry, and to him we owe the credit for the great American industrial system which is the envy of the world.

HILL: What about the quality of genius? Aren't the leaders in industry and business blessed with some form of genius which most people do not possess, Mr. Carnegie?

CARNEGIE: Now you are talking about a fallacy that has deceived more people than any other mistaken idea. The word "genius" is badly overworked. It is generally used to explain successful achievement because most people do not take the time to dig in and find out how men succeed.

Personally I do not know what a genius is. *I have never seen one!* But I have seen many successful men who are called geniuses. Analysis of the cause of their success would show that they are only average men who have discovered and applied certain rules which enabled them to get from where they started to where they wished to go.

Every normal person has within him the potentiality of that

which we call "genius," in one field of endeavor or another, depending upon the individual's preferences, his inborn traits of character, and his ambition. I would say that the nearest quality to genius that I could describe is an obsessional desire to do some one thing and do it well, plus the willingness to act on one's own initiative. From this point on, genius is only a matter of *Organized Individual Endeavor* persistently carried out.

The man who knows precisely what he wants and is determined to get it is about the nearest approach to that which some call "genius" that I can think of. Such a man has better than an average chance of success, and when he achieves success the world is apt to look at him in the hour of triumph and attribute his achievements to what they believe to be genius.

HILL: But, Mr. Carnegie, doesn't the question of education enter into one's personal achievements? Isn't it true that the educated man has a better chance of success than the man who lacks education?

CARNEGIE: Many men are schooled, but few men are educated. An educated man is one who has learned how to use his mind so that he can get everything he desires without violating the rights of others. Education, therefore, comes from experience and use of the mind, and not merely from the acquisition of knowledge. Knowledge is of no value unless and until it is expressed in some form of useful service. Here is where the subject of personal initiative begins to prove its importance as an essential of success.

To answer your question more specifically, an educated man has a better chance of success than one who is not educated only in the event that he applies his education in the achievement of some definite objective. All too often men rely upon their possession of knowledge to take the place of *Organized Individual Endeavor.* They expect to be paid for that which they know instead of that which they do with their knowledge. This point is important.

I have heard it said that some successful business men hesitate to employ men who have just graduated from college, for the reason that many college graduates "have too much they must unlearn" before they become useful in the practical affairs of business.

Speaking for myself, I would much prefer college-trained men for positions of responsibility, but I prefer them to come to me with an open mind, seeking more knowledge. I prefer those who have a sound knowledge of fundamentals rather than the tricks of the trade. I prefer those who know the difference between theory and practice.

There is one great advantage that most college graduates have over those who lack this training, and it is the fact that college training helps one to organize his knowledge. Disorganized knowledge is of very little value.

HILL: Do you believe that alertness in the application of individual initiative is an inborn trait? That one has it, or doesn't have it, according to the nature of his hereditary gifts?

CARNEGIE: My observation of people has forced me to the conclusion that personal initiative is largely based on personal desires and ambitions. The man who appears to have no individual initiative, awakens and moves under his own initiative in a hurry when he becomes obsessed with some definite strong desire or purpose.

HILL: Would you say, then, that personal desire is the beginning of all individual achievements?

CARNEGIE: Yes, without a doubt! Definiteness of Purpose is the result of desire. When a man's desires take on the proportion of an obsession, he usually begins to translate them into their physical equivalent through Definiteness of Purpose. Desire, therefore, is the starting point of all individual accomplishments.

As far as I know, there is no impelling motive other than desire which inspires a man to move on his own initiative.

Herein lies the secret of the influence some wives have over their husbands. When a man's wife desires riches or success, she may transplant that desire in the mind of her husband and cause him to move on it in a way that will enable him to succeed.

I have often known of this happening. But, in the last analysis, the desire for riches or success must become a definite motive on the part of the husband. The presence of a deeply seated desire in a man's mind has a tendency to stir him into action as nothing else can do.

HILL: Then you believe it is true, as one philosopher expressed it, that men's faults consist in low aim and not in the stars?

CARNEGIE: There is nothing that will take the place of high aim! When a man sets his mind upon the achievement of a definite purpose, the powers of the universe appear to be on his side. He begins to make use of every available means to attain the object of his desires. The first thing that comes to his aid is his right to the exercise of individual initiative. Personal desires can be attained only by the exercise of personal initiative. If initiative takes on the form of Organized Individual Endeavor, one's chances of success are greatly multiplied.

When you analyze individual achievement in this manner, you learn quickly enough that no great achievement is possible without the application of *Organized Individual Endeavor*. The use of this principle for the attainment of one's desires is not optional. *It is imperative!*

HILL: From your analysis of *Organized Individual Endeavor*, I assume that this principle can be applied by the man with little schooling as well as by the man with extensive schooling; that it is not essentially a part of one's education in the popular interpretation of the meaning of the word "education."

CARNEGIE: Lest you become confused on this point, let me make it clear that no man is educated, in the true meaning of that term, until he acquires a practical working knowledge of the principle of *Organized Individual Endeavor*. Moving in an orderly, well-organized manner, toward a definite end is precisely the procedure of an educated person. Go back to the definition of the word "education," and study it carefully. You will observe that the application of education leaves no alternative other than that of action based on *Organized Individual Endeavor*. You might properly say that *Organized Individual Endeavor is education*.

HILL: Mr. Carnegie, you said that the right time to begin a

thing is when one makes up his mind to do it. Now there must be some plan by which the public schools can be influenced to teach the Philosophy of American Achievement as soon as it has been published in textbook form. Therefore, I would like to know how you would go about introducing the philosophy in the public schools.

CARNEGIE: You have asked me to plan a job that will require many years for its completion, and many steps will have to be taken by you before the job is finished. Speaking in general terms, here is about the way you should proceed:

First, you will have to publish the philosophy in popular text-book style and introduce it through individuals who desire to get ahead by the application of definite rules. If you are fortunate enough to find a publisher who will push the sale of your books, you will be able to do a pretty good job of distribution within from three to five years.

Second, you should begin training lecturers who will be able to teach the philosophy, so that when the time comes you can supply the public schools with teachers. Meanwhile, before the public schools are ready for them these lecturers can make a good living by organizing private classes.

Third, you should organize your own private school for the purpose of teaching the philosophy by the home-study method, thereby placing yourself in a position to reach men and women in all parts of the country who want the philosophy.

Fourth, you should have your publisher arrange for the translation of the philosophy into foreign languages, so it will be available to the mixed population of the United States who do not speak the English language. They need such a lesson in American-ism. This plan will also provide you with the means of spreading the philosophy in foreign countries.

By the time you will have taken these steps, the general public will have become so success-philosophy "conscious" that the public schools will become attracted to it. The time required to bring all this about may be as much as ten years, depending, of course, upon what sort of a leader you prove yourself to be.

HILL: In other words, it is up to me to put into practice that which I am offering to teach others. Is that the idea, Mr. Carnegie?

CARNEGIE: That is exactly the idea! You wouldn't think much of a doctor who refused to take his own medicine if he were ill. You must become your own best advertisement of the Philosophy of American Achievement by demonstrating that you can make it work for you.

HILL: Do you mean that I must convert the philosophy into great riches to prove its soundness?

CARNEGIE: It altogether depends upon what you mean by the term "riches." There are many forms of riches, you know. As far as the accumulation of money is concerned, you can acquire all of that which you need, and much more, by applying the philosophy. But, I wish to call your attention to a form of riches available to you which transcends, by far, any that money represents.

The riches I have in mind are so stupendous in both quality and quantity that you may be surprised when I describe them. You may be still more surprised when I tell you that the riches I have in mind will not accrue to you alone, but they will become the property of the people of the world. If you recognize the far-flung possibilities of the picture I am about to draw for you, and follow the suggestions I offer, you may see the day when your riches will be vastly greater than any I possess.

THE STEEL MASTER'S CHALLENGE TO HIS PROTÉGÉ

So, here is the picture. I warn you before I describe it, that it will put you on the spot where your qualifications as a leader will be shown up for precisely what they are. But, I will also be on the spot, for I selected you, out of all the men I know, as the man most capable of taking the Philosophy of American Achievement to the people.

First: By the time you will have absorbed all the knowledge I shall pass on to you in connection with the philosophy of success which I have gathered from experience, you will be in possession of the greater portion of my riches. Add to this the value of the riches you will acquire from other successful men with whom I will arrange for their collaboration with you in the organization of the philosophy, and you will be in possession of the greater portion of the real riches represented by the American system. The sum total of these riches will be too fabulous for estimation, because they will be of such a nature that they may add to the riches of all the people of the United States, to say nothing of the people of other nations.

Second: You will have demonstrated the soundness of the principle of *Going the Extra Mile* by forcing the world to recognize you as the organizer of the first practical philosophy of individual achievement, an honor which is unusual, for no one before you has ever attempted to provide the people with such a philosophy, although the need for it has always existed.

Third: The time will come when the unity of purpose of the American people will be disturbed because of the infiltration of foreign-born ideas which do not harmonize with the American way of life, and the people will be prepared, through causes beyond your control, for a dependable philosophy through which harmony may be restored. At this point the Wheel of Fortune will turn up your number, and your big opportunity will have come. You will not have to induce people to accept the philosophy. They will do that voluntarily!

I can see this opportunity already in the making. The seed of it may be found in the growing spirit of greed through which men endeavor to get *something for nothing*. The seed is gaining ground in the disturbing elements which have begun to threaten the harmony between industry and its workers. Subversive philosophies will find a convenient soil for the germination of this seed, in the labor organizations. Here is where the discord will become first obvious.

Professional agitators will work their way into the labor organizations and use them as a means of undermining American Industry. The disturbance may result in some form of revolution that will strike at the very roots of the foundation stones of Americanism, but it will run its course and the American people will recover from the shock.

The people will begin to search for a way out, as the American people always do when overtaken by an emergency. *Then your big opportunity will have arrived!* The period of reconstruction of the American way of life will have begun, and the philosophy you will have organized by *Going the Extra Mile* will become, of necessity, the means by which harmony will be restored.

If you fail to see this picture as I have painted it, your failure will be mine also, because I have chosen you as my emissary to carry out the greatest assignment I have ever given to any man. If you do your work as I believe you can do it, the whole world will be richer because of your labor—richer not only in material things, *but richer in spiritual understanding,* without which no form of riches can long endure.

I hope you have recognized the fact that the Philosophy of American Achievement embodies not only the rules of material success, but also the principles expounded by the Master, in the Sermon On the Mount, "Whatsoever ye would that men should do unto you, do ye also unto them."

Unless you comprehend this broader meaning of the philosophy, you will miss the greater possibilities of your mission. The people of the world are becoming spiritually bankrupt. They are turning away from the principles of Christianity to embrace the principles of paganism. They can be led back to the true principles of civilization by converting their greatest weakness into an irresistible power of attraction. That weakness is their desire for material things.

Very well, the Philosophy of American Achievement provides the only known safe road to the accumulation of material riches. But it provides the means of spiritual recovery. Therefore, in giving the people that which they desire most, you will bestow along with it *that which they need most!* Surely you will not miss this point.

Thus, in the picture I have drawn for you, you have a clear description of an opportunity such as no other American philosopher has ever possessed. This is an opportunity which may make you a great servant of the American people. Now,

I have a parting word of advice: Acquire humility of the heart. Do not become over-impressed with your own importance. Accept your mission as a privilege for which to be thankful, and not as an advantage of which to boast. Remembering, always, that "The Greatest Among You Shall Be the Servant of All."

No man is a free man until he learns to do his own thinking and gains the courage to act on his own personal initiative.

Cultivate Creative Vision   *Chapter Seven*

A philosopher said, "The imagination is the workshop of man wherein is fashioned the pattern of all his achievements." Another thinker described it as "The workshop of the soul wherein man's hopes and desires are made ready for material expression."

This chapter describes the methods by which some of the great leaders of America have, through the application of Creative Vision, made the American way of life the envy of the world.

Observe the close relationship between this and the preceding chapter on Organized Individual Endeavor. All forms of organized effort must be planned through Creative Vision. The two principles are inseparable.

HILL: Mr. Carnegie, you have said that Creative Vision is the seventh principle of individual achievement. Will you analyze this principle and describe how one may make practical use of it?

CARNEGIE: First of all, let us have a clear understanding of the meaning of the term "Creative Vision," as we are here using it, by explaining that this is but another name for imagination.

There are two types of imagination. One is known as synthetic imagination and the other as creative imagination.

Synthetic imagination consists of the act of combining recognized ideas, concepts, plans, facts, and principles in new arrangements. The old axiom that "There is nothing new under the sun," grew out of the fact that the majority of things which seem to be new are nothing but a re-arrangement of that which is old.

Practically all the patents recorded in the Patent Office are nothing more than old ideas which have been arranged in a new order, or given a new use. Patents which do not come under this heading are known as "basic patents" and they are the work of Creative Imagination; that is, they are based on newly created ideas which have not been previously used or recognized.

Creative Imagination has its source, as far as science has been able to determine, in the subconscious mind, wherein exists, through some power unknown to science, the ability to perceive and interpret "basically" new ideas. It is believed, by some, that the faculty of Creative Imagination truly is "The workshop of the soul" through which man may contact and be guided by Infinite Intelligence. Of this, however, there is no conclusive evidence save only that which is circumstantial.

Let us, therefore, be content to accept the reality of Creative Imagination and make the best possible use of it, without endeavoring to define its source. Of one fact we can be sure, and that is the undeniable reality of the existence of a faculty of the mind through which some men perceive and interpret new ideas never before known to man. Later we shall cite well-known examples of such ability. Moreover, we shall endeavor to describe how this ability may be developed and made to serve practical ends.

HILL: Which of the two types of imagination is used more often in the field of industry, and in the ordinary walks of life?

CARNEGIE: Synthetic imagination is more commonly used. Creative Imagination, as the name implies, is used only by those who, generally speaking, have attained to some form of leadership or unusual skill.

HILL: Will you mention examples of the application of both types of imagination, giving as many of the details as possible in order that the practical methods of application of these principles may be understood?

CARNEGIE: Let us take the work of Thomas A. Edison, for example. By studying his achievements we shall see how he made use of both types of imagination, although he used the synthetic type more often.

His first invention to attract world-wide attention was created by bringing together, in a new combination, two old and well-known principles. I refer to the incandescent electric lamp, the perfection of which was attained only after Mr. Edison had tried more than ten thousand different combinations of old ideas without satisfactory results.

HILL: Do you mean, Mr. Carnegie, that Mr. Edison had the persistence to keep on trying in the face of ten thousand failures?

CARNEGIE: I mean just that! And I may as well here call your attention to the fact that men with a keen sense of imagination seldom quit trying until they find the answer to their problems.

As I was saying, Mr. Edison perfected the incandescent electric lamp by combining two well-known principles in a new way. The first of these principles was the established fact that by applying electric energy to both ends of a piece of wire a resistance is established through which the wire becomes heated to a white glow that will produce light.

That principle had been known long before the time of Mr. Edison's experiments with the electric lamp, but the trouble arose from the fact that no way had been found to control the heat.

Perhaps the facts would be better understood if I said that no form of metal or other substance had been found that would carry the necessary amount of heat to make a satisfactory light for more than a few seconds. The intense heat of the electricity soon burned out the metal.

After trying every known substance he could find, without discovering anything that would serve the desired purpose, Mr. Edison stumbled upon another well-known principle which proved to be the answer to his problem. I say he "stumbled" upon it, but perhaps that is not the precise way the principle came to his attention. Of that I shall have more to say later on. At any rate, there came into his mind the well-known principle by which charcoal is produced, and he recognized in it the answer to the problem that had caused him more than ten thousand failures.

Briefly explained, charcoal is produced by placing a pile of wood on the ground, setting it on fire and then covering the whole pile with dirt. The dirt permits just enough air to pass through to the fire to keep it alive and smouldering, but not enough to enable the fire to blaze. The smouldering process continues until the wood becomes charred through and through, leaving the log intact, in the form of a substance known as charcoal.

The reason the wood does not burn up entirely, as it would if left in the open air, is the fact that the dirt allows only enough oxygen to reach the fire, through the intake of air, to produce the smouldering condition, but not enough to cause the wood to burn up completely. You of course learned, in the study of physics, that where there is no oxygen there can be no fire; that by controlling the inflow of oxygen the amount of heat of fire can be controlled proportionately.

Mr. Edison had known of this principle long before he began experimenting with the electric lamp, but not until after he had gone through thousands of tests did he think of it as being the principle for which he was searching.

As soon as this principle was recognized as the one for which he was searching, he went into his laboratory, placed a coiled wire in a bottle, pumped out all the air, sealed the bottle with wax, applied the electric energy to the two ends of the wire, and lo! the world's first successful incandescent electric lamp was born. The crudely constructed lamp burned for more than eight hours.

Of course it is obvious as to what happened. By placing the wire in a vacuum that contained no oxygen it could be heated sufficiently to cause it to produce a light without its burning out entirely, as it had done when left in the open air. That same principle is used in the making of all incandescent electric lamps today, although the method has been greatly refined until the modern electric lamp is much more efficient than it was when Edison first discovered how to control the heat.

Now, let us go back to the question as to how Mr. Edison came to think of combining these two old principles in a new way. I said he "stumbled" upon the idea of using the charcoal principle as a means of controlling the heat of the electric energy. But that is not exactly the way this idea occurred to him.

Here begins, then, the entry into the picture of the principle of Creative Imagination. By his repetition of thought in connection with his problem, carried on over a long period of time, through thousands of experiments, Mr. Edison either consciously or unconsciously charged his subconscious mind with a clear picture of his problem, and, by some queer power which no one understands, his subconscious mind handed over to him the solution to his problem, in the form of a "hunch" that caused him to think of the charcoal principle.

In describing the experience many years afterward, Mr. Edison said that when the "hunch" came to him he recognized it immediately as being the missing link for which he had been searching. Moreover, he felt assured it would work, even before he tested it. He made the further significant statement that when the idea of using the charcoal principle "flashed into his mind" it brought with it a feeling of assurance of its suitability such as did not accompany any one of the other thousands of similar ideas he had tested, through synthetic imagination.

From this statement we may draw the conclusion that the subconscious mind not only has the power to create the solution to problems, but it also has a means of forcing one to recognize the solution when it is presented to the conscious mind.

HILL: From your last remark, Mr. Carnegie, I draw the conclusion that persistence was of the essence of Mr. Edison's success in the discovery of the solution to his problem.

CARNEGIE: Yes, and some other factors too. First of all, he began his research with definiteness of purpose, thus applying the first of the 17 principles of individual achievement. He knew the nature of his problem, but equally as important as this, he was determined to find its solution. Therefore he backed his definiteness of purpose with an *obsessional desire* for its attainment.

Obsessional desire is the state of mind which, as you will recall, serves to clear the mind of fear and doubt and self-imposed limitations, thereby opening the way for that state of mind known as Faith. By his refusal to accept defeat, through more than ten thousand failures, Mr. Edison *prepared his mind for the application of Faith.* We may reasonably assume that his Faith placed him in contact with Infinite Intelligence, wherein is known all facts and the solution to all problems which are capable of solution.

HILL: Were all of Mr. Edison's inventions created through the joint application of creative imagination and synthetic imagination, as in the case of the incandescent electric lamp?

CARNEGIE: Not by any means. The majority of his inventions were created solely through the aid of synthetic imagination, by the trial-and-error method of experimentation. But he did complete one invention solely through the aid of creative imagination, and as far as I know, this was the only invention he perfected through this principle alone. I have reference to the phonograph. That was basically a new idea. No one before Edison, as far as is known, had ever produced a machine that would record and reproduce the vibrations of sound.

HILL: What technique did Mr. Edison use in the application of creative imagination in perfecting the talking machine?

CARNEGIE: The technique was very simple. He impressed his subconscious mind with the idea of a talking machine and there passed over to his conscious mind a perfect plan for the building of such a machine.

HILL: Do you mean that Edison relied on creative imagination entirely?

CARNEGIE: Yes, entirely! And one of the strange features of this particular invention of Mr. Edison's is the fact that the plan which his subconscious mind yielded to him worked, almost from the first attempt to apply it. The idea of how such a machine could be produced "flashed" into Edison's mind. He sat down then and there and drew a rough picture of the machine, handed it to his model-maker and asked him to produce the machine, and in a matter of hours it had been finished, tested and lo! it worked. Of course the machine was crude, but it was sufficient to prove that Edison's creative imagination had not failed him.

HILL: You say that Mr. Edison "impressed his subconscious mind" with the idea of a talking machine. Now, how did he go about doing this, and how long did it require before his subconscious mind handed over to him the working principle of the machine?

CARNEGIE: I am not sure that Mr. Edison stated exactly how long he had been thinking of such a machine before his subconscious mind picked up his thoughts and translated them into a perfected plan, but I am under the impression it was not more than a few weeks, at most. Perhaps not more than a few days.

His method of impressing his subconscious mind with his desire consisted of the simple procedure of converting that desire into an obsession. That is, the thought of a machine that would record and reproduce sound became the dominating thought of his mind. He focused his mind on it, through concentration of his interest, and made it the major occupant of his mind from day to day until this form of auto-suggestion penetrated his subconscious mind and registered a clear picture of his desire.

HILL: Is that the way one connects the conscious mind with the subconscious, Mr. Carnegie?

CARNEGIE: Yes, that is the simplest known method. You see, therefore, why I have emphasized the importance of intensifying one's desires until they become obsessional. A deep, burning desire is picked up by the subconscious and acted upon much more definitely and quickly than an ordinary desire. *A mere wish appears to make no impression on the subconscious!* Many people become confused as to the difference between a wish and a burning desire which has been stimulated into obsessional proportions *by the repetition of thought* in connection with the desire.

HILL: If I understand you correctly, Mr. Carnegie, the element of repetition is important. Why?

CARNEGIE: Because repetition of thought creates "thought habits" in the mind which cause the mind to go right on working on an idea without one's conscious effort. Apparently the subconscious concerns itself first with those thoughts which have become habits and especially if the thoughts have been strongly emotionalized by a deep and burning desire for their realization.

HILL: Then anyone may make use of creative imagination by the simple process of charging his subconscious mind with definite desires?

CARNEGIE: Yes, there is nothing to hinder anyone from using this principle but you must remember that practical results are obtained only by those who have gained discipline over their thought habits, through the process of *concentration of interest and desire. Fleeting thoughts* which come and go intermittently, and mere wishes, which are about the extent of the average person's thinking, make no impression whatsoever on the subconscious mind. I will have more to say on this subject when we discuss self-discipline.

(Author's Note: The subject of habit, and its effect on individual achievement, will be covered thoroughly in another chapter of this book, under the title of "Cosmic Habit-force," a newly discovered law of nature which promises to become of the utmost importance in connection with the power of thought. Nothing was known of this law at the time Mr. Carnegie was analyzing this subject, although his description of the manner in which the subconscious mind can be reached and influenced harmonizes perfectly with the nature of "Cosmic Habit-force.")

HILL: Will you mention some additional examples of the practical application of the two types of imagination?

CARNEGIE: Well, take the experience of Henry Ford, in connection with his perfection of a self-propelled vehicle, for example. The idea of such a vehicle was first suggested to him by a steam-propelled tractor that was being used to haul a threshing machine. From the first time that he saw the tractor his mind began to work on the idea of a horseless buggy. At first he used only the principle of synthetic imagination by centering his mind on ways and means of converting the steam tractor into a rapid-moving vehicle for the transportation of passengers.

The idea became obsessional with him, and it had the effect of conveying his *burning desire* to his subconscious mind where it was picked up and acted upon. The action of the subconscious mind suggested to him the use of an internal combustion engine to take the place of the steam engine, and he went to work immediately on the creation of such an engine.

Of course he had the experiments of other men in connection with internal combustion gas engines as a guide, but his problem was to find a way to convey the power of the engine to the wheels of a vehicle. He kept his mind charged with his *Major purpose* until, step by step, his subconscious mind presented him with ideas with which he perfected the *planetary system* of power transmission which enabled him to perfect his first working model of an automobile. (Model T).

HILL: Will you describe the major factors which entered into the *modus operandi* of Mr. Ford's mind while he was perfecting the automobile?

CARNEGIE: That will be very easy. And when I describe them you will have a clear understanding of the working principles used by all successful men, as well as a clear picture of the Ford mind, viz.:

(a) Mr. Ford was motivated by a definite purpose, which is the first step in all individual achievements.

(b) He stimulated his purpose into an obsession by concentrating his thoughts upon it.

(c) He converted his purpose into definite plans, through the principle of *Organized Individual Endeavor,* and put his plans into action with *unabating persistence.*

(d) He made use of the Master Mind principle, first, by the harmonious aid of his wife, and secondly, by gaining counsel from others who had experimented with internal combustion engines and methods of power transmission. Still later, of course, when he began to produce automobiles for sale, he made a still more extensive use of the Master Mind principle by allying himself with the Dodge brothers and other mechanics and engineers skilled in the sort of mechanical problems he had to solve.

(e) Back of all this effort was the power of Applied Faith, which he acquired as the result of his intense desire for achievement in connection with his *definite major purpose.*

HILL: Summarized briefly, Mr. Ford's success was due to his having adopted a *definite major purpose* which he fanned into a white-heat flame of obsession, thus leading to the stimulation of both the faculties of synthetic imagination and creative imagination.

CARNEGIE: That tells the story in one sentence! The part of the story that should be emphasized is the fact that Mr. Ford moved with *persistence!* At first he met with one form of defeat after another. One of his major difficulties was lack of capital with which to carry on his research, before he perfected his automobile. After that came a still greater difficulty in connection with procuring the necessary operating capital to produce his automobiles in quantity production.

Then followed a series of difficulties, such as disagreements with the members of his Master Mind group, and other similar problems, all of which called for *persistence and determination.* These qualities Mr. Ford possesses, and I think we might say he owes his success to his ability to know exactly what he wants and his capacity to stand by his wants with *unrelenting persistence.*

If one single quality stands out in the Ford character, above all others, it is his capacity for persistence. Let me remind you, again, that definiteness of purpose backed with a form of persistence that assumes the proportion of an obsession, is the greatest of all stimulants of both the synthetic and the creative forms of imagination. The mind of man is provided with a power which forces the subconscious mind to accept and to act upon *obsessional desires that are definitely planned.*

HILL: Will you now cite some other examples of the practical application of imagination?

CARNEGIE: Take, for example, Dr. Alexander Graham Bell's research in connection with the modern telephone. Here we have an example of the use of creative imagination, for Bell's invention was basically new. Let us say that he, like Edison, "stumbled" upon the principle that made the telephone practical, while searching for some mechanical device with which he could create a hearing aid for his wife, whose hearing was impaired.

Here, again, we find a man who was inspired by a definite purpose which assumed *obsession proportions*. His keen sympathy for his wife was the factor that gave obsessional force to his purpose. In this case, as in all others where men give obsessional proportions to their desires, a *definite motive* was behind his desire. *Motive* is the beginning of all desires.

Through a long period of research that is too involved in details for description here, Dr. Bell's subconscious mind finally presented him with an idea which served his purpose. It became known to the scientific world as Bell's experiment, the substance of which was this:

A ray of light is cast upon a plate of selenium which sends the ray back to another plate—some distance away—of the same metal. This latter communicates with a galvanic battery, to which a telephone is attached. The words uttered behind the first plate are distinctly heard through the telephone at the end of the second plate. The ray of light, accordingly, has served as a telephone wire. The sound waves have become transformed into light waves, the latter into galvanic waves, and these have become once again sound waves.

Thus a basically new principle for conveying sound waves was uncovered. It has been claimed that the principle, in part, was suggested to Dr. Bell by the experiments of a man by the name of Dolbear. There was a lawsuit over the priority of right to the principle, but Mr. Dolbear lost the suit, and Dr. Bell was declared to have been the discoverer of the working principle of the modern telephone.

At any rate, Dr. Bell's desire for a mechanical hearing aid for his wife, backed by a *persistent search* for such a device, led to the discovery of the principle he needed. It must be remembered that the subconscious mind makes use of every practical means available for revealing knowledge to those seeking it with obsessional desire. It performs no miracles, but it makes intelligent use of all practical media available in carrying out its purpose.

HILL: Now, Mr. Carnegie, let us get away from the field of invention and see how the principle of imagination may be applied in the less complicated fields of endeavor.

CARNEGIE: Very well, take for example the first great mail-order house that was established in the United States. Here we have a fine example of synthetic imagination applied to merchandising.

A telegraph operator with whom I formerly worked found that he had extra time on his hands which he could not use in connection with his duties as a railroad telegrapher. Being a man with an inquisitive type of mind, he began to search for something he could do that would keep him occupied and at the same time add to his income. Here, again, the question of motive entered the picture. (The motive of financial gain.)

After having turned the matter over in his mind for several months, he envisioned a profitable outlet for his efforts by using the idle telegraph line for the purpose of selling watches to his fellow operators in his division; so he ordered half a dozen watches, at wholesale rates, and began to offer them for sale.

The idea caught fire from the very beginning. In a very short time he had sold all six of the watches. Then, spurred on by his success, his imagination began to expand until he took on other items of jewelry. Everything went well, and he was doing a land-office business, until his superintendent found out what he was up to and fired him on the spot.

Every adversity brings with it the seed of an equivalent benefit! Out of this telegrapher's adversity was born the first great *mail-order house*. He switched his method of selling from telegraphy to the mails, using at first a mimeographed catalogue of his wares. Moreover, he added others outside the field of telegraphers to his list of prospective buyers, mainly people living in the villages and rural districts.

In a little while his business had grown to where he could afford a printed catalogue illustrated with pictures of his merchandise. From that point on the story is known to millions of people throughout the United States who now purchase merchandise from the mail-order house he established.

He finally took a partner into the business with him, thereby making use of the Master Mind principle. This partner proved to be a veritable gold mine because he had a keen sense of advertising. Several years later the business was sold out to a corporation at a price which made its owners multimillionaires. That was the beginning of mail-order merchandising on a large scale.

Now, there was nothing very mysterious about this man's success. He simply put his mind to work on a definite purpose and kept behind that purpose until it made him rich. He did not create anything new. He merely put an old idea to a new use. In this manner many of the great fortunes have been accumulated.

HILL: If I understand you correctly, Mr. Carnegie, the telegraph operator applied only the principle of synthetic imagination.

CARNEGIE: Yes, that is it. You see, he did nothing except apply the principle of merchandising in a new way; but do not forget that this is about all that most successful men do. Rarely do men create basically new ideas, through the application of creative imagination, as Dr. Bell and Mr. Edison did.

Now let us take the modern railroad refrigerator car, for example. The man who first made practical application of this principle revolutionized the meat-packing business. He was a packer whose business was limited due to the fact that he could ship fresh meat only a short distance. Motivated by a desire to extend his business over a greater territory, he began to search for a suitable method. A man generally finds whatever he is looking for if he gives his desire obsessional proportions. Well, this packer was motivated by the desire for larger financial gains, so he kept his mind on his problem until it occurred to him to convert an ordinary railroad box car into an over-sized ice box.

There was nothing left to be done except to go to work and experiment with the idea, which he proceeded to do. The plan worked satisfactorily, although the first refrigerator car was a very crude affair. He kept on improving his idea until he had refined it into the modern refrigerator car, as we know it today.

His idea not only helped him to extend his meat business almost without limitation, but it gave a new impetus to the sale and distribution of other lines of merchandise, particularly fruits and vegetables, until today that single idea has added hundreds of millions of dollars of wealth to individuals, corporations, and the nation as a whole.

The refrigerator car was brought into existence solely by the application of synthetic imagination, through the simple process of placing an ice box on wheels, so to speak.

George Pullman performed a similar feat by placing beds in railroad coaches, thus converting them into sleeping quarters. There was nothing new about either the beds or the railroad coaches; but the idea of combining these two types of service was new.

The new combination made the man who created it an immense fortune, to say nothing of providing thousands of jobs for others and a desirable service for the traveling public, for which it continues to pay a huge sum annually. Ideas, such as these, are the products of imagination. The man who trains his mind to create ideas, or to give to old ideas a new and better use, is well on the road toward economic independence.

Back of these ideas was the personal initiative of the men who created them, plus the principle of Organized Individual Endeavor through which they were made practical. Both the sleeping car and the refrigerator car had to be promoted and sold, thus necessitating the investment of large amounts of capital. Both of these ideas, and all similar ideas that are made practical, require the application of some combination of the principles of individual achievement; but in the final analysis such ideas generally can be traced back to their originating source, in the imagination of one person.

HILL: Will you name the principles which are most commonly used by those who apply the principle of imagination?

CARNEGIE: Well, that depends somewhat on the nature of the application that is to be made of imagination, and the person making it; but generally speaking the following are the principles which are more often allied with imagination:

(a) *Definiteness of Purpose,* based on an obsessional desire growing out of one or more of the nine basic motives. (See list of the nine basic motives in Chapter Two.) The motive which more commonly serves to stimulate the imagination is that of a desire for financial gain. The profit motive has been without a doubt the greatest inspiration to the men who have developed industrial America.

(b) *The Master Mind* principle, through which men go into a huddle and frankly exchange thoughts with the object of solving business or professional problems, is also a great stimulation of the imagination. It was this principle, more than all others, through which the steel industry, of which I was the founder, became prosperous. The so-called "round table" is a great institution. When men sit down and begin to pool their ideas, in a spirit of harmony and oneness of purpose, they soon find a solution to most of the problems that confront them, no matter what business they may be engaged in, or what may be the nature of their problems.

(c) *Going the Extra Mile* comes in prominently for its share of credit as a stimulant to the imagination. When a man makes it a habit to do more than he is paid for, he generally begins to draw upon his imagination for new sources through which to render this sort of service. This fact alone would be sufficient compensation for Going the Extra Mile, even if there were not still greater benefits available.

(d) *Applied Faith* is a definite source of stimulation of the imagination. Moreover, it is an essential in connection with the stimulation and application of creative imagination. *Men with little or no faith will never receive the benefits of creative imagination.*

(e) *Organized Individual Endeavor* depends directly upon the application of imagination for its effectiveness, as all forms of definite planning are carried on through imagination.

There are many other sources of stimulation of the imagination, but these five are on the "must" list.

Fear sometimes stimulates the imagination, while of course at other times it paralyzes the imagination. When a man is in great danger his imagination often performs seemingly superhuman feats; especially where self-preservation is the motive.

Failure and temporary defeat sometimes have the effect of stirring one's imagination, although more often they have the opposite effect.

The question method which master salesmen often resort to, has the effect of arousing the imagination and putting it to work, and the reason for this is obvious. By asking questions the salesman forces his prospective buyer to think. *Moreover, he chooses the line of thought to be engaged in,* by the adroitness of his questions.

Curiosity often stimulates imagination to a high pitch. Curiosity, growing out of death and the uncertainty of life, and the unknown and perhaps unknowable facts of immortality, has been the chief source of inspiration out of which all the religions have grown.

Self-expression, through speaking and writing, is a never-ending source of stimulation of imagination, as are many other forms of action. The very moment a man begins to organize his thoughts for the purpose of expression, whether through words or deeds, he starts his imagination to work. For this reason children should be encouraged to give free expression to their thoughts, as this develops imagination early in life.

Hunger is a universal source of inspiration of imagination. When a man needs food his imagination goes to work automatically, without any form of urge. In the lower order of life, instinct goes to work in the face of hunger, and I have known of ingenious applications of instinct under such an urge.

Thus we see that wherever we touch life, whether in man or the lower orders of organic life, imagination and instinct may be found as essential parts of the individual's working equipment.

Concentration of attention on a definite problem or object tends to put the imagination to work immediately. Witness, for example, the astounding achievements of Dr. Elmer R. Gates, who created hundreds of useful inventions by "sitting for ideas." The same principle was used by Thomas A. Edison and Dr. Alexander Graham Bell. By fixing their minds on definite objectives, through definiteness of purpose, they put creative imagination to work with far-reaching results.

Scientists, and sometimes laymen, put their imaginations to work by setting up hypotheses of facts or ideas which, for the time being, they assume to exist. Scientific research and experiment would hardly be practical if hypothetical cases were not utilized, as often the facts for which they are searching are entirely unknown.

Lawyers and trial judges often resort to the use of hypothesis in order to establish facts that cannot be uncovered through any other source. The chemists and the physicists resort to the same method when searching for unknown facts. And so does the doctor, when other means of diagnosis of disease fail him. Detectives often work entirely through the aid of hypothesis in the solution of crime.

HILL: Why is it that so few people appear to have a well-developed imagination? Is the capacity for keen imagination a matter of heredity, Mr. Carnegie?

CARNEGIE: No, the faculty of imagination, like all other faculties of the mind, can be developed through use. The reason so many people seem not to have a keen imagination is obvious. Most people allow the faculty of imagination to atrophy, through neglect.

HILL: Inasmuch as everyone must use salesmanship, in one way or another, will you illustrate how imagination can be used in selling?

CARNEGIE: I can give you an endless number of examples of this sort. Take the case of a life insurance agent whom I know, for instance. He began selling insurance after an accident which incapacitated him for any sort of heavy manual labor, and within a year he became the high man for the entire United States, in the agency force of his company.

I will give you one illustration that will tell the story of his success. But, before I do so I think I should tell you that this man became a master at applying the Master Mind principle. He also became equally proficient in applying many of the other principles of achievement, among them Creative Vision.

One day he walked into the office of a very distinguished and wealthy lawyer and came out, within half an hour, with an application for a million-dollar policy on the lawyer's life, although the lawyer was known to have refused to purchase insurance from a half dozen or more of the ablest insurance men in the city in which he lived.

And this is the way he did it:

He carried with him a fully illustrated, newspaper feature story of the lawyer's activities, set in type with a heavy streamer headline which read, "Prominent Lawyer Insures His Brains for a Million Dollars!"

The story told how the lawyer had come up from the bottom, through his unusual skill as a corporation attorney, until he was in a position where he commanded the most select clientele in New York City. The story was well written. It carried pictures of the lawyer and the members of his family, including a picture of his Long Island estate.

He handed the story to the lawyer and said, "I have made arrangements for this story to be released in over a hundred newspapers the moment you prove that you can pass the necessary physical examination. I hardly need to suggest to a man of your intelligence that the story will bring you enough new clients to more than pay the premium on the insurance policy."

The lawyer sat down and read the story carefully. When he had finished, he asked how the insurance man had procured so much information about him, and how he managed to get those pictures of his family.

"Oh," replied the insurance man, "that was easy. I simply made arrangements with a newspaper syndicate to do the job."

The lawyer read the story a second time, made a few corrections in it, handed it back and said, "Let's have your application blank." The sale was closed in a few minutes, but more than three months of preparation went into it before the insurance agent made his call. He left no detail unattended. He made it his business to find out all about the lawyer before the story was written, and saw to it that the story was so prepared that it got under the lawyer's skin at his weakest point, which was his desire for publicity.

What he really sold the lawyer was not an insurance policy on his life, but an insurance policy on his vanity! That streamer headline turned the trick. Moreover, he not only earned a fat premium on the sale, but he received $500.00 from the newspaper syndicate for the exclusive use of the story.

Now that was imagination, or I miss my guess!

Salesmen with imagination often sell something entirely different from that which they appear to be selling. The experience of Dr. Harper, a former president of the University of Chicago, aptly illustrates what I mean.

Dr. Harper was one of the greatest "endowment getters" the educational world has ever known. He took a notion to build a new building on the campus that required a million-dollar endowment. If you wish to see imagination as it is employed by a master, observe the technique through which he got his million dollars. Observe, also, how many of the principles of individual achievement he applied in addition to imagination.

First of all, he chose his prospective donors with adroitness, confining the number to two well-known Chicago men, each of whom was quite able to donate a million dollars.

It could not have been purely accidental that these two men were known to be bitter enemies. One was a professional politician and the other was the head of the Chicago street railway system.

For years these two men had been fighting each other, a fact which would have meant nothing to anyone with less imagination than Dr. Harper possessed.

One day, precisely at twelve o'clock, Dr. Harper strolled into the office of the streetcar magnate, found no one on duty at the outer door (which was exactly as he expected the situation to be), and walked into the streetcar man's private office unannounced.

The magnate looked up from his desk, but before he had time to protest, the super-salesman said, "I beg your pardon for walking in unannounced, but I found no one in the outer office. My name is Dr. Harper, and I just called to see you for a minute."

"Please be seated," said the streetcar man.

"No, thank you," replied the educator, "I have only a minute, so I will tell you what I have in mind and then be on my way. I have been thinking, for some time, that the University of Chicago should do something to recognize you for the wonderful job you have done in giving the city the finest street railway system in America, and I had in mind honoring you with a building on the campus to be named for you. When I mentioned the matter to our board, one of the members had the same idea, but wanted us to honor _____ _____ (naming the streetcar man's enemy), so I just came in to tell you what had happened, with the hope that you might find some way to help me defeat this board member's plan."

"Well!" exclaimed the streetcar man, "that is an interesting idea. Do please be seated and let us see what we can work out, will you?"

"I am very sorry," the educator apologized, "but I have another engagement in a few minutes and I must hurry on to it; but I tell you what I suggest. You think the matter over during the night and telephone me in the morning if any plan comes to mind that might help me to get the right man's name on that building. Good day, Sir!"

Without leaving any opening for further conversation, the master of imagination bowed himself out.

The next morning when he arrived at his office at the university, he found the streetcar man awaiting him. The two men walked inside, remained there about an hour, after which they walked out again, both of them smiling. Dr. Harper carried a check in his hand, waving it back and forth in the air to blot it. The check was for one million dollars.

The streetcar man had found a way to beat his enemy to the draw, as the clever Dr. Harper figured he would do. Moreover, he had sealed the bargain by delivering the money with the understanding that Dr. Harper would become personally responsible for its acceptance.

Edison failed ten thousand times before he perfected the incandescent electric lamp. The average man would have quit after the first failure, which explains why there are so many "average" men and but one Edison.

Exercise Self-discipline

Perhaps there is no other word in the English language which describes the major requirement for individual achievement as does the subject of self-discipline.

This entire philosophy serves in the main to enable one to develop control over himself, this being the greatest of all the essentials of success.

In this chapter will be found a consolidation of the previous seven principles. In this chapter the way will be prepared for one to apply the seven principles previously described.

You have already observed how the principles of this philosophy blend with one another and are related, as are the links of a chain, in such a manner that not one of the principles could be omitted without weakening the philosophy. Through self-discipline the power available through each of the principles of this philosophy becomes condensed and ready for application in the practical affairs of daily life.

The effect of this condensation may be clearly described by comparing it with a group of electric batteries, each of the seventeen principles of the philosophy representing a separate battery. By connecting the batteries properly one has available the sum total of the power each individual battery contains. Self-discipline is the "master battery" through which the power of all seventeen of the principles may be applied.

It is necessary for the student of this philosophy to catch the full significance of the relationship between self-discipline and the other principles of the philosophy in order that he may avail himself of the entire power that is available through the seventeen principles, for the reason that self-discipline represents the "bottle neck" through which that power must pass.

Mr. Carnegie has taken great pains to emphasize the necessity of self-discipline, because he learned from his own experience in dealing with thousands of men that no one may hope to achieve noteworthy success *without gaining control over himself.*

He learned, from his own experience and from his observation of other people, *that when a man once takes possession of his own mind and begins to rely upon it* he has achieved a victory of the highest order, and one that places him within easy grasp of whatever he sets his heart and head upon.

Self-discipline, then, may be defined as the act of taking possession of one's own mind!

Self-discipline is something one cannot acquire as one learns the multiplication table; but it can be acquired through persistence, by following the procedure outlined in this chapter. The price of self-discipline, therefore, is eternal vigilance and continuous effort in carrying out these instructions. In no other way can it be acquired, and it has no other bargaining price. One gets self-discipline through his own efforts or he does not acquire it at all.

Without self-discipline an individual may be likened to a dry leaf that is blown hither and yon by the stray winds of circumstance, *with not the slightest chance of coming within sight of anything that even remotely resembles personal success.*

Men who take possession of their own minds and use them may set their own price tag on themselves and make life pay what they ask. Those who fail to do so must take whatever life tosses out to them, and we need offer no evidence that this always is barely more than the mere necessities of life.

In the private study of Andrew Carnegie, you will now be privileged to sit while he instructs his first student, on the subject of self-discipline.

HILL: Mr. Carnegie, you have designated self-discipline as the eighth principle of individual achievement. Will you begin this interview by describing the part that self-discipline plays in personal achievement, and indicate how this principle can be developed and applied in the practical affairs of daily life?

CARNEGIE: Let us begin by calling attention to some of the uses of self-discipline. After that we will discuss the methods by which this important principle may become the possession of anyone who is willing to pay the price.

Self-discipline begins with the mastery of one's thoughts. Without control over thoughts there can be no control over deeds! Let us say, therefore, that self-discipline inspires one to *think first* and act afterward. The usual procedure is just the reverse. Most people act first and think afterward (if and when they think at all).

Self-discipline gives one complete control over the fourteen major emotions, enabling one to eliminate or subjugate the seven negative emotions and exercise the seven positive emotions in whatever manner desired. The effect of this control becomes obvious when one recognizes that emotion rules the lives of most people, and largely rules the world.

Although we have described the fourteen major emotions in a previous interview, we are compelled to mention them again, for the reason that self-discipline must begin, if it begins at all, with a complete mastery of these emotions.

The Seven Positive Emotions:	The Seven Negative Emotions:
1. LOVE	1. FEAR (See 7 basic fears)
2. SEX	2. JEALOUSY
3. HOPE	3. HATRED (Prolonged)
4. FAITH	4. REVENGE
5. ENTHUSIASM	5. GREED
6. LOYALTY	6. ANGER (Temporary)
7. DESIRE	7. SUPERSTITION

All these emotions are states of mind, subject to control and direction. The seven negative emotions obviously are deadly if they are not mastered. The seven positive emotions may also be just as destructive as the negative emotions if they are not organized, mastered and guided under complete control.

In these fourteen emotions is the "Mental Dynamite" which may lift one to great heights of achievement or dash one to the lowest depths of failure, and no amount of education, experience, intelligence or good intentions can alter or modify this possibility.

HILL: It seems obvious that lack of control of the seven negative emotions may lead one to sure defeat, but it is not clear as to
how one may use the seven positive emotions for the achievement
of desirable ends.

CARNEGIE: I will show you exactly how the positive emotions may be transmuted into a driving power that can be used
in the attainment of any purpose. I can best do this by describing
the manner in which one man made effective use of his emotions.
That man is Charlie Schwab, and my analysis of his use of
emotions is based upon close association with him over a long
period of years.

Shortly after he began work with me he made up his mind
to become an indispensable part of my business family, thereby
directing to a definite end the emotion of desire. In carrying out
his desire he applied all the principles of achievement mentioned in previous interviews, *viz:*

(a) Definiteness of Purpose
(b) The Master Mind
(c) Attractive Personality
(d) Applied Faith
(e) Going the Extra Mile
(f) Organized Endeavor
(g) Creative Vision
(h) Self-discipline

Through the principle of self-discipline Charlie Schwab organized the other seven principles and brought them under his
control. Back of this self-control he placed all of his emotional
feeling and expressed it through his loyalty to his associates,
enthusiasm over his work, hope of successful achievement in
connection with his work, faith in his ability to achieve; and back
of all these emotions he was driven by the emotion of love for his
wife whom he was seeking to please by his achievements.

The motive which inspired him to organize and use his emotions for the attainment of a definite end was the twofold motive
of *LOVE* and *DESIRE FOR FINANCIAL GAIN,* these two
being at the head of the list of the nine basic motives.

Of course Mr. Schwab made use of all the other principles of
individual achievement which we have not yet mentioned, before

he finally attained his goal, and he continued to use all the principles of this philosophy after attaining it, but the eight principles
we have covered were the ones he used at the outset.

HILL: I think I understand what you mean, Mr. Carnegie.
Will you check me while I describe my understanding of Mr.
Schwab's rise to power?

First, he decided what he wanted, thus putting into use the
principle of *Definiteness of Purpose.* He adopted a plan for getting what he wanted and, judging by what you have said of him,
he began carrying out his plan by *Going The Extra Mile,* thereby
making use of the principle of *Organized Endeavor.*

By working in harmony with you and his other associates, he
made use of the *Master Mind* principle.

By his adoption of such a high aim he showed that he understood and used the principle of *Creative Vision,* and demonstrated
also his understanding and application of the principle of *Applied
Faith.*

By the pleasing, harmonious manner in which he related himself to you and his other associates, he indicated his understanding
and use of the principle of *Attractiveness of Personality.*

By the intelligent manner in which he used all these principles,
and by sticking persistently to his undertaking until he com-
pleted it, he demonstrated his understanding and use of *Self-
discipline,* through which he subordinated all his desires to the
one sole purpose of making himself an indispensable part of
your organization.

Back of all this endeavor were the two motives of *Love* for his
wife and his *Desire for Financial Achievement* through which
he harnessed and used all his positive emotions for the attainment
of a definite purpose.

Now, does that about state the case?

CARNEGIE: That was the procedure followed. And you will
notice that his chances of success would have been lessened had
he failed to use any of the principles mentioned. It was through
a carefully planned application of *all these principles* that he
attained success. The application required self-discipline of the
highest order.

If he had squandered any of his emotional power in any other direction whatsoever, the results might have been different, a fact of which I am reminded by the experience of another man who started out to attain the same relationship in my organization that Charlie Schwab successfully attained.

This man had everything that Charlie had, as far as ability was concerned. In addition to this he had a much better education, having graduated from one of the best-known colleges, where he specialized in industrial chemistry. He made just as effective use of every one of the principles mentioned as Charlie did, with one lone exception, and that was the *motive* by which he was inspired. His *motive* was a desire for financial gain, not as a means of expressing love for his wife, but to feed his own vanity.

He had a love for power, not as an expression of his pride of achievement, but as a means of lording his authority over other people. Despite this weakness, he climbed steadily until he became an official member of my Master Mind group. Then he took a tumble through which he dashed his hopes and his opportunity to pieces by his arrogance and vanity.

He was reduced in rank, out of necessity for us to maintain harmony in our Master Mind group, and wound up finally at the bottom of the ladder, right where he started. His demotion inflicted a wound to his vanity from which he never recovered.

HILL: What was this man's greatest weakness, Mr. Carnegie?

CARNEGIE: I can answer that in three words: *Lack of self-discipline!* If he had gained mastery over his feelings, he could have succeeded with much less effort than Charlie Schwab put into his job, because he had more education, and possessed every other attribute of success that Schwab possessed.

He failed to control and direct his positive emotions. When he saw himself slipping, he began to give way to many of the negative emotions, particularly to jealousy, fear and hatred. He was jealous of those who had succeeded, he hated them because they had excelled him, and he feared everyone, particularly himself. No man is strong enough to succeed with such an array of enemies as this working against him.

HILL: I judge, from what you have said, that personal power is something which has to be used with discretion, or it may turn out to be a curse instead of a blessing.

CARNEGIE: I have always made it a part of my business philosophy to caution my associates against the dangers of indiscreet use of personal power, and especially those who through promotions have but recently come into the possession of increased power. Newly acquired power is something like newly acquired riches; it needs watching closely lest a man become the victim of his own power. Here is where self-discipline gives a good account of itself. If a man has his own mind under complete control, he makes it serve him in a manner that does not antagonize other people.

HILL: If I understand you, Mr. Carnegie, self-discipline calls for a complete mastery of the seven negative emotions and a controlled guidance of the seven positive emotions. In other words, a man must stand with his foot on the necks of the seven negative emotions, while he organizes and directs to a definite end the seven positive emotions. Is that the idea?

CARNEGIE: Yes, but self-discipline calls for mastery over traits of character other than the emotions. It calls for a strict budgeting and use of time. It calls for mastery of the inborn trait of procrastination. If a man aims for a high station in life, he has no time to spend on non-essential activities other than those he needs for recreation, and these are not exactly non-essential.

HILL: Will you name the traits of character which most often stand in the way of self-discipline?

CARNEGIE: The list is rather long, and it will be covered in detail in the coming interview on *Learning from Defeat*. However, let us assume for the present that the major enemies of self-discipline are the seven negative emotions. These are the obstacles to which a man must give attention first, if he wishes to be sure of success.

Self-discipline begins with the formation of constructive habits; especially the habits connected with food, drink, sex, and the use of one's so-called "spare-time."

Generally speaking, when a man gets these habits under control, they help to regulate all his other habits, and you will observe that the mastery of the eight principles of this philosophy we have mentioned provides a man with everything he needs to shape his habits so they serve him constructively.

Consider, for example, what *Definiteness of Purpose* does to fix one's habits. When one begins to apply the principle of *Going the Extra Mile* he makes a long step forward in the establishment of constructive habits, for in doing more than he is paid for he is forced to budget his time to better advantage.

Consider, then, what happens when a man becomes obsessed with a strong *motive* which he begins to express through the principle of *Organized Endeavor,* in conjunction with the principle of Creative Vision. By the time he gets control of these principles he has already gone a long distance toward the adoption of habits which, of themselves, constitute the finest sort of *self-discipline.* Do you see how this works?

HILL: Yes, I do, and I can see, too, that everything a man does centers around the major motive behind his *Definite Major Purpose.* Motive really is the starting point of all achievement, is it not?

CARNEGIE: That is right; but you should take care to say that one's motive must be obsessional. That is, it must be so strong that it impels a man to subordinate all his thoughts and efforts to its attainment. Too often people become confused between motive and a mere wish. Wishing will not bring success. If it did everyone would be successful, because all people have wishes.

They wish for everything from the earth to the moon, but wishes and day dreams amount to nothing until they are fanned into a hot flame of desire based upon a definite motive, and this must become the dominating influence of one's mind; it must be given obsessional proportions sufficient to cause action.

Even a motive without organized endeavor behind it will be of no benefit, so I repeat what I have already suggested, that one should copy the nine basic motives and place them in a prominent place where they can be seen daily.

These motives which serve as a driving force behind one's chosen major purpose should be underscored and emphasized so they will not be overlooked. They should be included, also, in the written description of one's *Definite Major Purpose,* as suggested in a previous interview. A definite purpose without an obsessional motive back of it is as useless as a locomotive without any steam in the boiler. Motive is the thing that gives power and action and persistence to one's plans.

HILL: That reminds me to ask you, Mr. Carnegie, what is your motive in spending all this time coaching me to organize the Philosophy of American Achievement? You have more of the material riches than you need. You have recognition as the leading industralist of the world. Your life has been a stupendous success, and as far as I can see there is nothing you desire which you do not already possess.

CARNEGIE: That is where you are wrong. I do not have everything I wish. It is true I have more material riches than I need, as is evidenced by the fact I am giving my money away as rapidly as I can do so safely. But there is something I want more than all else, and it is an obsessional desire to provide the people of America with a safe and dependable philosophy by which they may acquire riches in their highest form; riches which will enable people to relate themselves to one another so that they may find peace of mind and happiness and joy in the responsibilities of life.

My obsessional desire grew out of my experiences with people, through which I have learned of the great need for such a philosophy. It is the exception rather than the rule when I find a man who is trying to benefit himself without damaging others. On every hand I see people unwisely trying to get something for nothing, although I know well enough that all they will get is grief and disappointment.

My motive in helping to organize a dependable philosophy of individual achievement is the same as that which prompts some men to erect great monuments of stone to mark the spot where their earthly remains will finally rest.

Monuments of stone crumble with time and go back to dust;

but there is a type of monument which can be made eternal, and it will last as long as civilization itself. It is the monument a man may build in the hearts of his fellowmen, through some form of constructive service which benefits mankind as a whole.

It is such a monument that I hope to build, through your co-operation, and may I suggest that in helping me to build it you may let it serve, also, as your own monument?

HILL: I see your point, Mr. Carnegie. Was that your motive at the outset of your career?

CARNEGIE: No, it was not. In the beginning I was motivated by a desire for self-expression and the desire for financial influence with which to make that expression widespread in its influence. But, in carrying out my original motive I happily hit upon a bigger and nobler motive—the motive of making men instead of making money.

I caught the vision of that greater motive as the result of my having discovered, in the process of making money, the great need for better men. If civilization is to evolve to still higher standards of living, or hold even the gains it has made, men must be taught higher standards of human relationship than those which now prevail.

And, above all, they must learn that there are riches vastly greater than any represented by material things. The need for this wider vision is sufficient to challenge even the greatest of men. It was this challenge to which I responded when my obsessional motive became that of giving the people a sound philosophy of individual achievement.

HILL: From all you have said, I deduce that self-discipline is largely a matter of the adoption of constructive habits.

CARNEGIE: That is precisely the idea! That which a man is, that which he accomplishes, both his failures and his successes, are the results of his habits. Fortunately, habits are self-formed. They are under the control of the individual. The most important of these are the habits of thought. A man comes finally to resemble, in his deeds, the nature of his thought habits. When he gains control over his thought habits, he has gone a long way toward the attainment of self-discipline.

Definite motives are the beginning of thought habits. It is not difficult for a man to keep his mind on the thing that serves as his greatest motive, especially if the motive becomes obsessional. Self-discipline without definiteness of motive is impossible. Moreover, it would be without value. I have seen fakirs in India who had such perfect self-discipline that they could sit all day long on the sharp points of nails driven through a board, but their discipline was useless because there was no constructive motive back of it.

HILL: Then self-discipline, in the sense that it is designated as one of the 17 principles of individual achievement, has reference to complete mastery of both one's thought habits and one's physical habits.

CARNEGIE: Self-discipline means exactly what the word implies; complete discipline over self! Now I must call your attention to the fact that self-discipline calls for a balancing of the emotions of the heart and the reasoning faculty of the head.

That is, one must learn to respond to both his reason and his feelings according to the nature of each circumstance calling for his decisions. Sometimes it will be necessary for him to set aside his emotions entirely, and allow his head to rule. In matters of love and sex, this ability becomes highly important.

I have known men who had so little control over their love emotions that they were as so much putty in the hands of a woman. Such men, needless to say, never accomplish very much that benefits them. On the other hand I have seen men who were so cold and unemotional that they were under the control of their heads entirely. They, too, miss the better things of life.

HILL: Would it not be safer if a man controlled his life with his reasoning faculty, leaving the emotions out of his decisions and plans?

CARNEGIE: That would be very unwise, even if it were possible, for the reason that the emotions provide the driving power, the action force, which enables a man to put his "head" decisions into operation. The remedy is control and discipline of the emotions, not elimination. Moreover, it is very difficult to eliminate the great emotional nature of man, if in fact it is not impossible.

The emotions of man are something like a river in that their power can be dammed up and released in whatever proportions and whatever directions one desires, but they cannot be eliminated. Through self-discipline a man can organize all his emotions and release them, in a highly concentrated form, as a means of attaining the object of his plans and purpose.

The two most powerful emotions are LOVE and SEX. These emotions are inborn, the handiwork of nature, the instruments through which the Creator provided for both the perpetuation of the human race and for social integration by which civilization evolves from a lower to a higher order of human relationship.

One would hardly wish to destroy so great a gift as the emotions, even if this were possible, for the reason that they represent man's greatest power. If you destroy hope and faith, what would you have left that would be of use to man? If you remove enthusiasm, loyalty and the desire for achievement, you would still have left the faculty of reason (the "head power"), but what good would it be? *There would be nothing left for the head to direct!*

Now let me call your attention to an astounding truth, *viz.:* The emotions of hope, faith, enthusiasm, loyalty and desire, are nothing but specialized applications of the inborn emotions of LOVE and SEX diverted, or transmuted, into different purposes! As a matter of fact every human emotion outside of LOVE and SEX has its roots in these two natural, inborn traits of man. If these two natural emotions were destroyed in a man, he would become as docile as an animal that has been desexed. He would have his reasoning faculty left, but what could he do with it?

HILL: Self-discipline, then, is the tool with which a man may harness and direct his inborn emotions in whatever direction he chooses?

CARNEGIE: That is correct. And now I wish to call your attention to another astounding truth, *viz.: Creative Vision* is the result of self-discipline through which the emotions of LOVE and SEX are transmuted into some specialized plan or purpose. *There has never yet been born a great leader in any form of human en-*

deavor who did not attain his leadership by mastery and direction of these two great inborn emotions!

The great artists, musicians, writers, speakers, lawyers, doctors, architects, inventors, scientists, industrialists, salesmen, and the outstanding men and women in all walks of life attain their leadership by harnessing and directing their natural emotions of LOVE and SEX as a driving force behind their endeavors. In most instances the diversion of these emotions into specialized endeavor is done unconsciously, as the result of a BURNING DESIRE for achievement. In some instances the transmutation is deliberate.

HILL: Then it is no disgrace for one to be born with great capacity for the emotions of LOVE and SEX?

CARNEGIE: No, the "disgrace" comes from the abuse of these natural gifts of the Creator! The abuse is the result of ignorance, the lack of training as to the nature and potentialities of these great emotions. To say that the medium by which the Creator perpetuates the species is a disgrace is the same as saying that man himself is a disgrace, for there is but little left in man except about sixteen dollars' worth of chemical matter, if you remove from him the *creative power* of emotion!

HILL: I get the impression that the most important application of self-discipline is that through which one takes possession of his sex emotion and transforms it into whatever form of endeavor he desires. Is that true?

CARNEGIE: Yes and I may add that when a man once acquires discipline over his sex emotion he will find it easy to discipline himself in all other directions, and this for the reason that the emotion of sex reflects itself, either consciously or unconsciously, in practically everything a man does.

Failure to gain control over the emotions of LOVE and SEX generally means failure to gain control over other traits. Take the case of Charles Dickens, for example. Early in life he met with a great disappointment in love. Instead of allowing his unrequited love emotions to destroy him, he transmuted that great *driving force* into a novel called *David Copperfield,* which brought him fame and fortune and led him into the creation of other literary works which made him a master in this field.

Abraham Lincoln was a mediocre lawyer who had failed dismally at everything he had undertaken until the deep wells of his emotion were opened wide by his great sorrow over the death of Anne Rutledge, the only woman he ever truly loved. He converted his sorrow into a public service that made him one of America's immortals. It is regrettable that none of his biographers caught the significance, or made explanatory references to the tragedy which marked the turning point of the great statesman.

Napoleon Bonaparte's creative genius as a military leader was largely an expression of his Master Mind alliance with his first wife. Observe, with profound significance, the tragedy that overtook this man after his "head" overruled his heart, and he put his first wife aside in furtherance of the ambitions of his head.

In your research, as you organize the philosophy of individual achievement, observe carefully and you will discover that *somewhere in the life of all great men will be found the influence of a woman!* Observe, too, that wherever a man and a woman pool their emotions in a spirit of harmony, for the attainment of a definite end, they become almost invincible against all forms of discouragement and temporary defeat.

It is through man's harmonious alliance with woman that he comes into possession of his greatest spiritual power! Perhaps the Creator willed it so, but be that as it may, the fact remains that the world has record of no great men whose lives had not been definitely influenced through the emotions of LOVE and SEX.

Let it be clearly understood that in speaking of SEX I have reference to that inborn creative emotion which gives man his creative ability, and *not merely to the physical expression of that power*. It is the wrong use and the burlesque connotations of this great emotion which have sometimes degraded it to the lowest levels. In this respect man has degraded himself as no animal of of the order lower in intelligence than man has done.

HILL: From your analysis of the emotion of sex, I get the impression that this emotion may be either man's greatest asset or his greatest liability, according to his understanding and application of the emotion.

CARNEGIE: You are exactly right in your assumption. And now I wish to call your attention to another significant fact, *viz.:* The emotion of sex, without the modifying emotion of love, as it is expressed in "illicit" sex relationships, is man's most dangerous influence. When these two great emotions are expressed jointly, they become a creative power which savors of a spiritual nature.

HILL: Then I take it, from your remarks, that the emotion of sex, without the modifying influence of the emotion of love, is purely a biological force that may be disastrous if it is not controlled.

CARNEGIE: You have the idea. But let me tell you something about the method by which this emotion should be *controlled*. The safety valve consists in the principle of transmutation through which this great driving power may be converted and placed back of one's *Definite Major Purpose*. When used in this manner it becomes a priceless asset, even without the modifying influence of the emotion of love.

The emotion of sex will not be denied some form of expression. As I have stated, it resembles a river in that it can be dammed up and its powers diverted into whatever forms of action one desires, but it cannot be shut off from expression without great damage. Like the water of a river that has been dammed, if it is not released under controlled conditions it will break out, by the sheer force of its own inherent power, in ways that are destructive.

This is a fact well known to all doctors and psychiatrists. Uncontrolled emotions of love and sex are responsible for most of the mental disorders and many forms of insanity. So, you see that self-discipline, through which these powers are guided into safe channels of human endeavor, is the only sensible solution of the problem they present.

HILL: Inasmuch as the emotions of love and sex appear to have first place in the powers over which one should exercise self-discipline, will you now analyze their influence in the practical affairs of daily life? I wish further enlightenment as to the part these emotions play in the essential factors of human relationship, in all walks of life, as far as you can describe them.

CARNEGIE: That is a sensible request, so let us deal with it frankly, keeping in mind that any philosophy of individual achievement which is of practical value must enable people to surmount the practical problems of daily life; *and I mean all the problems!*

As we have already seen, all human activity is based upon *motive*. It was not by chance that the motives of LOVE and SEX were placed at the head of the list of the nine basic motives. That is precisely where they belong, because these two motives inspire more action than all other motives combined.

The greatest literature, poetry, art, drama, and music have their roots in the love motive. In Shakespeare's works you will observe that both the tragedies and the comedies are highly colored with the motives of LOVE and SEX. Remove these motives from the Shakespearean plays and you would have nothing left but commonplace dialogue, no better than that of an ordinary playwright. You see, therefore, that these creative emotions can serve the highest purpose in literature.

The accomplished orator, in whatever field of endeavor he may be engaged, gives color and magnetic force to his words by transmuting the emotions of LOVE and SEX into enthusiasm, and thus does he impart feeling through the spoken word. I have heard orations which were masterpieces in both their theme and their perfect English, yet they failed to impart feeling because the orator marshalled his thoughts from his head instead of his heart. He put no feeling into his words because he either lacked emotional capacity or was ignorant as to its use.

No author ever writes a line in which he does not convey to the reader the exact state of his own mind, whether he writes from his "head" or his "heart," and all the king's horses and all the king's men could not prevent the reader from detecting in his writing the presence of emotion, or the lack of it. Perhaps the greatest example of this truth, in all literature, may be found in the Bible. No one can read a single paragraph from the Bible without catching something of an emotional feeling of its writer, although the actual meaning is sometimes beyond the possibility of accurate interpretation.

No two people have ever been known to interpret the meaning of most of the contents of the Bible in exactly the same manner, but everyone who reads the Bible recognizes the power of the emotional feeling it conveys.

In ordinary conversation everyone imparts, through the spoken word, the exact coloring of his own feelings, or his lack of feelings, and it is by this means that experienced observers of human character arrive at the actual state of mind of the speaker. As we all know, words often are used, not to convey one's thoughts, but to conceal them! Therefore, the experienced analyst of human character judges people, not by their words, but by the feeling or lack of feeling they unconsciously impart with their words.

It is by this method that a woman's so-called "intuition" may, if she will be guided by it, enable her to distinguish the real from the false in man's words of proclaimed affection. When a man speaks from his "heart" instead of his "head," his words carry connotations which no experienced woman will misunderstand, but she relies upon the feeling imparted by the words rather than the words.

In view of these well-established truths, consider how important it is for one to understand and to use deliberately the power of emotion in speech and in writing, for it is a truth indeed that no man ever speaks a word or writes a line without consciously or unconsciously betraying the presence of his feelings or the lack of feelings, no matter what the construction of his words may be intended to convey.

HILL: If I understand you, Mr. Carnegie, one's words are colored by the nature of emotions, whether the emotions are positive or negative.

CARNEGIE: That is true, but I wish to call your attention to the fact that the negative emotions, such as fear, jealousy, and anger, can be controlled and transmuted into a constructive driving force. It is through this sort of self-discipline that the negative emotions may be shorn of their dangers and made to serve useful ends. Sometimes fear and anger will inspire actions in which a man would not otherwise engage, but all actions growing out of negative emotions should have the modifying influence of the "head" so they may be guided to constructive ends.

HILL: Should one submit both the negative and the positive emotions to the modifying influence of the reasoning faculty, or the "head," as you express it, before expressing the emotions in action?

CARNEGIE: Yes, that is one of the major purposes of the reasoning faculty. No one should ever, at any time, act on his emotions without first modifying his impulses of thought by submitting them to his reasoning faculty. This is the major function of self-discipline. As I stated at the beginning, self-discipline consists of a proper balancing of the powers of the "head" and the "heart."

The human ego, consisting, as Webster defines it, of "the entire man considered as union of soul and body," should be the judge whose influence should be the determining factor as to the circumstances and the extent that either the "head" or the "heart" should be given the greater influence in forming plans and making decisions. Self-discipline, then, should include a working arrangement through which the ego may throw its weight on the side of either the emotions or the reasoning faculty, in connection with all expressions of either of these.

Chapter Nine

Organize Your Thinking

HILL: You have explained that the ninth principle of individual achievement is Organized Thought. You have stated, also, that no one may be sure of success without the ability to organize his thinking habits. Therefore, will you go ahead, Mr. Carnegie, and explain the meaning of the term "organized thought"? I have a general idea what it means, but I would like to have a detailed statement of its meaning—also a clear understanding of how this principle is applied in the practical affairs of life.

CARNEGIE: Before discussing the organization of thought, let us examine thought itself. What is thought? With what do we think? Is thought subject to individual control?

Thought is a form of energy that is distributed through the brain, but it has one peculiar quality unknown in connection with all other forms of energy; it has *intelligence!*

Thought can be controlled and directed toward the attainment of anything man may desire. In fact thought is the only thing over which any person has complete, unchallenged control. The system of control is so complete that no one may penetrate the mind of another without his consent, although this system of protection often is so loosely guarded that one's mind may be entered at will by any person skilled in the art of thought interpretation.

Many people not only leave their minds wide open for others to enter and interpret their thoughts, but they voluntarily disclose the nature of their thoughts by unguarded expressions of speech and their personal conduct, their facial expression and the like.

HILL: Is it safe for one to leave his mind open to free entry by others?

CARNEGIE: Just about as safe as leaving the door to one's house unlocked, with all of one's valuables left inside the house, except that the loss of purely material things is as nothing compared with the loss one may suffer by leaving his mind open to entry by any stray tramp who may wish to go in and take possession.

You see, the habit of leaving one's mind open and unguarded not only permits other people to enter and become familiar with one's most private thoughts, but this habit permits all sorts of "tramp" thoughts, released from the minds of others, to enter one's mind.

HILL: You believe, then, the thoughts do pass from one mind to another, through the principle of telepathy?

CARNEGIE: That fact has apparently been established by men of science, but I have evidence of its existence, from my own personal experience. Yes, one's mind is being constantly bombarded with the impulses of thought released from the minds of others—especially those with whom we come into close contact daily. As I have stated before, one negative-minded workman, if left to associate with other workmen, will pass on his negative thoughts to every person within the range of his influence, although he never speaks a word or makes a single move indicating his state of mind. I have seen this very thing happen so often that I could not be mistaken about it.

HILL: And that is why you emphasize, so strongly, the necessity of harmony between men associated in a Master Mind alliance?

CARNEGIE: That is one of the major reasons why I have emphasized the importance of harmony. The "chemistry" of the brain is such that the mind-power of a group of men can be organized so it functions as one unit of power only when there is perfect rapport between the minds of the individuals.

HILL: One of the important steps, in organized thought, seems to be that of the Master Mind alliance, through which men pool their mind-power, their experience, education and knowledge, and move in response to a common motive. Is this the right idea, Mr. Carnegie?

CARNEGIE: You have stated the matter perfectly. You might have said that the Master Mind alliance is the most important step one may take in connection with organized thought, for that is true. But, organized thought begins with the organization of the individual's *thinking habits*.

To become an effective member of a Master Mind alliance an individual must first form definite, *controlled habits of thought!* A group of men working together under the Master Mind principle, each of whom has so disciplined himself that he controls his *thought habits,* represents organized thought of the highest order. As a matter of fact, there never can be full assurance of harmony in a Master Mind group unless each member of the group is so self-disciplined that he can control his own thoughts.

HILL: Do I understand you to say that an individual may actually discipline himself so that he controls the nature of his thoughts?

CARNEGIE: That is true, but remember that one gains control over his thoughts by forming definite *thought habits.* You know, of course, that when habits are once formed they function automatically, without any voluntary effort on the individual's part.

HILL: But, isn't it very difficult for one to force his mind to function through definite habits? How may one go about this sort of self-discipline?

CARNEGIE: No, there is nothing difficult about the formation of habits. As a matter of fact the mind is constantly forming thought-habits without the conscious knowledge of the individual, responding, as the mind does, *to every influence that reaches it from one's daily environment.*

Through self-discipline one may switch the action of his mind from the response to the casual influences around him, to subjects of his own choice. This is accomplished by setting up in the mind a definite motive, based on a definite purpose, and intensifying that purpose until it becomes an obsession.

Stating the matter differently, one may fill his mind with a definite purpose that is so interesting it leaves him no time or opportunity to dwell upon other subjects. In this manner he forms definite thought-habits. The mind responds to whatever stimuli one feeds it. When a man is driven by a strong desire to achieve success in any given direction, his mind responds to that desire and forms definite thought-habits connected with the attainment of that desire.

HILL: Then organized thought begins with definiteness of purpose?

CARNEGIE: Everything man achieves begins with definiteness of purpose. Name a single instance, if you can, where a man has achieved any form of success without a definite motive, based on a definite purpose, carried out through a definite plan.

But, you must remember that there is one more factor that must be considered in connection with definiteness of purpose. The purpose must be expressed in terms of intense action. Here is where the power of the emotions gives an account of itself. The emotional feeling of desire for the attainment of a definite purpose is the power that gives life and action to that purpose, and influences one to move on his own initiative.

To insure satisfactory results, one's definite purpose should be given obsessional proportions. It should be backed by a *burning desire* for its attainment. Desires of this sort take full possession of one's mind and keep it so fully occupied that it has no inclination or opportunity to entertain stray thoughts released by the minds of others.

HILL: I believe I see what you mean. For example, a young man who is in love has no difficulty in keeping his mind on the object of his love, and not infrequently his mind works out ways and means of inducing a response to his affections, from the woman of his choice. In this sort of circumstance one has no difficulty in forming *controlled thought habits*.

CARNEGIE: A good illustration. Now switch it over to some other sort of purpose such, for example, as the development of a business, or a profession, or the attainment of a definite position, or the accumulation of money, and you will have an idea of how these ends are attained, through *obsessional* desire for their attainment.

HILL: But, Mr. Carnegie, one usually cannot put the same sort of emotional desire into the attainment of material things that he experiences in his love for the woman of his choice.

CARNEGIE: Of course not; but there are other emotions with which he can stimulate his desire for material things. Study the nine basic motives and you will observe that any sort of a desire is emotional in its nature. There is the desire for material riches, and it is a rather universal and well-developed desire with most people; the desire for personal expression leading to recognition and fame; the desire for self-preservation; and the desire for freedom of body and mind.

All of one's emotions, including, of course, the emotion of love, can be converted to the attainment of any desired end. The desire for the accumulation of material riches may, for example, be combined with one's love for the woman of his choice, where the desire for money is associated with one's desire to provide the woman of his choice with the comforts that money will buy. In such a circumstance one would have a double motive for the accumulation of money.

HILL: I see what you mean. As a matter of fact one might be influenced by all of the seven positive motives, as a driving force behind one's major purpose in life, could he not?

CARNEGIE: Yes, by the seven positive motives and, through transmutation of emotion, by the two negative motives as well. You know, of course, that any emotion, whether positive or negative, may become an inspiration to action that can be directed to the attainment of any desired end. The motive of fear, for example, often serves as a powerful inspiration to action. To benefit by it one has only to control his *action habits,* until those habits become automatic.

HILL: Do you mean that habits function voluntarily, without any effort on the part of the individual?

CARNEGIE: Yes, that is exactly what any habit does when it becomes fixed.

HILL: You say "when it becomes fixed"? What fixes a habit? Must an individual do that, and if so, how does he proceed to make a habit permanent?

CARNEGIE: Habits become fixed by some unknown law of nature which causes the impulses of thought to be taken over by the subconscious mind and voluntarily carried out. This law

does not make habits. It only fixes them so they operate automatically. The individual begins a habit by repeating a thought
or a physical act. After a time (depending upon the emotional
feeling that goes into the thought) one's thought habits are taken
over and followed voluntarily.

HILL: Then the formation of habits is something an individual
may control?

CARNEGIE: Oh, Yes! and may I remind you that the control
of habit forming is an important part of *organized thinking?* If
you overlook this fact, you will have missed the most important
thing in this interview. You see, an individual may set up any
sort of habits he chooses, go through them for a while, very much
in the same manner that one would go through a physical culture setting-up exercise, after which the habits will become automatically perpetuated without his conscious attention to them.

HILL: And you say that some unknown law of nature fixes
one's habits so they perpetuate themselves?

CARNEGIE: That is an established fact. It is one of the most
important facts in the entire field of mental phenomena, for it is
literally the medium by which an individual may *take possession
of his own mind!* Think that over before you pass on, and remember that the man who uncovers the secret by which nature
fixes man's habits, will have made a stupendous contribution to
science—a greater contribution, perhaps, than that made by Newton, who discovered the law of gravitation.

Perhaps when the discovery is made, if it ever is made, it will
be revealed that the law which fixes men's habits and the law of
gravitation are closely related, if not actually one and the same.

(This remark by Carnegie planted in his protege's mind the
seed which developed thirty years later into the revelation of the
law of Cosmic Habit-force described in a later chapter.)

HILL: Your hypothesis intrigues me, Mr. Carnegie! Could you
elaborate upon it?

CARNEGIE: Not very much. Your question reminds me of a
story I heard. After he had preached a two-hour sermon on
"sins," a colored preacher was requested, by a member of his
flock, to elaborate on the subject. "Well," said the Reverend,

"sin am de thing we have de most of and knows de least about!"

All we know definitely about habit is the fact that any thought or physical act that is repeated tends to become perpetuated, through some force which carries on the habit automatically. We know that habits can be changed, modified or eliminated altogether, by the simple process of voluntarily adopting opposing habits of a stronger nature.

For example, the habit of procrastination (a habit with which everyone is more or less afflicted) can be mastered by setting up definite habits or prompt initiative, based on a sufficiently strong motive to insure the new habits a dominating influence in the mind until they become automatic in their operation. Thus, you see that *motive* and *habit* are twin brothers! Almost every habit one adopts voluntarily is the result of a definite motive, or purpose.

You see, therefore, that one may establish any habit he desires, or eliminate any undesirable habit, by applying enough self-discipline to fix his habits, until they become automatic. If habits are not fixed voluntarily, they develop without one's conscious help. It is in this manner that most undesirable habits are formed.

HILL: It is obvious, then, that the principle of self-discipline is a necessary tool in the formation of habits one deliberately forms?

CARNEGIE: *Self-discipline* and *organized thinking* are almost synonymous terms. There can be no organized thinking without strict self-discipline, for after all, organized thought is nothing but carefully chosen thought. *Thought habits* can be established only through strict self-discipline. Motive, or obsessional desires, make self-discipline very easy. It is no trouble at all to form thought-habits if one has a definite motive, backed by a strong emotional desire for the attainment of the object of the motive.

HILL: Do you mean that it is easy for one to form thought habits in connection with subjects in which one has a keen personal interest?

CARNEGIE: That's the idea. The procrastinator drifts through life, a failure, because he has no obsessional motive for doing anything in particular. His thinking is not organized because he has chosen no specific calling for organized planning.

HILL: Will you briefly describe the major benefits of organized thinking, from the viewpoint of the man who wishes to make the best use of his time and ability?

CARNEGIE: The benefits are so numerous that it is difficult to decide where to begin or where to stop, but these are some of the more obvious advantages of this habit:

(a) Organized thinking enables one to become the master of his own mind. This he accomplishes by training his faculty of will to control his emotions, turning them on and off as occasion may require.

(b) Organized thinking forces one to work with definiteness of purpose, thereby enabling him to set up a habit that prohibits procrastination.

(c) It develops the habit of working with definite plans instead of blundering ahead by the hit or miss method.

(d) It enables one to stimulate the subconscious mind to greater action and more ready response, in the attainment of desired ends, instead of allowing the subconscious mind to respond to the "tramp" thoughts and destructive influences of one's environment.

(e) It develops self-reliance.

(f) It gives one the benefit of the knowledge, experience and education of others, through the medium of the Master Mind alliance, which is an important medium used by all able thinkers.

(g) It enables one to convert his efforts into greater material resources and larger income, since an organized mind can produce more than one that is not organized.

(h) It develops the habit of accurate analysis, through which one may find the solution to his problems instead of worrying over them.

(i) It aids in maintaining sound health, because mind power that is organized and directed toward the attainment of desirable ends has no time to be wasted in connection with self-pity or imaginary ailments. Idle minds tend to develop ailing bodies.

(j) Last, but by no mean least, organized thinking leads to peace of mind and that form of permanent happiness which is known only to the man who keeps his mind fully occupied. No one can be either happy or successful without a *planned program* for the use of his time. Planned programs are based on organized thinking.

As I have stated before, the brain is something like a rich garden spot in that it will voluntarily grow a fine crop of weeds if it is not organized and kept busy growing a more desirable crop. The weeds are represented by the stray thoughts that take possession of the unorganized, idle mind, as the result of one's daily environment.

Study this list of benefits carefully and you will reach the conclusion that any one of them offers sufficient reward to justify all the effort one puts into organizing his thinking habits. The sum total of all these benefits represents the difference between success and failure. Success is always the result of an ordered life. An ordered life comes through organized thinking and carefully *controlled habits*.

HILL: I take it, from what you have said, that work and organized thinking are essentially related.

CARNEGIE: Nothing can take the place of work, as a part of organized thinking. You see, work is thought power translated into physical action! Organized thinking can never be relied upon to become a habit until it is expressed in some form of action.

HILL: You have stated that organized thinking begins with the adoption of a Definite Purpose; that the purpose must be followed by a plan, expressed in action until the action becomes a habit. Now, will you state whether or not one may work as effectively in expressing a plan of action in connection with some form of labor he does not like to perform as he can if he performs work that he likes?

CARNEGIE: A man will always be more effective when engaged in the sort of work he likes best. That is why one's major purpose in life should be of his own choice. People who drift through life, performing work they do not like, merely because they must have an income as a means of living, seldom get more than a living from their labor. You see, this sort of labor does not inspire one to perform service in an obsessional desire to work.

It is one of the tragedies of civilization that we have not found a way to give every man the sort of work he likes best to do. That sort of work is never a drudgery.

HILL: Then it would be proper to say that organized thinking can best be done when a man moves with a definite motive, in the performance of work of his own choice, under conditions that inspire him to make his work an obsessional desire?

CARNEGIE: That would be one way of stating the matter. You will observe, as you begin to analyze men who succeed and those who fail, that the successful men always are engaged in work they like to perform. Hours mean nothing to them. They consider the joy of their labor to be an important part—perhaps the most important part—of their compensation.

HILL: Do you think the time will ever come when ordered society will find ways and means of aiding everyone to do that which he likes best to do?

CARNEGIE: Yes, I think that time will come, because that sort of a system would be not only economical, but it would do away with much of the misunderstanding that now prevails between employers and employees. The man who is engaged in work of his own choice is worth much more than the man who performs work that he does not like, no matter what the wage scale may be.

HILL: Isn't it the responsibility of the employers to find a way to assign all workmen to the sort of work they like best?

CARNEGIE: Perhaps it is, but our present system of industry does not always make this an easy matter. You see, there are only a certain number of jobs of each class of work to be performed in a business or industry, and generally the ones men like best to do are those of which there are the fewest number.

The solution of this problem will call for an improved system of employment—one that will enable an employer to select men who are suited for each particular job, with reference to their native ability, training, and preference for jobs. It will also call for a different system of compensation—a system that will give men an opportunity to earn more money when performing work that is less desirable, thereby establishing a motive for their putting more into such work.

HILL: I can see that the analysis of this subject leads one, immediately, into deep water. It seems that the solution of the problem will have to begin while the individual is being educated, through a system that will prepare him to perform work of his own choice. Then, all educational institutions should coordinate their efforts in such a manner that they would not turn out too many men for some types of work and too few for other types. This would require a periodic survey of business, industry and the professions, to enable educational institutions to determine how many men of each classification could be absorbed in employment.

CARNEGIE: Yes, the system would have to be conducted in some such manner. Right now, for example, the schools are turning out doctors, teachers, and lawyers in greater numbers than are needed in these fields, with the result that some of the members of these professions have a hard time making a living.

HILL: I take it, from your analysis, that *organized thinking* should begin with those engaged in educational work and those who manage industry and business.

CARNEGIE: That is one place where it should begin, but do not overlook the fact that the habit of organized thinking is also an individual responsibility, and the individual who overlooks it must accept from life whatever he can get. The better things of life go always to men who form habits of organized thinking. It has always been this way. It always will be. Thinking constructively is one responsibility which no one can delegate to another. *It is an individual responsibility.*

HILL: Granted, Mr. Carnegie, that organized thinking is an individual responsibility, there must be a starting-point from which one begins to acquire the ability to organize his thinking, and at least a few simple rules by which one may be guided in this business of organizing his thoughts. Could you name some of the rules?

CARNEGIE: The first thing one must recognize, in order to become an accurate thinker, is the known fact that the power with which we think is "mental dynamite" that can be organized and used constructively for the attainment of definite ends, but if it is not organized and used, through *controlled habits,* it may become a "mental explosive" that will literally blast one's hopes of achievement and lead to inevitable failure.

Stating the matter in another way, one should recognize that the power of thought is probably a projected portion of Infinite Intelligence, but every individual has been given the privilege of appropriating and using this power for the attainment of ends of his own choice; that the medium of appropriation and control is *voluntary habits!*

One cannot control Infinite Intelligence, but one can control his own mental and physical habits, thus indirectly he may appropriate and use Infinite Intelligence, because Infinite Intelligence fixes one's habits and makes them permanent and automatic in their operation.

Next, the accurate thinker must learn how to avail himself of reliable sources of information; where to obtain dependable facts which he will need in connection with organized thinking. Guesswork and hopeful wishing (the most common sources of information to a majority of the people) can never be relied upon to supplant accurate sources of facts.

Here is where the Master Mind principle becomes indispensable, as it enables one to supplant his own stock of knowledge with the knowledge, education, experience and native ability of all others with whom he has a Master Mind alliance. If one chooses his Master Mind allies wisely, as most successful business and industrial leaders choose theirs, one may have at his command the most reliable sources of knowledge that schooling and human experience have to offer. Thus, in his business of thinking, planning and organizing he has not merely his own brain to guide him, but the brains of each member of his Master Mind alliance.

There is no escape from the fact that the formation of a Master Mind alliance is one of the most important major steps one must take in order to organize his thinking, evidence of which may be found in the fact that all successful people are allied, in one way or another, with others whose knowledge they use freely. Without such an alliance there can be no such reality as effective organized thinking, and this for the reason that one brain (no matter how capable it may be) is never complete by itself.

When we speak of a man's wife as his "better half" we generally express much more of the truth than we realize, for it is a well-known fact that no man's mind is complete without a harmonious alliance with the mind of a woman. Therefore, every man should include at least one woman in his Master Mind alliance.

When the minds of male and female are combined, or blended, in a spirit of harmony, the alliance tunes in and appropriates a much greater proportion of that force which we call "spiritual power" than either can appropriate when operating independently. The man who overlooks this truth will suffer an irreparable loss of potential mind power, as there is nothing that can take the place of spiritual power.

Now I cannot tell you what "spiritual power" really is, but I assume that it is simply a greater volume of Infinite Intelligence than that which is available where the feeling we describe as "spiritual" is not present.

There are certain emotions which lift one into this exalted feeling, such as the emotion of love and the emotion of faith. While one's mind is stimulated by this exalted feeling, the faculty of the imagination becomes more alert, one's words take on a magnetic influence that makes them impressive, fear and self-limitation disappear, and one dares to undertake tasks he would not think of beginning when his mind is stimulated only by the purely mental processes of enthusiasm and desire.

HILL: Do you mean, Mr. Carnegie, that one may so relate himself to others under the Master Mind principle, that he may lift himself above the ordinary processes of mental operation of the mind, and place himself under the guiding influence of that power known as spiritual? And this, too, is a part of organized thinking?

CARNEGIE: I mean precisely that! The term "organized thinking" means everything the two words connote; that is, thinking based on every known advantage, every known mind stimulant, every known source of accurate knowledge, and the highest form of ability, whether it be native ability or acquired ability; whether it be individual ability or the ability available to one through the minds of others.

HILL: Pardon my seeming facetiousness, but I take it from what you have just said that a man who is highly skilled as an organized thinker is a sort of super-man!

CARNEGIE: To be candid, you are correct! And I am glad to know that you have at last caught the full significance of what I have been trying to tell you; namely, that the power of thought is an irresistible force; that it has no limitations save those set up by the individual, either by his lack of understanding of the possibilities of thought-power, or lack of knowledge as to how to organize, appropriate and supply this power.

HILL: What about the man who acquires great knowledge in connection with organized thinking, but uses his power unfairly, to gain advantage over others? Is there not a danger in teaching men how to become super-men, in view of the fact that some men have great capacity to use their minds, but lack a well-grounded sense of moral obligation to others?

CARNEGIE: An all-wise Creator has provided for such a circumstance, evidence of which may be found in the fact that the man who uses his mind-power to damage or destroy others soon eliminates himself by the loss of his power, and the Creator has also very wisely provided that this sort of power is something that cannot be passed on from one to another, through physical heredity. *It is a power that each individual must acquire for himself, or he does not become privileged to benefit by it.*

Go back into history and examine the records of those who have undertaken to become world conquerors, and observe what happened to them! Nero, Alexander the Great, Julius Ceasar, Napoleon Bonaparte and others of similar determination made great strides toward world domination; but look what happened to them and their achievements. Not one of them accomplished his aim, not one of them passed on to his followers any means by which his gains could be maintained; but these selfish leaders did pass on to their followers a curse that wiped out all the gains they made.

Apply the principle anywhere you choose, at any period of civilization, and observe that the effect is the same. Only the gains of men who use their mind-power beneficially have been preserved. Study the gains made by the Nazarene, for example, and observe that although they were infinitesimal during His lifetime, they have lived and spread down through nineteen centuries until the influence of Christianity is now a recognized force in every part of the world.

Give yourself no worry over the man who uses his mind power for the detriment of others, for he has fixed his own destiny by the nature of his deeds. If he is not cut down sooner, he will be wiped out within the accepted three score and ten years of average age that men live. The trend of civilization is upward, and though the line may zig-zag upward and downward at given periods, it moves eternally upward, as a whole. Wise men recognize this truth and adapt themselves to it.

HILL: I agree with what you have said, Mr. Carnegie, but there are so few wise men! The world seems populated with too many who either fail to recognize the advantages of relating themselves to others helpfully, or grossly neglect to do so, believing, no doubt, that they are smart enough to make their own rules of life and get by with them. What should be done with, or for, such people? Should they not be either taught, or forcefully made to conform to the rules of decent human relationship?

CARNEGIE: Yes, they are forced to conform, to a certain extent. Practically every man-made law that exists is evidence of the recognition of the need of a means of restraint. If everyone understood and respected the laws of nature there would be no need for man-made laws. But force is not enough to bring men into an understanding of the laws of nature. Education is also necessary. That is why you were chosen to organize the Philosophy of American Achievement. In this philosophy you have the necessary motives and inducements, in the form of promise of individual benefits, to influence people to apply the philosophy voluntarily and of their own free will. This sort of effort is far superior to that which is produced through force. *Men do best that which they wish to do!*

The most beneficial of all prayers are those we offer as an expression of gratitude for the blessings we already have.

Learn from Defeat   Chapter Ten

Two important facts of life stand out boldly!

One is the fact that the circumstances of life are such that everyone inevitably is overtaken by defeat, in many different ways, at one time or another. The other is the fact that *every adversity carries with it the seed of an equivalent benefit!*

Search where you will but you cannot find a single exception to either of these circumstances, either in your own experience or in the experiences of others. The burden of this chapter, therefore, is to describe how defeat may be made to yield "the seed of an equivalent benefit," how to convert it into a stepping stone to greater achievement, and that it is not necessary to accept defeat as a handy excuse for failure.

HILL: Mr. Carnegie, you have stated in previous interviews that there are no limitations to mental capacity except those which an individual sets up in his own mind, and you have explained this by saying that defeat can be converted into a priceless asset if one takes the right attitude toward it. Will you now explain what is the right attitude?

CARNEGIE: First of all, let me say that the right attitude toward defeat is that which refuses to accept it as anything more than temporary, and this is an attitude that one can best maintain by so developing his will-power that he looks upon defeat as a challenge to test his mettle. That challenge should be accepted as a signal that has been deliberately hoisted to inform him that his plans need mending.

Defeat should be looked upon in precisely the same manner that one accepts the unpleasant experience of physical pain, for it is obvious that physical pain is nature's way of informing one that something needs attention and correction. Pain, therefore, may be a blessing and not a curse!

The same is true of the mental anguish one experiences when

overtaken by defeat. While the feeling is unpleasant it may be, nevertheless, beneficial, because it serves as a signal by which one may be stopped from going in the wrong direction.

HILL: I see your logic, but defeat sometimes is so definite and severe that it has the effect of destroying one's initiative and self-reliance. What is to be done in such a circumstance?

CARNEGIE: Here is where the principle of self-discipline comes to one's rescue. The well-disciplined person allows nothing to destroy his belief in himself, and permits nothing to stop him from rearranging his plans and moving ahead when he is defeated. You see, he changes his plans, if they need change, but not his purpose. If one has mastered the principle of Organized Thought one knows that the power of will is equal to all the circumstances of life, and he allows nothing to destroy his *Will to win.*

HILL: You mean, I assume, that defeat should be accepted as a sort of mental tonic that can be made to serve as a means of stimulating one's will-power.

CARNEGIE: You've stated it correctly. As I told you previously, every negative emotion can be transmuted into a constructive power and used for the attainment of desirable ends. Self-discipline enables one to change unpleasant emotions into a driving power, and every time this is done it helps to develop one's power of will.

You must remember, also, that the subconscious mind accepts and acts upon one's "mental attitude." If defeat is accepted as permanent, instead of being regarded as a mere stimulant to greater action, the subconscious mind acts accordingly and makes it permanent.

You see, therefore, how important it is that one form the *habit* of searching for the good there is to be found in every form of defeat. This procedure becomes the finest sort of training of the will-power and serves, at the same time, to bring the subconscious mind into action in one's behalf.

HILL: Yes, of course! You mean that the subconscious mind carries out one's mental attitude to its logical conclusion, regardless of the nature of the circumstance which brings it into action.

CARNEGIE: Yes, but you have hardly stated the matter fully. The subconscious mind responds always to the dominating thoughts in one's mind. Moreover, it gets into the habit of acting quickly on the thoughts which are repeated most often. For example, if one falls into the habit of accepting defeat as a negative circumstance, the subconscious mind makes the same mistake and forms similar habits. That is why I stress the importance of *controlled habits.*

One's mental attitude toward defeat becomes, eventually, a habit, and this is one habit that must be controlled if one is to acquire the ability to make defeat an asset instead of a liability. You have no doubt seen men and women who by their immediate reactions seem to automatically accept defeat and who thus become confirmed pessimists.

HILL: I see what you mean. The "seed of an equivalent benefit" that is to be found in every adversity consists in the opportunity one has to use the experience as a means of developing his will-power, by accepting it as a mental stimulant to greater action. Is that your idea, Mr. Carnegie?

CARNEGIE: That states the idea in part, but you omitted saying that by accepting defeat in a positive mental attitude one thereby influences the subconscious mind to form the habit of doing the same thing. In time this habit becomes permanent, after which the subconscious mind will be reluctant to accept any experience in any except a positive attitude. In other words the subconscious mind can be trained to convert all negative experiences into an inspirational urge to greater effort. Now, that is the point I wish to emphasize.

HILL: Apparently there is no escape from the law which fastens habits upon one. If I understand you correctly, Mr. Carnegie, failure can become a habit.

CARNEGIE: Not only can failure become a habit, but the same thing applies to poverty, and worry, and pessimism of every nature. Any state of mind, whether positive or negative, becomes a habit the moment it begins to dominate the mind.

HILL: I never thought of poverty as being a habit.

CARNEGIE: Then, you must think again, because it is a habit!

When anyone accepts the condition of poverty this state of mind becomes a habit, and poor he is and so remains.

HILL: What do you mean by "accepting poverty"? How does one signify his acceptance of so undesirable a condition as poverty, in a country like ours, where there is an abundance of riches of every nature?

CARNEGIE: A man *accepts* poverty by neglecting to create a plan to acquire riches. His act may be, as it usually is, entirely negative, consisting of nothing but the lack of a definite purpose. He may not be conscious of his acceptance, but the result is the same. The subconscious mind acts on one's dominating "mental attitude."

HILL: From what you say about habits, I reach the conclusion that success is a habit.

CARNEGIE: Now you are getting the idea! Of course success is a habit. It is a habit that one forms by adopting a Definite Major Aim, laying out a plan for the attainment of that aim, and working the plan for all he is worth. Beyond that the subconscious mind comes to one's rescue and helps by inspiring one with ideas through which the object of one's aims may be acquired.

HILL: It is true, then, that one who is born in an environment of poverty, where he sees nothing but poverty, hears nothing talked of but poverty, and associates daily with those who have accepted poverty, has "two strikes" on him to begin with.

CARNEGIE: That's precisely right, but do not assume that there is nothing one can do about such a circumstance, for it is a well-established fact that most of the successful people of America began under just such a condition as you have described.

HILL: What is one going to do to master a condition which brings the majority of the children into the world in an environment of poverty, in a country like ours, where there is plenty for everyone? Is there not a responsibility resting upon someone to help correct such a condition? Are helpless children to be left to their own fates merely because they selected the wrong environment in which to be born?

CARNEGIE: Now you are getting at the very heart of what I had in mind when I gave you the job of organizing the Philosophy of American Achievement, and I am happy to see you becoming fired with enthusiasm in connection with this vital subject. What I propose to do about poverty I am doing right now, by preparing you to help people master poverty.

As I have already told you, I am giving away the money I have accumulated, but this is not the solution of any part of the problem you mention. What the people need is not a gift of money, *but a* gift of knowledge with which they may become self-determining, including not only the accumulation of money, but the more important matter of learning how to find happiness in their relationships with others.

America is the most desirable country that civilization has ever created, but there is plenty of work yet to be done before it becomes the paradise on earth that it may become. *Paradise and poverty do not mix!* Men's souls cannot grow while their stomachs are empty.

The march of human progress cannot move rapidly where a majority of the people suffer with inferiority complexes growing out of the fear of poverty. And I may as well call your attention, here and now, to the fact that there can be no enduring happiness for the few who have wealth as long as a majority of their neighbors have less than the minimum necessities of life.

Now do not falsely conclude that I am advocating any system whereby we will all turn socialistic and divide up our possessions with our neighbors. That would not change the condition of poverty, for you must remember that *poverty is a state of mind, a habit!* No, gifts of material things will never save anyone from poverty.

The place to begin changing poverty is in the individual mind, and the way to begin is by inspiring the individual to use his mind, to become creative, to render useful service in return for that which he desires. That is one sort of gift that cannot damage anyone, and it is precisely the sort of gift that I am preparing you to take to the American people.

HILL: Then you believe that a man cannot get the most out of material wealth unless he earns it, himself.

CARNEGIE: That's it! The highest aim of human beings is a

state of mind known as happiness. I have never heard of any-one finding enduring happiness except by *some form of personal action of benefit to others.* You see, the business of accumulating riches, if it is carried on in the right spirit, not only provides a man with the necessities and the luxuries his nature requires, but he also finds happiness in his activities.

It is a part of the inherent nature of mankind to wish to build and create and indulge in personal expression, to own material wealth beyond the actual necessities of life, and to attain happiness in proportion to the service performed.

HILL: You are leading me into pretty deep water, Mr. Carnegie, but I can see the soundness of your viewpoint. You mean that the possession and ownership of material things cannot, of themselves, give one happiness, but the usage of these things can. Is that your belief?

CARNEGIE: Not merely my belief, but the existing fact! I ought to know, because I have been on both sides of the fence. I began in poverty and worked my way into riches. Therefore, I speak from experience when I say that real riches consist not in material things, but in the use one gives to material things. That is why I am divesting myself of most of my material wealth. But, mind you, I am not giving it away to individuals, but I am placing it where it may inspire individuals to help themselves.

HILL: It is your intention, then, to provide the people of America with a practical philosophy that will help them to acquire riches the same way you acquired them, through self-effort?

CARNEGIE: That is the only safe way for anyone to acquire anything!

It is my aim to provide the American people with a philosophy that will make them success-conscious. This is the only possible way, as far as I know, in which the poverty-consciousness you mentioned can be mastered. It certainly cannot be eliminated through any system of gifts of material things.

That sort of system would only soften the people and make them more dependent. What this country needs is a philosophy similar to that of the pioneers who settled the country—a philosophy of self-determination which gives every individual both an incentive to acquire wealth for himself, and a practical means of accomplishing this end.

HILL: Do you mean that you do not believe in charity, Mr. Carnegie?

CARNEGIE: Surely I believe in charity, but do not overlook the fact that the soundest of all forms of charity is that which helps a man to help himself. That form of help begins by aiding a man to organize his own mind.

Every normal mind has within it the seed of both success and failure. My idea of charity is a system that will encourage the growth of the seed of success and discourage the growth of the seed of failure. I believe in personal gifts of material things only where individuals are unable, through physical or mental disability, to help themselves.

But, we often make mistakes in this sort of charity, by recognizing physical disability through gifts while ignoring the possibilities of encouraging those who are physically disabled to begin using their minds.

I know many people whose physical afflictions are sufficient to justify them in expecting charity, but they refuse such help because they have found ways of earning a living through the use of their minds. In this way they escape the humility of the acceptance of help from others.

HILL: But you do believe in the maintenance of poorhouses for the indigent and aged who are unable to support themselves, do you not?

CARNEGIE: No! emphatically I do not! The very word "poorhouse" carries connotations that lead to the development of inferiority complexes. But I do believe in a system of compensation for the aged and the indigent, provided it allows the individual to live his own life, in an environment of his own choice.

The proper way to handle such cases is by a carefully supervised system of monthly or weekly allowance which permits the individual to maintain his own home environments. I do not think the system should end with the mere donation of money. It should provide for some form of mental activity, where the individual is mentally fit, if it is nothing more than reading.

The greatest of all curses is that which deprives a person of "mental food" and consigns him to eternal idleness. I never hear of a man "retiring" from active life that I do not feel sorry for him, for I know that man was not created to remain idle as long as he has a mind with which to think. I know, too, that no idle person is happy.

HILL: Then you do not believe in the prison system that deprives men of liberty without providing them with adequate constructive opportunity to use their minds and bodies?

CARNEGIE: No, I do not! Such a system is brutal, and it is none the less so because some men have criminal tendencies and cannot be trusted at large. Every prison should provide ample activity for both the body and the mind of prisoners. Men cannot be reformed by punishment, nor by idleness.

Reformation can come only through properly guided activity, by force if necessary, which results in the development of the right sort of habits. The curse of our prison system is the fact that it is generally conducted as a form of "punishment" and not as a system of *restoration!* If you restore a man to normalcy you do it by changing the *habits of his thinking.* And that applies to those who are out of prison the same as those who are in.

There are millions of people in an imaginary prison who have been charged with no crime. They are prisoners in their own minds, consigned there by their own self-imposed limitations, through the acceptance of poverty, and the acceptance of temporary defeat. It is this sort of prisoner that I hope to release, through the Philosophy of American Achievement.

HILL: I never thought of free men as being prisoners, but I can see from your analysis that many are.

CARNEGIE: And the worst part of the story is the fact that millions of these unfortunates are little children who were born to such imprisonment. Children who did not ask to be brought into the world, but find themselves here, in a prison as strong and as deadly as any that is built of iron bars and stone walls. These little prisoners must be rescued! The rescue must begin by awakening them to the realization of the power of their own minds.

HILL: Where and how is this awakening to take place, Mr. Carnegie?

CARNEGIE: It should begin in the home and be carried on, also, as a part of the public school system. But nothing along this line will happen until someone comes forth with a practical plan that has public support.

HILL: And you think there is a nation-wide need for some supplementary form of training through which school children may be taught the fundamentals of individual achievement, based on personal initiative?

CARNEGIE: That is one of America's greatest needs. Remember what I tell you: if such a system is not introduced, the time will come, and very soon, when this country will cease to be the nation of pioneers it has been in the past. People will become indifferent to opportunity; they will cease to act on their own initiative; they will become easy victims of even the slightest form of defeat.

HILL: You believe, then, that thrift and the spirit of self-determination are qualities that should be taught in the public schools?

CARNEGIE: Yes, and in the home as well. But the trouble with most homes is the fact that the parents are as much in need of this sort of training as are the children. As a matter of fact parents are the worst offenders in the matter of influencing children to accept poverty, for it is but natural that children accept whatever conditions of life their parents accept.

HILL: Then you believe that self-discipline should begin in the home, and it should be demonstrated by the parents, in the form of thrift, ambition and self-reliance?

CARNEGIE: The home is the first place where a child gets its impressions of life, and it is here that the child often acquires habits of failure that endure throughout life. Trace the record of any successful person and you will find that somewhere, probably during his early childhood, he came under the influence of some success-conscious person, perhaps a member of his own family, or a near relative. When a person once acquires a success-consciousness, he seldom allows it to be stifled through defeat.

You might say that success-consciousness gives one a sort of immunity againt all forms of defeat.

HILL: Now, Mr. Carnegie, you must have learned, from your wide and varied experience with people, what are the major causes of failure. Will you mention the outstanding causes?

CARNEGIE: Yes, I was coming to that in a few minutes, because it is essential that a practical philosophy of individual achievement include both the causes of success and the causes of failure. You may be surprised to learn that there are more than twice as many major causes of failure as there are causes of success.

HILL: Will you name these causes in the order of their importance?

CARNEGIE: That would not be practical, but I will name some of them and place at the head of the list the most common of all causes of failure, *viz:*

1. The *habit of drifting through life,* without a Definite Major Purpose. This is one of the key-causes of failure in that it leads to other causes of failure.

2. Unfavorable physical hereditary foundation at birth. Incidentally, this is the only cause of failure that is not subject to elimination, and even this can be bridged, through the principle of the Master Mind.

3. The habit of meddlesome curiosity concerning other people's affairs, through which time and energy are wasted.

4. Inadequate preparation for the work in which one engages, especially inadequate schooling.

5. Lack of self-discipline, generally manifesting itself through excesses in eating, drinking intoxicating beverages, and sex.

6. Indifference toward opportunities for self-advancement.

7. Lack of ambition to aim above mediocrity.

8. Ill health, often due to wrong thinking, improper diet and exercise.

9. Unfavorable environmental influences during early childhood.

10. Lack of persistence in carrying through to a finish that

which one starts (due, in the main, to a lack of a definite purpose and self-discipline).

11. The habit of maintaining a negative "mental attitude" in connection with life generally.

12. Lack of control over the emotions, through *controlled* habits.

13. The desire for something for nothing, usually expressed through gambling and more offensive habits of dishonesty.

14. Indecision and indefiniteness.

15. One or more of the seven basic fears: (1) poverty (2) criticism (3) ill health (4) loss of love (5) old age (6) loss of liberty (7) death.

16. Wrong selection of a mate in marriage.

17. Over caution in business and occupational relationships.

18. Excess tendency toward chance.

19. Wrong choice of associates in business or occupational work.

20. Wrong choice of a vocation, or total neglect to make a choice.

21. Lack of concentration of effort, leading to dissipation of one's time and energies.

22. The habit of indiscriminate spending, without a budget control over income and expenditures.

23. Failure to budget and use TIME properly.

24. Lack of controlled enthusiasm.

25. Intolerance—a closed mind based particularly on ignorance or prejudice in connection with religion, politics and economics.

26. Failure to cooperate with others in a spirit of harmony.

27. Craving for power or wealth not earned nor based on merit.

28. Lack of a spirit of loyalty where loyalty is due.

29. Egotism and vanity not under control.

30. Exaggerated selfishness.

31. The habit of forming opinions and building plans without basing them on known facts.

32. Lack of vision and imagination.

33. Failure to make "Master Mind" alliance with those whose experience, education and native ability are needed.

34. Failure to recognize the existence of, and the means of adapting one's self to the forces of Infinite Intelligence.

35. Profanity of speech, reflecting, as it does, evidence of an unclean and undisciplined mind, and an inadequate vocabulary.

36. Speaking before thinking. Talking too much.

37. Covetousness, revenge, and greed.

38. The habit of procrastination, often based on plain laziness, but generally the result of lack of a definite major purpose.

39. Speaking slanderously of other people, with or without cause.

40. Ignorance of the nature and purpose of the power of thought, and lack of knowledge of the principles of operation of the mind.

41. Lack of personal initiative, due, in the main, to the lack of a definite major purpose.

42. Lack of self-reliance, due, also, to absence of an obsessional motive founded on a definite major purpose.

43. Lack of the qualities of a pleasing personality.

44. Lack of faith in one's self, in the future, in one's fellow-men, in God.

45. Failure to develop the power of will, through voluntary, controlled habits of thought.

These are not all the causes of failure, but they represent the major portion of them. All these causes, except number two, can be either eliminated or brought under control, through application of the principle of definiteness of a major purpose and mastery of the will-power. You might say, therefore, that the first and last of these causes of failure control all the others except one.

HILL: Do you mean that if one masters the first and the last of these forty-five causes of failure he would be well on the road toward success?

CARNEGIE: Yes, if a man is working toward the attainment of a definite major purpose, and has his will-power so organized that he is using it to best advantage in directing the forces of his mind, I would say that he is well within the sight of success.

HILL: But, these two principles alone are not sufficient to save a man from defeat, are they, Mr. Carnegie?

CARNEGIE: No, but they are sufficient to enable him to make a comeback and go ahead with his plans. As I have stated, self-discipline means that a man will not accept any circumstance of defeat as being more than a temporary experience which serves as a challenge to greater effort.

HILL: Suppose the defeat is of a nature that it seriously impairs a man's use of his physical body, such, for example, as the loss of his legs, or hands, or a stroke of paralysis which limits or deprives him entirely of the use of his physical body? Wouldn't that seriously handicap one?

CARNEGIE: To be sure, it would handicap one, but it need not necessarily be accepted as permanent defeat. Some of the most successful men the world has ever known attained their greatest success after having been physically afflicted. Here, again, let me remind you that the Master Mind principle is sufficient to provide a man with every sort of knowledge that is available to mankind and it can be used to take the place of all physical effort.

HILL: Then if a man fails to apply the Master Mind principle he may be defeated because of his own neglect, since there is a remedy available to him.

CARNEGIE: You have the idea correctly. The Master Mind principle can be used as a substitute for everything save only the use of the brain. As long as a man can think, he can use this principle, and it sometimes happens that men do not discover the possibilities of their own minds until they are deprived of the use of some essential portion of their physical bodies. In such cases it may be generally said that their physical handicap becomes a blessing in disguise.

I know a blind man who is one of the most successful teachers of music in the United States, if not in the entire world. Before he was overtaken by this affliction he earned only a modest living, as the member of an orchestra. His affliction had the effect of introducing him to a wider field of opportunity, with a much greater financial income. Helen Keller used her affliction to make her one of America's great women.

Helen Keller has proved that the loss of two of the most important of the five senses need not necessarily condemn one to failure. Through the use of her will-power she has very definitely bridged both of her physical impairments. With the aid of the Master Mind principle, she is rendering useful service by teaching the whole world the needed lesson that the mind need not remain imprisoned, even though the physical body be greatly impaired.

Beethoven made a similar demonstration. Sometimes the loss of physical qualities only tends to strengthen one's mental qualities, and I have yet to know of the first man who attained great success without having met and mastered great difficulties, in the form of temporary defeat. Every time a man rises from defeat, he becomes mentally and spiritually stronger. Thus, in time, one may actually find himself—his true, inner self—through temporary defeat.

Two kinds of people never get ahead. Those who do only that which they are told to do and those who will not do what they are told to do.

Seek Inspiration
(*Applied Enthusiasm*)

"Inspiration," as used here, has reference to that combination of emotions usually known as "enthusiasm," but *inspired feeling* has a deeper meaning because it is related to the spiritual powers of man, and has its source in the subconscious mind.

Inspiration—the emotions put into action through spiritual power—is the beginning of all great achievements of whatever nature!

Everyone desires to achieve personal success, in one form or another, but only those who acquire the habit of fanning the fire of enthusiasm into a white heat of *obsessional desire* ever attain noteworthy success.

More than forty years ago the step-mother of a young mountaineer called him into the family living room, excluded the other children of the family from the conference, and said something which changed his entire life for the better, and at the same time planted in his mind a desire which he has transplanted into thousands of other minds—the desire to become self-determining through the rendering of useful service.

This boy was only eleven years of age, but he was known among the mountain folk as the "worst boy in the county!" This is what his step-mother said to him:

"People misjudge you. They call you the worst boy in the county, but you are not the worst boy; you are the most active boy, and all you need is a definite purpose to which you can direct the attention of your inquiring mind. You have a keen imagination and plenty of initiative. Therefore I suggest that you become a writer. If you will do this, and give as much interest to reading and writing as you have been devoting to playing pranks on the neighbors, you may live to see the time when your influence will be felt throughout this state."

There was something in the step-mother's tone of voice which registered effectively in the "bad" boy's mind. He caught the spirit of enthusiasm in which his step-mother had spoken to him, and began, immediately, to act on her suggestion.

By the time he was 15 years of age he was writing newspaper and magazine stories that were being published in small newspapers and magazines. His writing was not brilliant, but it carried a spirit of enthusiasm which made it readable.

At the age of 18 he was assigned, by the editor of Bob Taylor's Magazine, to write the story of Andrew Carnegie's achievements in industry. That assignment was destined to bring another change in his life, for it led not only to an opportunity to write books that would make his influence felt throughout the state, as his step-mother had suggested, but that influence now extends throughout a major portion of the world, and it is obviously destined to render useful service in helping to save the American way of life from annihilation.

In the interview with Andrew Carnegie, this young writer was moved by Mr. Carnegie's enthusiasm. He acquired the spirit of that enthusiasm, and it has been that spirit which has made his books "best sellers" for many years.

Mr. Carnegie has emphasized the importance of initiative, definiteness of purpose, persistence and organized endeavor. We come, now, to the chapter in which an analysis will be made of the power behind all these—the power that gives life and action to these qualities. That power is known as inspiration.

HILL: I am ready, Mr. Carnegie, for your analysis of the eleventh principle of individual achievement, which you call inspiration. I wish you to define the meaning of this term and describe how one may develop enthusiasm at will.

CARNEGIE: Inspiration can be developed by stimulating the faculty of the emotions, through any of the fourteen major emotions we have mentioned in previous interviews, or any other emotion.

HILL: Then inspiration is emotion in action?

CARNEGIE: That is the brief way of stating it. Perhaps it

would be more correctly stated if one said that inspiration is voluntary emotion—a feeling that one initiates at will. But, you have overlooked one very important factor in your question, the question of *control* of inspiration. It is just as important to know how to modify, control, or shut off entirely, the action of the emotions as it is to know how to start them into action.

Before we go into the discussion of emotional control, however, let us take inventory of the benefits available through inspiration. To begin with, let us be reminded that inspiration is the result of desire, expressed in terms of action, and based upon motive. Inspiration is a form of animation which creates enthusiasm. No normal person ever goes into a heat of enthusiasm without a motive. It is obvious, therefore, that the beginning of all enthusiasm is desire based on motive.

There are two types of enthusiasm, passive and active. Perhaps it would be more accurate if I said that enthusiasm may be expressed in two ways: passively, through the stimulation of emotional feeling, and actively, by the expression of feeling, through words or deeds.

HILL: Which is the more beneficial of the two—the active expression or the passive?

CARNEGIE: The answer to that depends upon the circumstances. Of course passive enthusiasm always precedes the expression of active enthusiasm, as one must feel it before he can express it in any form of action or words.

There are times when the expression of enthusiasm may be detrimental to one's interest, as it may indicate over-eagerness, or disclose one's state of mind under circumstances when he does not wish to have it known to others. It is highly important, then, that one learn how to withhold the expression of his feelings under all circumstances. It is also important that one acquire the ability to give open expression of his feelings at will. In both instances, the control is the important factor.

Now let us briefly describe some of the benefits of both passive and active enthusiasm. First of all, let us remember that enthusiasm (which may be an expression of one or more of the emotions) stimulates the vibration of thought and makes it more intense, thus starting the faculty of the imagination to work in connection with the motive which inspired the enthusiasm.

Enthusiasm gives tone quality to one's voice and makes it pleasing and impressive. A salesman or public speaker would be ineffective without the ability to turn on his enthusiasm at will. The same is true of one who engages in ordinary conversation. Even the most prosaic subjects can be made interesting if they are expressed with enthusiasm. Without it the most interesting subjects can become boresome.

Enthusiasm inspires initiative, both in thought and in physical action. It is very difficult for one to do well, that in which he has no feeling of enthusiasm.

Enthusiasm dispels physical fatigue and overcomes laziness. It has been said that there are no lazy men. What appears to be a lazy man is one who is moved by no motive over which he becomes enthusiastic.

Enthusiasm stimulates the entire nervous system and causes it to perform its duties more efficiently, including, in particular, the function of digestion of food. For this reason the meal hour should be the pleasantest hour of the day, and it should never become the occasion for settling personal or family differences of opinion, nor should it become the time for the correction of the faults of the children.

Enthusiasm stimulates the subconscious section of the brain and puts it to work in connection with the motive which inspires enthusiasm. In fact there is no known method of stimulating the subconscious mind voluntarily except that of inspired feeling. Here let us emphasize the fact that the subconscious mind acts upon all feeling, whether it is negative or positive. It will act on the emotion of fear as quickly as it will act on the emotion of love. Or, it will go to work on the worry over poverty as quickly as it will act on the feeling of opulence. It is important, therefore, to recognize that enthusiasm is *the positive expression* of feeling.

Enthusiasm is contagious! It affects everyone within its range, a fact that is well known to all master salesmen. Moreover, one may influence others through either the active or the passive expression of enthusiasm, as passive enthusiasm stimulates one's brain so that it sends out highly intensified thought vibrations that may be picked up by others.

Enthusiasm discourages all forms of negative thought, and dispels fear and worry, thus preparing the mind for the expression of faith.

Enthusiasm is the twin-brother of the faculty of the will, *it being the major source of sustained action of the will!* It is also a sustaining force in connection with persistence. We might say, therefore, that will power, persistence and enthusiasm are triplets which give one sustained action with a minimum loss of physical energy. As a matter of fact enthusiasm converts fatigue and static energy into active energy.

Emerson spoke a deeper truth than most people recognize when he said that "Nothing great was ever achieved without enthusiasm." He must have known that enthusiasm gives quality to every word a man speaks, to every task at which he sets his hands.

HILL: I have heard it said that writers unconsciously project their enthusiasm, or the lack of it, in every word they write, so that even the casual reader may interpret the writer's mental attitude as he wrote. Is this a sound theory?

CARNEGIE: Not just a sound theory, but a fact. Try it out yourself and be convinced. A man's writing may be translated into other languages, but it will very largely carry with it the same tempo of enthusiasm the writer felt when writing.

I have heard it said that the writer of advertisements who feels no enthusiasm in connection with his copy, writes poor copy, no matter how many facts he may describe. I have also heard it said that the lawyer who feels no enthusiasm over his case fails to be convincing to judges and juries.

And there is plenty of evidence that the enthusiasm of a doctor is his greatest remedy in the sick-room. Enthusiasm is one of the greatest builders of confidence, for everyone knows that enthusiasm and faith are closely related.

Enthusiasm denotes hope and courage and belief in one's self. I do not recall ever having promoted a man to a higher position, or ever having employed a man for a responsible position, who did not first demonstrate his enthusiasm over the possibilities of the position. I have observed that the young people who have gone to work in our offices, as clerks and stenographers, have promoted themselves into more responsible positions in almost exact ratio to the enthusiasm they displayed in their work.

HILL: Is it not possible for one to display too much enthusiasm for his own good?

CARNEGIE: Yes, uncontrolled enthusiasm often is as detrimental as no enthusiasm. For example, the man who is so enthusiastic over himself and his own ideas that he monopolizes the conversation when conversing with others is sure to be unpopular, not to mention the fact that he misses many opportunities to learn by listening to others.

Then, there is the man who becomes too enthusiastic over the roulette wheel or the horses, and the man who becomes more enthusiastic over ways and means of getting something for nothing than he does over rendering useful service, not to mention the woman who becomes more enthusiastic over card parties and society than she does over making her home and herself attractive to her husband. This sort of uncontrolled enthusiasm may be very detrimental to all whom it affects.

HILL: Is enthusiasm of any value to the man engaged in manual labor?

CARNEGIE: I can best answer that by calling your attention to the fact that most of the higher officials of my own organization began in the humblest of positions. The man who made the greatest progress of all my associates began as a stake driver, and he formerly worked as a teamster. His boundless enthusiasm was the quality that first attracted my attention to him, and it was this same quality that lifted him, step by step, into the highest position we had to offer.

Yes, enthusiasm can be of value to anyone, regardless of his occupation, for it is a quality that attracts friends, establishes confidence, and breaks down the opposition of others.

HILL: What part, if any, does enthusiasm or lack of it play in the relationship of the home?

CARNEGIE: Let us go back a little way, and consider the part that enthusiasm plays in bringing men and women together in a bond of marriage. Did you ever hear of a man winning the woman of his choice without displaying considerable enthusiasm over her? And, it also works the other way around. A man will not be inclined to propose marriage to the woman who shows no enthusiasm over him.

Mutual enthusiasm, therefore, is usually the basis of marriage, and woe unto the party to the marriage who allows that enthusiasm to wane afterward. We speak of the relationship as love, but what is love but mutual enthusiasm of two people over each other?

HILL: Under what circumstances does enthusiasm reach its highest degree of personal benefit?

CARNEGIE: In a Master Mind alliance, two or more people work together, in a spirit of perfect harmony, for the attainment of a definite purpose. Here the enthusiasm of each member of the alliance projects itself into the minds of all the other members, and the sum total of enthusiasm thus created, by the harmonious blending of a group of minds, becomes available to and influences each individual member.

HILL: You mean, for example, where there are, let us say, a dozen men allied in a Master Mind group, each man in the alliance has his own enthusiasm supplemented by that of all the others. Therefore, his enthusiasm becomes multiplied by twelve. Is that the idea?

CARNEGIE: That is the general idea, but it often happens that the enthusiasm of one or more members of such an alliance is increased much more than the sum total of the entire group. One of the strange effects of a Master Mind alliance is the fact that it brings into operation the principle of increasing returns, in connection with the stepping up of the vibrations of the mind, so that one person may feel the effects of enthusiasm to an extent that produces the state of mind known as faith.

Theoretically, what happens is this: The influence of the Master Mind alliance of minds steps up the rate of thought vibration to where it reaches the level of Infinite Intelligence on the part of one or more members of the alliance. Under such a condition I have known men to create ideas they were not capable of creating alone, under the ordinary circumstances of thought— *ideas far beyond the range of knowledge of all the members combined.*

HILL: I can see that enthusiasm is a greatly misunderstood word, judging by what you have just said.

CARNEGIE: It is perhaps the most misunderstood word in the English language, for there are but few who recognize that the so-called genius is only a man who, because of his great capacity for enthusiasm, steps up the vibrations of his mind until he is enabled to communicate with a source of knowledge not available to him through his faculty of reason alone.

Most so-called enthusiasm is nothing but an uncontrolled expression of one's ego—a state of mental excitement which is easily recognized as nothing but a meaningless expression of personal vanity. That sort of enthusiasm may be very detrimental to those who indulge in it, as they usually express themselves in some form of exaggeration.

HILL: Will you give more details concerning your statement that many of your employees have promoted themselves through the expression of enthusiasm? Just what effect did their enthusiasm have on their jobs that entitled them to promotion?

CARNEGIE: It not only had an effect on their own jobs, *but it affected those who worked with them!* You recall my statement to the effect that a man with a negative mind, working in a plant where he may contact hundreds of other workmen, may influence all the others to become also negative to a greater or lesser degree. Well, the same principle applies where one has a positive mind and expresses enthusiasm in connection with his work.

Any state of mind is contagious!

There is a law of nature which tends to make men's thought-habits permanent. That same law may also be related to the principle of telepathy, through which thought passes from one brain to another. At any rate, the person with an active mind, whether it be negative or positive, will influence every person within range of that mind so that he acquires a portion of it.

Now you can see why an employee with a positive mind is worth more than one with a negative mind. The employee who thinks in terms of enthusiasm naturally is one who is happy in his work. He therefore radiates a wholesome mental attitude that spreads to those around him and they, too, take on a part of his attitude. Accordingly, they become more efficient workers.

But that is not the only reason why the person who expresses enthusiasm as a habit promotes himself into the more desirable positions of life. Enthusiasm, as I have already stated, gives one a keener imagination, increases his initiative, makes him more alert of mind, gives him a more pleasing personality, and thereby attracts the cooperation of others. These traits of mind make it inevitable that one promotes himself into any position which he may become capable of filling.

Every thought one releases becomes a definite part of one's character! This transformation takes place through the principle of auto-suggestion. One does not have to be a mathematician to figure out what will happen to the person whose dominating thoughts are positive, in view of the fact that such a person is adding power to his own character with every thought he releases.

Thought by thought he builds a personality that provides him with a strong will, a keen imagination, self-reliance, persistence, initiative and the courage and ambition to *desire and to acquire* whatever he wants. An employer has but little to do with the promotion of such a person. If one employer neglects to recognize his ability, he finds another who will, but he manages to keep growing and advancing in any direction he chooses.

HILL: I get the idea, Mr. Carnegie. An employee whose mind is dominated by the spirit of enthusiasm is beneficial to an employer, not only by his influence on other employees, but because of his own acquired strength of personality. Is that what you mean?

CARNEGIE: That's what I mean. And the principle applies to everyone; not merely to an employee. Take the owner of a retail store, for example, and you will find that his mental attitude is definitely reflected in every person who works in the store. I have heard it said that a skilled psychologist can walk through any retail store, study the employees a few minutes, and then give a surprisingly accurate description of the owner or the dominating head of the store, without ever seeing him or hearing a word spoken of him.

HILL: Then one might say that a store, or a business, has its own "personality" consisting of the dominating influence of the personnel of the business. Is that true?

CARNEGIE: Yes, and it is true of the home, or any place where people gather regularly. The psychologist with a keen sense of perception can walk into any home, get the "mental feel" of the place, and tell precisely whether the home is dominated by the spirit of harmony or the spirit of bickering and friction. The mental attitude of people leaves its permanent influence on the very atmosphere of their environment.

Every city, for example, has its own rate of vibration, made up of the dominating influences and the mental attitudes of the people who live there. Moreover, every street, and every block in every street, has its own "personality," each being so different from the others that the trained psychologist can walk down any street, blind-folded, and pick up enough information from the "mental feel" of the street to give an accurate description of the people who live there.

HILL: That seems almost incredible, Mr. Carnegie.

CARNEGIE: Perhaps it may, to the inexperienced person, but not so to the skilled interpreter of people's "mental attitude." If you wish convincing evidence of the accuracy of what I have said, make an experiment of your own.

Take a walk down Fifth Avenue, in New York City, and observe the feeling of opulence you pick up as you go along. Then go across to the tenement section, take a stroll down that thoroughfare, and observe the feeling of defeatism and poverty that you will pick up. The experiment will provide you with undeniable evidence that the vibrations of Fifth Avenue and the vibrations of the tenement street are direct opposites, one negative, the other positive.

Carry the experiment still further by going into private homes. Choose a home where you know there is domestic harmony and cooperation. Study carefully the "mental feel" you pick up in this home, without anyone speaking a word to you. Then, go into a home where you know the domestic relationship is disturbed by inharmony and family friction. Study the "mental feel" you pick up there. By the time you have made a dozen such experiments, you will know from first-hand experience that every home has a "mental atmosphere" that harmonizes perfectly with the "mental attitude" of those who live there.

This experiment will also convince you that there is some unknown law of nature which fixes the habits of thought and tends to give them permanency. The law not only gives permanency to thought, in the mind of the individual, but it extends the influence of that thought to the environment in which one lives.

It will pay anyone to stand on the side lines of life and watch himself go by so he may see himself as others see him.

Control Your Attention *Chapter Twelve*

HILL: Mr. Carnegie, you have named the twelfth principle of the philosophy of individual achievement, Controlled Attention. Will you describe how this principle can be applied in the practical affairs of life?

CARNEGIE: Very well; let us take note, first of all, of the fact that Controlled Attention is directly related to all the previous eleven principles we have analyzed. As a matter of fact, there is a portion of each of these eleven principles combined with the principle of Controlled Attention.

From this you will observe that the proper approach to mastery of the principle of Controlled Attention is by mastery and application of the eleven principles previously covered.

Now let us define the term Controlled Attention, and make sure we understand exactly what it means. It is the act of combining all the faculties of the mind and concentrating them upon the attainment of a definite purpose. The time involved in the act of concentration of thought on a given subject depends upon the nature of the subject and upon that which one expects in connection with it.

Take my own case, for example. The dominating forces of my mind are, and have been for many years, concentrated upon the making and marketing of steel.

I have others allied with me who likewise concentrate their dominating thoughts upon the same objective. Thus we have the benefit of Controlled Attention in collective form, consisting, as it does, of the individual mind power of a great number of people, all working toward the same end, in a spirit of harmony.

HILL: Could you not have carried on other business activities just as successfully as you conducted the steel industry, and at the same time? Wouldn't the Master Mind principle have made this possible?

CARNEGIE: I have known men to conduct many separate, unrelated businesses successfully, with the aid of the Master Mind; but I have always believed they would have done much better had they confined their efforts entirely to one line of business. Splitting one's attention has the effect of dividing one's powers. The best plan for anyone to follow is to devote all his energies to some specific field. This concentration enables one to specialize in that field.

HILL: But what about doctors who engage in general practice? Do they not have a better opportunity to add to their income than those who specialize in one particular branch of medicine?

CARNEGIE: The exact opposite is true. If you ever have occasion to engage a specialist to remove your appendix, as I have had, you will learn that specialization in medicine pays. When I was a small boy the old family physician who used to look after the health of the people of our neighborhood, would have removed an appendix for $25.00, and I suspect he could have done the job about as well as the specialist who charged me more than ten times that amount. But, I called in the specialist just the same.

HILL: Does this same rule apply in the field of retail merchandising?

CARNEGIE: It applies in every line of business and every calling. Modern merchandising has practically made the old-fashioned general store obsolete. While the most prosperous stores are departmentalized, they are not the same as the old general merchandise stores, because each department is managed by a specialist who devotes all his time to that department. You might say that a modern department store is nothing but a group of highly specialized stores, all operating under one roof and one general overhead, but possessing increased buying power that gives the store a tremendous advantage over smaller stores.

HILL: You would say, then, that the department store is managed under the principle of Controlled Attention?

CARNEGIE: That and other principles of the philosophy of individual achievement, especially the Master Mind principle and Definiteness of Purpose.

HILL: What about the banking business? Is it managed, also, by application of the principle of Controlled Attention?

CARNEGIE: Very much so! Every department of a large bank, and practically every individual position in each department, is highly specialized. The same is true of railroading. Practically every position in the railroad business is specialized. Promotions are from the bottom upward, and the men holding the more responsible positions have had training in nearly all the subordinate positions; but they never undertake to hold two jobs at the same time.

It is the same in the steel industry. Men become highly skilled by confining their efforts to specialized work. Here, too, promotions are from the bottom upward. All of our head men have served their apprenticeship in subordinate jobs in the operating end of the business.

HILL: You believe, then, that the better opportunities of the future will be available to those who concentrate their efforts along some specialized lines?

CARNEGIE: It has always been that way. Perhaps it always will be.

HILL: What about the profession of teaching? Is it not possible for a teacher to prepare himself to teach many different subjects?

CARNEGIE: It is possible, but not advisable. The big universities are nothing but a group of associated colleges, each specializing in some particular branch of education. If it were practical for a teacher to do better work by devoting his efforts to a diversity of subjects, the universities would have discovered this long ago.

HILL: What about the student who is preparing himself for a life work? Should he specialize in some particular branch of education?

CARNEGIE: Yes, if he knows what his Definite Major Purpose in life is to be. Otherwise he should confine his efforts to a general educational course until such time as he chooses a goal. Then he should continue his education through specialized training. The lawyer, for example, usually takes a course in general education, then specializes in law. The doctor usually does likewise. General education gives one an approach to organized thinking, self-discipline and self-reliance—all essential qualities for success in any calling.

HILL: What about the stenographer? Should he or she concentrate on one line of work?

CARNEGIE: The stenographer must specialize, obviously, before procuring a position. After that he may have to engage in general service for a time, but the stenographer who does not wish to remain in that sort of work takes stock of his opportunities while engaged in general office work, and sooner or later specializes in some particular department through which he can promote himself to a better position.

Many of the more successful business and industrial leaders of our times got their start through stenographic positions, where they had an opportunity to study the methods of their superiors. This is among the finest of all types of office work as far as preparation for executive responsibilities is concerned. The stenographer literally goes to school to highly skilled executives and is paid for doing so.

HILL: What about the farmer? Should he specialize, also?

CARNEGIE: Yes, he should; but usually he does not. This is one of the major weaknesses of agriculture. The men who are making the most money from the soil are those who specialize in certain crops, such as wheat, rye, barley, and trucking. The farmer who raises a little of everything very seldom receives much for anything he raises.

HILL: What about the bookkeeper? Should he specialize, too?

CARNEGIE: Yes, unless he is contented to remain always a bookkeeper, and even then he will make more from his work if he specializes in some particular branch of accounting. The better paid men in this field usually branch out from general bookkeeping to auditing and the installation of accounting systems. A clever man in this field finds it quite profitable, for every business beyond the one-man size needs dependable records of its transactions.

HILL: Now, I am going to give you a hard one, Mr. Carnegie!

What about the young woman who intends to marry? What chance has she of specializing, unless it is in connection with pots and pans and the rearing of babies?

CARNEGIE: That's not as hard as you imagine. Of all the people who should specialize for a life work I can think of no one who might do so to better advantage than the woman who intends to make marriage a career. Sure! she should specialize. She should specialize, first, in the psychology of managing a husband, by learning how to inspire a man to do his very best. After that she should specialize in household economy, so she may contribute her part in managing the home. She should specialize, also, in dietetics, so she will know how to feed a family the sort of food that aids in the maintenance of sound health.

HILL: But, Mr. Carnegie, this looks like a lot of specializing! Wouldn't that make a housewife a sort of maid-of-all-work?

CARNEGIE: It need not! It all comes under the heading of preparation for the career of marriage, the greatest of all careers. The woman who completes a college course can plan her education so she will learn how to manage a home, and if she intends to marry that is precisely what she should do. If she wishes to become a career woman, of course she should plan her education accordingly.

HILL: So, there seems to be no way out of the responsibility of concentrating one's efforts if one is to succeed?

CARNEGIE: No, the jack-of-all-trades usually is good at none! There is some part that everyone can take in the scheme of affairs —some part through which he can render useful service and gain his just compensation. It is everyone's responsibility to find out what his part is, and to prepare himself for it. *A well-ordered life requires preparation.* Before one begins to prepare, he should know for what he is preparing himself. That, within itself, is concentration of effort.

The man who has no definite purpose in life, who cannot do some one thing and do it well, is like a dry leaf on the bosom of the wind. He will be tossed here and there, wherever the winds of chance carry him, but like the rolling stone, he will gather no moss. Unfortunately, the majority of people spend their lives in thus rolling!

HILL: Do you mean that a man should choose his Definite Major Purpose before beginning his education, and prepare himself to specialize in connection with that aim?

CARNEGIE: Not always. Seldom is a very youthful person, who has not finished his basic education, in a position to adopt a Definite Major Purpose. In that case he should complete his essential education through the grades and high school. If he still is unable to choose a major purpose in life he should either go to work and learn, from experience, of the possibilities of different occupations, or go to college and take a general liberal arts educational course. After that one should be able to decide what calling he wishes to follow.

HILL: Suppose that a person chooses a Definite Major Purpose, but finds, after he pursues it for awhile, that he dislikes it, or he finds something he likes better? Should he make a change?

CARNEGIE: By all means! A man will succeed best in that which he likes best, all else being equal. It is advisable for one to change provided he does not get into the habit of changing every time the work he has chosen becomes difficult, or he meets with temporary defeat. Changing from one line of work to another involves a tremendous loss. It is something like an industrial plant, the management of which changes from one product to another. The successful person must reach the stage of specialization, sooner or later; the sooner the better.

HILL: Is it advisable for a business man to engage in politics?

CARNEGIE: Not if he wishes to succeed in business. Politics is a profession unto itself, and not a very dependable one at that. But it is a profession, and those who succeed best at it are those who do nothing else.

HILL: What sort of career would you advise a young man to choose? A professional career or a business career?

CARNEGIE: That depends upon the young man, his likes and dislikes, his native ability, his physical conditions, etc. Generally speaking I would say that business and industry offer much broader opportunities than do the professions, because the professions are overcrowded already. This is essentially an industrial nation. Industry is the back-bone of our economic structure.

I have never seen the time when a reliable, loyal, and capable man could not find his place in industry. Here is where most of the larger fortunes are made, which, within itself, partly answers your question, since most people choose a career with the object of earning a living and accumulating as much wealth as possible. There always has been a shortage of capable men at the head of industry, but never a shortage in the professions.

HILL: What about the army or the navy, or the government service as a career? Are there desirable opportunities in any of these three branches of service?

CARNEGIE: Again I must say that this depends very largely on the person who is choosing the career. If a man wishes an opportunity to engage in a creative effort, he would not choose government service as a career, since his chances there would become a matter of the whims of politicians. He would fare better in either the army or the navy, since these are somewhat further removed from political influence.

Some have made commendable records in both of these fields of the service, but generally they were men who liked that sort of life. The line of promotion in both the army and the navy is rather long and by no means easy. Military service calls for concentrated effort and a definite limitation of ambition, as the possibilities of advancement are known in advance.

Some men are not suited, by nature, to limit themselves in this manner. They prefer to take their chances in business or industry, where the risks may be greater and the work harder, but the possibilities of achievement are without any fixed limits.

HILL: Would you recommend that an ambitious woman undertake to divide her attention between marriage and a personal career?

CARNEGIE: No, under no circumstances. Career women seldom make successful wives. Conversely, successful wives seldom make efficient career women. It should be one or the other. I have known of many marriages resulting in failure because of this very situation, where the wife endeavored to divide her attention between her home and a career. It may happen, and it sometimes does, that a married woman is forced to take up a career because of the illness of her husband, or his death, but the division of attention between home and career should never be a matter of choice.

HILL: Then you recommend *concentration of effort,* through specialization, in all callings? You believe, obviously, in a "one-track" mind?

CARNEGIE: Specialization, through concentration of effort, gives one greater power. It saves lost motion in both thought and physical action. It harmonizes with the principle of Definiteness of Purpose, the starting point of all achievement.

I believe in a one-track mind if you allow me to describe it in this way: A wide range of knowledge based on facts related to one's major purpose, but expressed through organized plans for the attainment of that purpose.

I might make my meaning better understood if I stated it this way: A man should have a multiple-track mind for the accumulation of knowledge, but a single-track mind for the expression of that knowledge, which is about the same as saying that one should have a reserve of both general and specific knowledge, but he should concentrate its use upon the attainment of a Definite Major Purpose.

We have already discussed the fact that knowledge gives one no power until it is organized and expressed in action! That requires concentration of effort. A man may be a walking encyclopedia of general knowledge—and I have known such people —but his knowledge will be practically useless until he organizes it and gives it some form of expression, through definiteness of purpose.

HILL: I see what you mean. Definiteness of purpose implies concentration of effort. When a man decides to attain any definite end, he must of necessity concentrate his thoughts and his physical action upon that purpose.

CARNEGIE: That's the idea. You see, therefore, that the person who has mastered and begun to apply the eleven principles of this philosophy previously discussed, has begun, at least, to acquire the habit of *controlled attention*. I call your attention to the fact that the principles of this philosophy are so inter-related that the mastery and application of any one principle leads to the application of combinations of the other principles.

HILL: You mean, for example, that when one adopts a Definite Major Purpose as his life work, and begins to carry out that purpose, he automatically begins also to make use of *controlled attention, self-discipline, organized individual endeavor, organized thought,* and *self-reliance,* as a very minimum. He may, of course, be under the necessity of using many of the other principles, depending upon the nature of his purpose.

CARNEGIE: That's exactly what I mean! You see, therefore, how impossible it would be for one to single out a Definite Major Purpose and begin carrying out his plans for attaining it, without concentrating his attention on that purpose.

Carry the analysis a step further and imagine, if you can, anyone mastering and applying the eleven previously mentioned principles of this philosophy without the aid of *Controlled Attention.*

This principle is an indispensable part of the philosophy of individual achievement. If I had overlooked including it as one of the seventeen principles *it would have projected itself into the philosophy* wherever one began to apply the philosophy. Thus you may acquire an understanding of the importance of Controlled Attention. Without its application, success in the broader sense is an impossibility.

A rudderless ship and a purposeless man
are eventually stranded on a desert sand.

Apply the Golden Rule　　　*Chapter Thirteen*

CARNEGIE: We come, now, to the thirteenth principle of individual achievement, the Golden Rule Applied—the principle which nearly everyone professes to believe, but few people practice, due, I suspect, to the fact that so few people understand the deep underlying psychology of this principle. Too many people interpret the Golden Rule, not to do unto others as if they were the others, but to do others and do them plenty before others do them.

Of course this false interpretation of this great rule of human conduct can bring nothing but negative results!

The real benefits of the Golden Rule Applied do not come from those in whose favor it is applied, but they accrue to the one applying the rule, in the form of a strengthened conscience, peace of mind, and the other attributes of sound character—the factors which attract the more desirable things of life, including enduring friendships and fortune.

To get the most from the Golden Rule, it must be combined with the principle of Going the Extra Mile, wherein consists the *applied* portion of the Golden Rule. The Golden Rule supplies the right mental attitude, while Going the Extra Mile supplies the action feature of this great rule. A combination of the two gives one the power of attraction which induces friendly cooperation from others as well as opportunities for personal accumulation.

HILL: I assume, from your remarks, that there are few benefits to be acquired through a mere belief in the Golden Rule?

CARNEGIE: Very few! Passive belief in this rule will accomplish nothing. It is the application of the rule that brings benefits, and they are so numerous and varied that they touch life through almost every human relationship. These are some of the more important of the benefits:

(a) The Golden Rule Applied opens the mind for the guidance of Infinite Intelligence, through faith.

(b) Develops self-reliance, through a better relationship with one's conscience.

(c) Builds a sound character sufficient to sustain one in times of emergency. Develops a more attractive personality.

(d) Attracts the friendly cooperation of others in all human relationships.

(e) Discourages unfriendly opposition from others.

(f) Gives one peace of mind and freedom from self-established limitations.

(g) Gives one immunity against the more damaging forms of fear, since the man with a clear conscience seldom fears anything or anyone.

(h) Enables one to go to prayer with clean hands and a clear heart.

(i) Attracts favorable opportunities for self-promotion in one's occupation, business or profession.

(j) Eliminates the desire for something for nothing.

(k) Makes the rendering of useful service a joy that can be had in no other way.

(l) Provides one with an influential reputation for honesty and fair dealing, which is the basis of all confidence.

(m) Serves as a discouragement to the slanderer and a reprimand to the thief.

(n) Makes one a power for good, by example, wherever he comes into contact with others.

(o) Discourages all the baser instincts of greed and envy and revenge, and gives wings to the higher instincts of love and fellowship.

(p) Brings one within easy communicating distance of the Creator, through the medium of an undisturbed mind.

(q) Enables one to recognize the joys of accepting the truth that every man is, and by right should be, his brother's keeper.

(r) Establishes a deeper personal spirituality.

These are no mere opinions of mine. They are self-evident truths, the soundness of which is known to every person who lives by the Golden Rule as a matter of daily habit.

HILL: It is apparent, from your analysis, that the Golden Rule is the very foundation of all the better qualities of man; that the application of this rule provides one with a powerful immunity against all destructive forces.

CARNEGIE: Your definition is good. It does provide immunity against many of the ills which beset the path of mankind, but immunity is negative; it provides, also, the positive attracting power by which one may acquire whatever he demands of life, from peace of mind and spiritual understanding on down to the material needs of life.

HILL: Some people claim that they would like to live by the Golden Rule but find it impossible to do so, due to the fact that those who do not live by this rule would take advantage of them. What has been your experience on this point?

CARNEGIE: When a man says he cannot live by the Golden Rule without suffering damage from others, he shows clearly his lack of understanding of this principle, albeit a common misunderstanding. If you will study carefully the benefits I have enumerated, which one may enjoy from application of the Golden Rule, you will observe that they are benefits of which no one can be deprived.

I think this common misunderstanding of the working principle of the Golden Rule grows out of the belief that the benefits from applying the rule must come from those who receive the benefits, whereas they may come from entirely different sources. Also, the misunderstanding arises from the false belief that the benefits consist only of material gains!

The greatest of all benefits attained through application of the Golden Rule are those which accrue to those who apply it, in the form of harmony within their own minds which leads to the development of sound character. There is no asset comparable in value with sound character, and this is something that an individual must build for himself through his thoughts and deeds. Character is of definite, practical value.

HILL: It is not true, Mr. Carnegie, that some people do take advantage of the man who lives by the Golden Rule, viewing this habit as a weakness to be exploited instead of a virtue to be rewarded?

CARNEGIE: Some people do this, but the percentage who regard the rule in this manner is so incomparably small that it becomes insignificant, by the law of averages. I would estimate that for every person who refuses to respond in kind, when dealt with on the Golden Rule basis, ninety-nine will respond. Thus, by the law of averages, you can see that it pays to overlook the damage that the one may cause.

Moreover, the law of compensation enters into the transaction and by some strange plan of nature with which man is not familiar, even the damage suffered from the short-sighted one is offset by the ninety-nine who do respond in kind. Emerson gave a very clear account of this in his essay on Compensation.

HILL: But there are so few people who are acquainted with Emerson's essay, or the law of Compensation. And many of those who are acquainted with it look upon it as a mere preachment by a moralist, without any real value in the practical affairs of modern life. Will you, therefore, give your views as to the practicability of the law of Compensation, in the modern affairs of business and industry, such as you have experienced?

CARNEGIE: My entire experience, in business and all other relationships, has forced me to accept the soundness of the law of Compensation as an eternal verity from which no man can escape, no matter how smart he may be or how hard he may try to avoid it. There is always some compelling circumstance which raises or lowers a man substantially to where he belongs in life, according to his *thoughts* and *deeds!*

A man may escape the influence of this law for a time, but viewed over a period of an average lifetime, *the law forces everyone to gravitate to the exact position where he belongs.* His own thoughts and deeds establish the space he may occupy and the influence he may wield in his relationships with others. Man may temporarily dodge his responsibilities to his fellowmen, but he cannot permanently dodge the consequences of dodging his responsibilities.

HILL: Then it is not sound expediency to adopt the policy of applying the Golden Rule when its application obviously will bring immediate returns, while failing or refusing to apply it when obviously to do so will mean temporary disadvantage?

CARNEGIE: No, that would be suicidal, although many people make the mistake of choosing the circumstances under which they apply the rule. To get the fullest benefit of this rule one must apply it as a matter of habit, in all human relationships. There are no exceptions!

HILL: That is a pretty conclusive statement; it gives one no leeway in which to temporize with the Golden Rule. One must either go the whole way or suffer the results of his neglect.

CARNEGIE: You have the idea. And here let me warn you that everyone is confronted with circumstances which tempt one to neglect the application of the Golden Rule as a means of temporary expediency. It is fatal to yield to the temptation.

Others may not know of the yielding, but one's own conscience knows. If the conscience is over-ridden, it becomes weak and fails to serve the purpose of guidance for which it was intended.

No man should deliberately try to deceive others; and what is more important, *he cannot afford, under any circumstances, to try to deceive his own conscience,* since this can serve only the purpose of weakening the source of his guidance. The man who tries to deceive himself is as unwise as the person who would slip poison into his own food.

HILL: Obviously you believe, Mr. Carnegie, that a man can apply the Golden Rule in all his human relationships and still prosper, in this age of materialism?

CARNEGIE: I would not state it just that way. I would make the statement stronger by saying that the man who lives by the Golden Rule—mind you, lives by it as a matter of principle—will be bound to prosper within the limits of his own individual capacity, whatever that may be. The results of application of the rule will accrue automatically, and from sources that are often the least expected.

HILL: That is a pretty definite statement, Mr. Carnegie. Coming from a man with your broad experience in dealing with all types of people, I have no choice but to accept it as sound. Your own achievements prove that the Golden Rule can be applied, in a material age such as this, with profit. I am assuming, of course, that you have always lived by the Golden Rule, but I should like to have an expression from you as to this.

CARNEGIE: He is a poor teacher, indeed, who teaches one thing and practices the opposite. My first understanding of the Golden Rule was acquired from my mother at an early age, before I came to America. My real knowledge of its soundness came from my experience in applying it to the best of my ability and understanding.

HILL: Have you ever suffered temporary loss by applying the Golden Rule?

CARNEGIE: Many times! But I am glad you said "temporary" loss, because I cannot truthfully say that, on the whole, I have ever lost anything from living by the Golden Rule. Such losses as I have sustained from an occasional circumstance under which the rule was applied without a direct response, have been repaid many times from other circumstances where the response was abundant.

Let me give you an example of what I mean:

When I first entered the steel manufacturing business, the price of steel, as I have mentioned before, was around $130.00 per ton. That price seemed much too high, so I began to look for ways and means of lowering it.

At first I lowered the price below the then cost of production, although my competitors complained that I was dealing unfairly with them by the practice. Very soon the increased business that came as a result of the lowered price enabled me to make still further reductions. I soon discovered that lowered prices meant bigger production, and bigger production meant lower unit costs and made lowered prices possible.

I kept up this policy until we finally got steel down to around $20.00 per ton. Meanwhile, the lowered price of steel led to the use of steel in many new forms, and after a while my competitors discovered that instead of damaging them I had actually benefitted them by forcing them to lower their prices. Thus, the public benefitted, the workers in the steel plants benefitted, and the manufacturers of steel benefitted from a business policy which, at first, had meant a definite loss to the manufacturer of steel.

Today steel is being used for the manufacture of a great variety of articles which could not have been manufactured from it at the old prices, and on the whole I have never lost anything by forcing the price down. My temporary losses were more than offset by my permanent gains, and I think this fairly well demonstrates how the Golden Rule works. It may, and oftentimes it does, cause temporary losses, but over a period of time the gains are greater than the losses.

HILL: You mean that the Golden Rule philosophy harmonizes, in every particular, with sound business economy.

CARNEGIE: That's the idea, and if you wish to see how it works out, keep your eye on Henry Ford and watch what happens to his business. He has adopted a policy of giving the public a dependable automobile at the lowest price at which automobiles have been sold.

He is putting fine materials and workmanship into his product, and you may depend upon it that the public will reward him with its patronage, no matter how many competitors he may have, and he will prosper beyond the expectations of most of those who are now criticizing him.

This is a prophecy, but you watch it and see for yourself that it is a sound prophecy. Mr. Ford will be likely to dominate the automobile industry, and he will be sure to do so unless some other far-sighted manufacturer comes into the field and follows his example.

(Author's note: This statement, by Mr. Carnegie, was made in 1909, and every student of this philosophy who is familiar with the astounding Ford achievements will recognize the wisdom with which Mr. Carnegie spoke.)

HILL: Would it not be impractical for certain types of professional men to live by the Golden Rule—lawyers, for example, whose profession makes it necessary for them to prosecute cases which makes the application of the rule difficult?

CARNEGIE: I could preach you a sermon on this subject, for I have had a great deal of experience with many types of lawyers, but I confine myself to the mention of but one lawyer whose professional policy, and its results, should be sufficient answer to your question.

This lawyer will not accept a case unless he is convinced that he is being retained on the *right side*. That is, he will not accept a case that is without merit, and I hardly need to tell you that he turns away far more prospective clients than he serves. But I must also tell you that he is busy all the time, and his income, judging from all I know about him, is approximately ten times that of the average type of lawyer.

I pay this lawyer a substantial sum annually, for his counsel alone, quite aside from any other service he renders me. A great many of my friends do the same. We employ him because we have confidence in him, and our confidence is based mainly on our knowledge that he will not mislead a client in order to earn a fee, nor will he accept a case that is unjust or unfair to anyone.

HILL: I see your point. A lawyer can live by the Golden Rule and prosper provided he is willing to forego the handling of cases that have no merit. But, what about the client who comes with the other sort of case—the type that is unjust? It seems that this sort of case is more prevalent than the other type.

CARNEGIE: In every profession, and every business, and every occupation there are ways to make money through unfair practices, and I must confess that there are individuals who are willing to earn money unfairly; but all of them are surrounded by hazards which, sooner or later, dry up the source of income or bring with it evils, if not losses, out of proportion to the gain.

It is true there are many legal cases which have no merit; some of them are out and out attempts to get something for nothing, through fraud and deceit. It is a lawyer's privilege to accept this sort of case if he chooses, but I stand on my original statement that such cases bring with them evils out of proportion to the gain to the lawyer.

Money obtained unjustly, through the tricks of the legal profession, may appear to be as good as any other sort of money, but there is a strange influence which accompanies such money which some people do not wish to be burdened with.

Somehow it has a way of becoming quickly dissipated without serving its greatest worth, just as does money that is stolen by highwaymen and thieves. Have you ever heard of a successful highwayman, or thief? I have known of many of them getting away with large sums of money. Most of them are now residing in prison.

All natural law is moral! The whole universe frowns upon immoral transactions of whatsoever nature they may be. And the man has not yet been born who can successfully run counter to the trend of natural law for more than a brief period.

It is my belief that the secret of the great power of the Golden Rule consists in the fact that it is in harmony with moral laws. It represents the positive side of human relationships. Therefore, it has moral law back of it.

HILL: Let us consider the young man or young woman just beginning a career. In what ways may he or she profit by the Golden Rule?

CARNEGIE: The first essential for success, in any calling of merit, is sound character. The Golden Rule applied, develops sound character and a good reputation. You perhaps wish a more concrete example of how young people may profit materially by application of the Golden Rule, so let us combine the principles of the Golden Rule and Going the Extra Mile and see what result we get. Let us go one step further and add the principle of Definiteness of a Major Purpose. We now have a combination which, if persistently and sincerely applied, will be sufficient to give any young person more than an average start in life.

HILL: Of course this combination would serve adults as well as youths, would it not?

CARNEGIE: Yes; if a man knows what he wants, makes up his mind to acquire it, forms the habit of Going the Extra Mile in order to get it, and relates himself to other people on the Golden Rule basis, he cannot be ignored by the world. He will attract favorable attention, no matter how humble his beginning may be.

HILL: Wouldn't these three principles be a pretty good combination for one to apply while going through high school or college, in preparation for a life-work? Wouldn't they give one a definite advantage over those who fail to apply these principles?

CARNEGIE: Yes, they would. As I have stated previously, it is one of the weaknesses of most people, during their school days, that they study for "credits" and to pass examinations without knowing what they are going to do with their schooling after they acquire it. It is my notion that most purposeless action is wasted, no matter when or where it is performed. The "go-getters," as the world calls alert, dynamic, successful people, move with a definite purpose in practically all that they do. They move by a definite motive, a definite plan, and they generally reach their destination because they know where they are going and are determined not to be stopped until they get there.

HILL: You believe that those who relate themselves to others on the Golden Rule basis, and make it a habit to Go the Extra Mile, will have less opposition from others, do you not?

CARNEGIE: Generally speaking, they will have practically no opposition from others. On the contrary, they will have the willing and friendly cooperation of others. That has been the history of those who live by these two rules.

HILL: Then we may say that these two principles not only serve as a moral guide, but they clear one's path of the usual forms of opposition?

CARNEGIE: That's the story. Now, I must call your attention to another benefit one may enjoy by living by these two principles. It consists of the fact that those who live by these principles, as a matter of daily habit, will profit by contrast with others who neglect to apply the principles.

Chapter Fourteen

Cooperate

HILL: Inasmuch as you have stated that team-work is the fourteenth principle of the Philosophy of American Achievement, will you name its major benefits, as it may be applied in the practical business world?

CARNEGIE: To begin with, let us realize that industrial America, as we know it today, could not carry on its vast operations without the principle of team-work.

Every industry you can name is manned by a group of men who coordinate their efforts in a spirit of friendliness, all working together for a common benefit. Small individual businesses may be operated by one man, but any business that takes on the proportion of an industry must embrace and use the principle of team-work.

You see, therefore, that *industry and team-work are synonymous terms!* And you recognize, of course, that a successful industry calls for efficient, harmonious cooperation among those who operate it.

HILL: Wouldn't that same statement apply as well to the management of a household?

CARNEGIE: Yes, but we shall come back to that later on. Right now let us confine our analysis to the larger operations of business and industry.

Take the subject of transportation, for example, and you will readily recognize that it calls for team-work on a huge scale. In railroading the team-work principle is so well-organized that all major operations are carried out on written orders. Verbal instructions will not do, because the hazards of the railroad business are such that it must be possible to fix responsibilities on all individuals engaged in the operations.

The operation of a modern railroad train is one of the finest examples of team-work. Every train moves on written orders. The orders originate in the office of skilled executives who plan the moves of trains. They are conveyed to trainmen by a dispatcher who, in turn, is responsible to the operating executives for their correct delivery and interpretation.

The train is in charge of a conductor who moves his train on written orders, except under certain conditions where he may move a limited distance without such orders. All members of the train crew are directly responsible to the conductor and carry out his instructions without question.

Every man working for a railroad, from the humblest track-walker to the president of the road, is related to the other workers in a spirit of team-work that cannot be violated without possible injury to someone.

HILL: Would you say, Mr. Carnegie, that the modern railroad executive makes perfect application of the principle of team-work?

CARNEGIE: As far as the relationship of the workers of the road is concerned, there is almost perfect coordination of effort, allowing for the unavoidable human weaknesses, and even these are largely safe-guarded by mechanical equipment and signal devices which work automatically.

But, the principle of team-work should not stop with the mere coordination of effort between the railroad workers themselves, for there is the public served by the railroad, which must be considered, because the public pays the salaries of the men who operate the roads. Therefore, the public is the real employer of all railroad men.

HILL: But isn't it true, Mr. Carnegie, that the public is forced to patronize railroads, whether people like the employees of railroads or not?

CARNEGIE: That is the general attitude of many people, including some railroad employees, but it is an erroneous viewpoint, and if it is adopted generally by railroad employees the time will come, and not very far in the future at that, when the railroads will find their business being taken away from them by other forms of transportation, such as automobiles and airplanes.

HILL: Automobiles and airplanes are not as efficient as railroads, and they cannot carry the heavier types of freight. How, therefore, can they ever compete successfully with the railroads?

CARNEGIE: Just remember this: The human element is the controlling factor in all business, including transportation. When enough people cease to wish to patronize the railroads because of the mental attitude of railroad employees, you may be sure that other competitive systems will come into existence to take over the business of the railroads. Airplanes will be refined and made to carry bigger loads. Automobiles will be designed to carry freight and passengers. But, more important than these, modern salesmanship will be applied so as to win the public over to these newer methods of transportation.

HILL: But, Mr. Carnegie, the railroad executives can use salesmanship also, can they not?

CARNEGIE: They can; but, will they? That's the question. The railroads have had a monopoly on the carrying of freight and passengers for so long that they may be slow to grasp the changing times quickly enough to adjust themselves to the more advanced methods. That is a common error of many people— failure to recognize facts in time to profit by them.

Monopolies often lead to indifference and deterioration in human relationships. The fact that all nature discourages monopolies should be a warning to men to avoid them.

Under the American system of free enterprise we have a form of friendly competition through which we keep the system active, alert and highly efficient, which amounts to cooperation, considering the system as a whole.

HILL: Do you mean that, although the American system of free enterprise is competitive, the various factors of the system are coordinated in a way that gives it power?

CARNEGIE: Yes, that is what I mean. Take the relationship between the system of free enterprise and the American form of government, for example, and observe that both the government and American industry benefit by the coordination of effort between the two. The government protects industry and industry, in return, helps to support the cost of government, through the taxes and wages which it pays to the workers.

As long as this system of coordination is carried on in a friendly manner the American form of government will survive and American industry will prosper, because the combined results of this sort of cooperation represent the American standard of living which is the most prosperous the world has yet known.

HILL: Then the government and industry are practically partners in the economic structure of the United States?

CARNEGIE: Yes, and as such they are subject to all the rules and regulations necessary to make any partnership a success. Both must give in order to receive. Both must work in a spirit of friendliness. Both must recognize the rights and the privileges of the general public, and both must become efficient in serving the public. Here, as in all other human relationships, failure to serve will result in the breaking down of the system.

The government must prevent monoplies in industry, but in doing so it must not become a competitor of industry, and it must not burden industry with unreasonable taxes, nor interfere with industry through unsound arbitrary rules of regulation which discourage the exercise of personal initiative and the use of accumulated capital.

On the contrary, it is the proper function of the government to encourage personal initiative through the fullest exercise of individual cooperation between those who carry on industry and the public they serve.

HILL: What would happen if the government became a competitor of industry, or burdened industry with regulations and taxes which made it unprofitable for industry to operate?

CARNEGIE: Precisely the same thing that would happen if individuals engaged in industry neglected to cooperate on a friendly basis for a common purpose. This happens sometimes, but it always leads to failure.

HILL: You mean that friendly coordination of effort is a requirement for success in all human endeavor?

CARNEGIE: Personal power is acquired through friendly coordination of effort, and in no other way. In this country we have an economic system based upon this sort of cooperation. That is why ours is the richest and most powerful nation of the world. We have found a practical way of coordinating the efforts of groups of individuals in all walks of life, and this coordination has given us great power.

If you are a close observer you will have noticed that the individuals who have attained the highest degree of cooperation in their relationships with others are those who have achieved the greatest success in their chosen callings.

HILL: You believe, then, that government regulation of industry is for the common good of all! Why?

CARNEGIE: Because regulation, within the bounds of reason, discourages the greedy and the selfish individuals from seeking monopolies, and protects the public against unfair practices in business.

Just as there must be unbiased umpires in athletics who see that the rules of the game are observed for the benefit of all the players, there must also be an unbiased governmental umpire who will see that the sound rules of industry are carried out for the benefit of all.

Every well-managed business has executives who see to it that all individuals work together in a spirit of team-work. These executives serve as the umpires who coordinate all factors essential for the successful operation of the business. Their sense of fairness and their wisdom determine the degree of success the business enjoys.

HILL: And you believe that a business cannot be successful without the aid of unbiased coordinators known as management?

CARNEGIE: That is the idea. Small one-man businesses may operate successfully without a coordinator, but the moment any business requires more than one man for its operation some individual must assume the responsibility of coordinating the factors which affect the business or it will not succeed.

Business is a science requiring accuracy of judgment, experience and a sense of fairness. All these factors must be coordinated and applied in accordance with carefully laid plans. Human nature is such that not all men are suited to serve as coordinators. Some men—in fact most men—will not accept the responsibility of efficiently directing themselves, let alone the responsibility of guiding others. Yet, without practical guidance of the workers, no business can succeed.

HILL: You mean, then, that the services of a coordinator in

business are beneficial to all workers—especially those who will not assume the responsibility of self-direction?

CARNEGIE: Yes, and I may add that an able coordinator not only serves the interests of a business as a whole, but he aids the individuals who work in the business to so direct their efforts that they can earn more than they would be worth if they lacked this guidance. Men require discipline, guidance and supervision, in order to make their efforts of the greatest value to themselves and to others. If you doubt this, observe what happens when the management of any business becomes inefficient, selfish or dishonest.

HILL: Summed up in a few words, what you are saying is that the coordination of individual efforts is essential for success in any business, and the majority of men lack the ability or the inclination to cooperate with others in an efficient, friendly manner?

CARNEGIE: That is precisely what I have been saying, and it is supported by the experience of all able business leaders. The best evidence of its soundness may be found in the well-known fact that while ordinary manual labor is always plentiful, managerial ability always is scarce. This is because men with the temperament, education, experience and personal inclination to coordinate the efforts of others are scarce. This scarcity accounts for the fact that able managerial ability always commands its own price, because here, as elsewhere in the field of economics, the law of supply and demand obtains.

HILL: In view of your analysis may I ask your opinion as to which type of man is the more essential to a well-organized business—the managerial types or the worker who carries out his instructions?

CARNEGIE: Both types are essential, but I may add my personal opinion that, as a whole, the managerial type is worth more to the worker than the worker is to the manager, since sound management enables a worker to earn more than he could earn if he worked independently! The ideal set-up, of course, exists where the coordinator and the worker recognize the necessity of each other and work together in a spirit of friendliness, as they do in all successful business.

HILL: Then there is no sound reason for discord between management and the workers?

CARNEGIE: No, and I may add that where such discord prevails both the management and the workers suffer, no matter what may be the cause of the discord. Any circumstance which injures either the management or the workers, damages proportionately, the whole business with which they are connected.

Friction between management and workers in industry can result only from unwillingness on the part of a few or of many to cooperate in a spirit of helpfulness. Such friction usually is the outcome of meddling by professional agitators who profit by causing friction among workers.

HILL: Inasmuch as the American system of free enterprise is inseparably a part of the American way of life, and one of the major foundation-stones of Americanism, is it not true that injury or destruction of our system of free enterprise would be the equivalent of an unfriendly thrust at our entire form of government?

CARNEGIE: That is true. The power that maintains the American way of life, or what we call "Americanism," is a coordination of many factors, the major one of importance being our industrial system, and this for the reason that our industrial system is our major source of exchange for commodities and personal services.

The greater portion of all money that changes hands in the United States passes through the industrial system in payment for commodities or wages. Therefore, the industrial system pays a major portion of the taxes needed for the operation of the government. Without this source of income the government would soon become bankrupt, as it produces nothing and earns no direct income.

HILL: If the American form of government is ever destroyed, or substantially changed so as to limit the personal liberty of the people, from what source do you believe the change will come?

CARNEGIE: If any such change ever takes place it will undoubtedly come as the result of interference with our industrial system. Our system of industry is, at one and the same time, our greatest asset and our most vulnerable point. It is the very hub of the American way of life, around which all the lesser factors revolve. It will continue to prosper as long as the government functions in the capacity for which it was created, namely, *as a friendly coordinator of all the factors of the American way of life!*

The government gets its power from the voluntary cooperation of the States, and the States get their power from the voluntary cooperation of the people who live within their borders, and the people get their power from friendly cooperation with one another, as expressed in terms of free enterprise. You see, therefore, that in final analysis the power of the United States comes from friendly cooperation among the people.

If the government is ever radically changed or destroyed, it will be the result of discord among the people, beginning at first, perhaps, in disagreement between small groups and blocs who are motivated by selfish reasons for individual aggrandizement. As long as the people work together in a friendly spirit there can be no change in our form of government, unless the people desire it. And even then the change will come from within, and it will not be forced upon the people from the outside.

You should remember that the power with which the people of America have become prosperous may serve, also, as a means of self-defense with which they may defend their rights and privileges, including their system of free enterprise.

Chapter Fifteen

Budget Your Time and Money

Andrew Carnegie directed his entire life by a strict budget that covered both his time and his financial resources. His achievements qualified him to speak as an authority on this subject, for America has never produced a man who made better use of his opportunities under the American way of life than did he.

Economic and social conditions have changed greatly since Mr. Carnegie's day, but the principles of personal achievement have not changed. They are the same today as they were when he was working his way up from the bottom to an enviable position, and they will serve as effectively today as they did when he was building his career.

HILL: Mr. Carnegie, you have named the *Budgeting of Time* as one of the essentials for individual achievement. Will you indicate what methods one should adopt to make the best use of his time?

CARNEGIE: Every successful person plans his life as carefully as a successful business man plans his business. He begins by adopting a *Definite Major Purpose,* and he follows through by devoting a definite proportion of his time to attaining the object of that purpose.

HILL: What proportion of one's time should be devoted to the attainment of his major purpose?

CARNEGIE: To begin with let us recognize that the average person comes into the world with *nothing but time* as an asset!

Each person has twenty-four hours of time each day—no more, no less.

When a person reaches the age of personal responsibility he should divide his time into three periods, (1) one for sleep, (2) one for work, and (3) one for recreation.

The usual distribution of this twenty-four hours per day period is (1) eight hours for sleep, (2) eight hours for work, and (3) eight hours for recreation. Some people, perhaps a majority of them, find it necessary to work ten hours per day in order to maintain the present standard of living, while they devote but six hours per day to recreation. The average person cannot get along on less than eight hours of sleep.

HILL: Which of these three periods of the day do you consider to be the most important?

CARNEGIE: That depends altogether on what you consider to be important. Sound health demands at least eight hours of sleep. An average living, under our present standard of living, demands at least eight to ten hours a day for work. This leaves from six to eight hours a day of free time which one may use as he pleases, and I would say that it is the most important period of the day, as far as personal achievement is concerned, because it provides one with an opportunity to acquire additional education, plan new means of rendering service, and create goodwill.

HILL: What about the person who uses this period for none of these purposes, but devotes it entirely to personal pleasure which in no way brings him additional influence or friends?

CARNEGIE: The person who uses his free time in this manner will never be a success in anything, except by some rare stroke of good fortune which favors him without his own efforts.

The sleep period produces no results except that of maintaining sound health. Therefore one can take no liberties with it, and it holds no seed of opportunity for self-promotion, or for the accumulation of material things.

The work period requires all of one's thoughts and efforts for specific duties. Therefore it holds but slight opportunities for extra effort, although one may so use it as to lay the foundation for opportunities by modifying the quality and the quantity of the work he performs.

The free-time period is just what its name implies—time that one may use as he pleases. Therefore, it is properly called one's "opportunity" time. During this period one may not only plant the seed of opportunity, but one may also cause the seed to germinate and grow, by carefully regulating his association with others, and by exercising strict discipline over his own thoughts.

The more successful people combine their free-time with their work-time, by devoting all of it to some sort of action which aids them in attaining the object of their major purpose. Thus, they work about two-thirds of their time and sleep the other third.

HILL: But, isn't it necessary for a man to take time off for recreation and play if he is to maintain sound health?

CARNEGIE: Yes, sound health demands a change of physical and mental habits, but successful people have learned how to make these changes by so arranging their work-time and their free-time that the free-time provides recreation along lines that contribute to and harmonize with the duties they perform during their work-time.

HILL: I see what you mean. A man may so use his free-time that it brings him opportunities definitely related to his work, such as association with people who can be of benefit to him in connection with the attainment of his major purpose, although his relationship with them may be entirely of a social nature from which he gets his recreation.

CARNEGIE: That's the idea, precisely! But, you should recognize the fact that most people do not spend their free-time in this manner. They use it for excitement, which too often they mistake for pleasure, and for association with people who influence them by destructive habits, such as drinking and gambling, or people who influence them by just plain laziness.

While one's free-time may be properly called "opportunity-time," it usually proves to be one's "misfortune-time," for it is during this period that most people acquire negative habits which vitally affect their work-time. Such habits, for example, as cutting into their sleep-time and thereby reducing the efficiency of their work-time as well as impairing their physical health.

HILL: I see the logic of your argument, Mr. Carnegie, but is it not true that a well-rounded life calls for play and recreation? That old saying that "all work and no play makes Jack a dull boy" seems to be sound.

CARNEGIE: That may be a sound saying, but there are many

misconceptions. Speaking for myself, and from my observations of the successful people I have known, I can say that there is no better form of play than that which is associated with the planning and attaining of one's major purpose. It would be a mistake to say that I work *hard!* for the truth is that I look upon my work as the finest sort of play. So does every other man who is succeeding in the true sense of that term.

A man's work can be a recreation if he does it in a spirit of intense enthusiasm, and likes what he is doing. Enthusiasm recreates and interest in one's work may therefore be recreation.

HILL: I recognize the truth of what you have stated, but what of the man who does not like his work—the man who is forced to labor in order to have the bare necessities of life? What motive has he for enthusiasm over his work?

CARNEGIE: I thought you would get around to that question. It is the very question I needed in order to make clear to you the full benefit of the free-time period.

It is true that a man may not always become enthusiastic over the work which yields him nothing but a bare living, but the more he dislikes his work the more reason he has to take the necessary steps to get out of it into something he likes better.

In most cases his only hope lies in the possibilities of his free-time, when he may prepare himself for the sort of work he does like, and form alliances with others who can and will aid him in getting into that sort of work. If he wastes his free-time in riotous living, or idleness, or in association with people who lead him into negative habits, obviously he must remain in the sort of work he does not like!

I didn't like the work I was forced to do during my youth!

It was hard, and it paid only enough for a bare living of the plainest sort. I got out of that sort of work by using my free-time to prepare myself for something better. The preparation consisted of reading, going to school, and especially the formation of friends among a class of people who could be of use to me. It was these very friends, whom I first contacted during my free-time, that came to my aid later in life when I needed working capital to enter the steel business.

You see, now, why I called free-time "opportunity-time!"

In a strict sense one should have no such thing as free-time, *for all of one's time, outside of that required for sleep, should be so used as to bring one some form of benefit.*

I can truthfully say that I never, in my entire life, spent a second of time voluntarily with anyone whom I did not believe could and would be of benefit to me! Of course I made the most of my associates, not merely by using them for my own benefit, but by carefully cultivating them, and serving them.

HILL: But, Mr. Carnegie, wouldn't some people consider it selfish for one to cultivate only those whom he desired to use?

CARNEGIE: No matter how one may view this habit, it is an essential for personal achievement. Personally I see nothing selfish about it, provided one so relates himself to others that he GIVES as well as receives, and I have made it clear that I have always followed this practice.

I can truthfully say for every benefit I ever received from another person I have rendered that person an equivalent benefit, or more; and, for every dollar I have accumulated I have helped others—many others—to accumulate.

So, where has the selfishness on my part come in? And, to top off my career I am now engaged in giving all my wealth to other people, in ways I think best suited to aid them.

HILL: I am glad I asked that question, for it is one that many another person will ask without an opportunity to get the correct answer had I not asked it.

From what you have said I have reached the conclusion that the question of the value of time boils itself down to where one is forced to recognize that the most important portion of one's time is his free-time, because the other periods of the day must, of necessity, remain routine periods during which one may not always have control over them.

CARNEGIE: You now have the viewpoint I wished you to get. Free-time is exactly what its name implies, for it is the starting-point of all individual freedom of both body and mind! There is but one thing over which anyone has greater control than he has over his free-time, and that is the nature of his thoughts. And, strangely enough, one's free-time is the most favorable of all times for one to organize and direct his thoughts along the lines of his own choice. *It provides one with an opportunity to withdraw his thoughts from the pressing obligations of life, and direct them to the source of that secret power from within which holds the answer to all human problems.*

Here, then, is the greatest of all reasons why one should organize his free-time and make deliberate, constructive use of it instead of wasting it in association with idlers and those who lack ambition.

And I conceive it to be true that the man who organizes and guards his free-time by a careful choice of associates, far from being a selfish person, thereby demonstrates the utmost of unselfishness, for only in this way can a man become the greatest benefit to himself and to others. If you wish to find the really selfish man, you may find him wasting his time—time that may belong to his family, or his creditors—in association with idlers who unwisely believe they are having a good time.

You will find the selfish man in the saloons and the gambling dens, or in worse places, in company with those who believe that free-time is something a man has a right to waste. Look around, observe people carefully, and the truth of what I have said will become obvious. Selfish men are those who live only for self, and usually they prefer to live their lives in company with others who, likewise, believe in living only for self.

I hope I have set you right on this subject, for there is much misunderstanding as to what constitutes selfishness.

Unselfishness manifests itself by the respect for and the constructive use of time. Selfishness manifests itself by a wanton disregard of time, one's own and the time of others. No man has the right to live unto himself alone. Civilization places on every man a responsibility to others, in one form or another. But, too many men wish to benefit by the advantages of civilization without contributing anything to the source of these advantages. That is selfishness in its most malignant form, or I have totally misinterpreted the meaning of the word selfishness.

My emphasis of this subject is not intended as a rebuke to you for asking the question that prompted it, but it is intended to inspire thought on the part of those who will need straight thinking on this subject, of whom there are millions. Selfishness is one of the fundamental evils of the world, and its true nature needs analysis such as I hope I have given it.

HILL: Granted that a man makes efficient use of his work-time by relating it to his free-time, and so combines the two periods that he is able to procure whatever he desires; that he has a *Definite Major Purpose* and, by the efficient use of his time attains that purpose, or is well on the way toward its attainment; is that enough to insure his success, Mr. Carnegie?

CARNEGIE: No! Assuming that you have reference to material things—money or its equivalent—when you speak of success, let me call your attention to the fact that neither the ability to procure money easily, nor the actual temporary possession of it will mean much to the man who does not learn how to USE riches.

The value of all riches, money included, consists in the use one makes of them; not in their mere possession!

The successful man (the one who attains economic success) budgets the use of his money and material assets as carefully as he budgets his time. He sets aside a definite amount of his income (usually determined on a definite percentage of the total) for (1) food, clothing, and household expense; (2) life insurance; (3) savings which he puts to work in some form of investments; (4) charity and recreation.

All four of these items are controlled by a strict budget from which no deviation is made except in the rarest cases of emergency. This insures the saving of a definite percentage of one's income, and leads to economic security.

What difference would it make whether a man's income were $100.00 a month or $1,000.00 a month, if he allowed it all to go for living expenses, or spent it for recreation, or for any other purpose that did not yield a material return of some sort?

I must tell you, however, that the majority of the American people make this very mistake. No matter how much they earn, it all goes out, in one way or another, because they have no established budget system for saving and properly *using* a percentage of it. I have known men to receive salary increases which they promptly spent—every cent of it—on living expenses. Now, if a man is getting a hundred dollars a month, and he receives an increase of twenty-five dollars a month, under ordinary circumstances he could save the entire amount of his increase, because if he could get along on a hundred dollars a month before the increase, he could get along on the same amount afterward, just as well.

Economic security is attained by careful management of one's income, and it calls for strict self-discipline in the matter of spending. The trouble with most Americans is that they have acquired the spending habit during their childhood, because of the lack of proper self-discipline on the part of their parents, and this habit has become a sort of mania with them. The habit of saving carries with it just as great a thrill as does the habit of spending, once it has been developed through self-discipline. And, need I mention that it is a much more desirable habit?

HILL: When you speak of "saving" you do not mean the mere hoarding of money in a savings account, or a safety-deposit box, do you, Mr. Carnegie?

CARNEGIE: No, I do not mean that. Intelligent saving calls for the USE of one's savings. *Money should be put to work earning more money!* And if it is not put to use one might as well not have any more than enough for actual living expenses.

HILL: What percentage of a man's income should he set aside as a savings fund?

CARNEGIE: That depends upon many things. The percentage should vary, according to whether a man were married or single, and depending upon the number of people dependent upon him for a living or an education. A single man should save a much larger percentage of his income than a married man, since generally speaking he has fewer dependents. He should save in anticipation of the day when he will have a family, as well as to provide himself with economic security in old age.

But, every man should save a definite percentage of his gross income, even if it is no more than five percent, in order that he may develop the *habit* of saving. The amount actually saved is not as important as the habit itself, because the savings habit connotes *self-discipline* that is of great value in other directions. Without self-discipline no man can be sure of ever attaining economic security, or of becoming successful in the attainment of his major purpose, no matter how much ability he may have, or what his opportunities may be. *The habit of saving is self-discipline of a high order!*

HILL: What do you consider to be the most important item on a man's savings plan?

CARNEGIE: Life insurance! That should take precedence over everything else, whether a man is married or single. In the first place, life insurance forces one to adopt the savings habit, because the premiums have to be paid annually. And this is a form of savings which one cannot draw out and spend as easily as if it were placed in a savings bank. It is also a great builder of self-reliance, and it provides one with peace of mind and freedom from worry over what may happen to his dependents if he dies, or to himself in old age.

Silence has one major advantage: it gives no one a clue as to what your next move will be.

Make Health a Habit Chapter Sixteen

The physical body is a "house" which the Creator provided to serve as a dwelling place for the Mind! It is the most perfect mechanism ever produced, and it is practically self-maintaining.

It has a brain which serves as the center of the nervous system, the coordinator of all bodily activity, and the receiver of all sense perceptions. The brain is the organ which—by means as yet unexplained by science—coordinates all perception, knowledge and memory into new patterns which we know as *thought*.

The brain is the commander of all voluntary movements of the body, the controller of all involuntary movements carried on through the subconscious section, such as breathing, the heartbeat, digestion, circulation of the blood, distribution of nervous energy and the like. It is the storehouse of all knowledge, the interpreter of the influences of environment and thought. It is the most powerful and the least understood organ of the body.

The brain is the housing place of the subconscious section of the mind as well as of the conscious section; but the energy and the intelligence with which thought is produced flow into the brain from the great universal storehouse of Infinite Intelligence, the brain serving only as a receiver and as a distributor of this energy.

Among its other duties, the brain operates a first-class department of chemistry through which it breaks up and assimilates the food taken into the stomach, liquefies the food and distributes it, through the blood stream, to every part of the body where it is needed for maintenance and repair of the individual cells. All of this service is performed automatically, but there are certain simple aids which the individual can give the brain that will help it to maintain sound physical health. The burden of this chapter is that of describing these aids, viz:

1. MENTAL ATTITUDE:

Inasmuch as the brain is the unchallenged boss of the entire physical body, we should recognize at the outset that sound physical health demands a *positive mental attitude.*

Sound health begins with a *sound health consciousness,* just as financial success begins with a *prosperity consciousness!* And let it be here emphasized that no one ever succeeds financially without that prosperity consciousness, nor does one enjoy sound physical health without a health consciousness. Ponder this statement, for it conveys a truth that is of paramount benefit in the maintenance of sound physical health.

To maintain a health consciousness one must think in terms of sound health, not in terms of illness and disease, for *we must emphasize that whatever the mind dwells upon the mind brings into existence,* whether it be financial succcess or physical health.

Emil Coue, the French psychologist, gave the world, in one sentence, a very simple but practical formula for the maintenance of a health consciousness: "Day by day, in every way, I am getting better and better." He recommended that this sentence be repeated thousands of times daily, until the subconscious section of the mind picked it up, accepted it and began to carry it out to its logical conclusion, in the form of sound health.

The "wise" ones smiled, not too tolerantly, when they heard of the Coue formula. The not-so-wise (?) accepted it in good faith, put it to work in earnest, and discovered that it produced marvelous results, for it started them on the road toward the development of a health consciousness.

And here is the reason why a positive mental attitude is essential for the maintenance of sound health:

(a) All thought energy, whether it is positive or negative, is carried to every cell of the body and there deposited as energy on which the cells operate.

(b) The energy of thought is carried to the cells of the body through the nervous system and the blood stream, for it is a known fact that the body chemist mixes the energy of thought with every particle of food that is assimilated and made ready for projection into the blood stream.

Positive evidence that this is true may be found in the fact that the mother who nurses her child from the breast may poison her milk by worry or fear, so that her child will become ill within a few minutes after taking the milk.

And again, it is well known that any form of worry, fear, anger, jealousy or hatred that one may experience while eating will cause the food to ferment in the stomach without assimilating, and "indigestion" is the natural result.

To maintain a positive mental attitude suitable for the development and maintenance of a sound health consciousness, the mind must be kept free of negative thoughts and influences through self-discipline and established habits.

There must be no "crabbing" or fault-finding. That hurts the digestive organs.

There must be no sustained hatred, for hatred attracts reprisals in kind and upsets digestion.

There must be no fear; it indicates friction in human relationships, lack of harmony and understanding within one's mind, and discourages digestion.

There must be no talk about illness and disease! for that leads to the development of the worst of all diseases—a disease known to the doctors as "hypochondria," which means, in the language of the layman, *imaginary illness.* It has been established that three-fourths of all patients who visit doctors' offices for treatment are suffering with nothing more than imaginary illnesses.

2. EATING HABITS:

This subject is worthy of an entire book, but inasmuch as there are many well written books on the subject we shall here confine ourselves to a few simple recommendations which are on the "must" list of all who would enjoy sound health.

The "MUSTS" of Correct Eating

(a) First, there must be no over-eating! It over-works the heart, liver, kidneys and the sewer system. A simple way to observe this admonition is the habit of getting up from the table before one is thoroughly satisfied. The habit will be a little difficult to acquire, but once it has been developed it will pay off in big dividends, consisting in many benefits—among them a great saving in doctors' bills.

Over-eating is a form of intemperance which may be, and it

often is, just as injurious as intemperance in drinking alcoholic beverages, or the taking of narcotics.

(b) One must eat a *balanced* ration, consisting of at least a fair proportion of fruits and vegatables, because these contain the sixteen major mineral elements which nature requires in the building and maintenance of the physical body. No vegetable contains all of these elements; therefore, in order to provide the body with the building material it requires one must eat a variety of food that is produced by nature from the soil of the earth.

Moreover, one must be sure that the vegatables he eats contain all the mineral elements that nature demands, which is something that cannot be determined by the appearance of the vegatable alone.

In most parts of the United States the soil has been so long abused by neglect, in not giving back to it the proper kind of fertilization, that it no longer contains all of the elements it needs for the production of healthful food. Particularly is this true in the South, where the soil has been "milked" for generations by the growth of corn and cotton, until it is deficient in many of the minerals nature orginally provided.

This deficiency reveals itself most disastrously in the lackadaisical movements and mental attitude of many of the people of the South. Of course they move slowly and with indifference because much of the food they eat is not of the right quality to give them vim and vigor.

Dr. Charles Northen, of Tampa University, Tampa, Florida, who is probably the ablest scientist in the field of soil feeding, has made astounding discoveries concerning the production of food. Through the application of colloidal chemistry, Dr. Northen has compounded a fertilizer which contains *all the mineral elements* needed by the soil for the production of healthful fruits and vegetables. He first analyzes the soil that is to be fertilized, discovers which minerals are lacking, then compounds a fertilizer containing those minerals.

As a demonstration of his ideas he planted two rows of bunch beans, fifty feet in length, side by side in the same soil. One row he fertilized with a compound containing all the necessary minerals for the production of healthful beans. The other row contained no fertilizer. The row that had been properly fertilized grew perfect beans *which were not molested by bugs or insects,* while the other row was literally eaten down to the stem of the beans by bugs and beetles.

He discovered by his experiments that fruits and vegetables containing all of the minerals which nature intended them to contain, developed within them a perfect immunity against attacks by insects. Moreover, he reasoned that the physical body which is supplied food containing all that nature requires for the maintenance of sound physical health, will likewise repel disease germs and everything else that is deleterious to health.

What a different system is Dr. Northen's scientific soil feeding from that of the average farmer who, if he fertilizes his soil at all, merely goes down to the retail fertilizer dealer and orders whatever the dealer may have on hand, not knowing whether or not it contains the mineral elements his soil lacks.

Healthful food must be grown to order from soil that has been analyzed and is known to contain all the mineral elements which nature needs in the production of healthful food.

Food that is lacking in the necessary mineral elements ferments in the alimentary canal, decays and sets up a condition known as toxic poisoning. Thus, deficient food not only fails to supply the body with the mineral elements it needs to carry on its maintenance work, but it actually creates a poison which may provide the beginning of a great variety of diseases. Some doctors have frankly admitted that most diseases begin in the alimentary canal, because of improper digestion.

(c) There must be no gulping of food nor fast eating. Such methods prevent the proper mastication of the food, and also indicate a nervous mental attitude which becomes a part of the food and is carried into the blood stream.

(d) There must be no eating between meals of tidbits, such as candy-bars and other sweets. If any eating between meals is done it should consist of ripe fruits, berries or raw vegetables. The better plan is to avoid between-meal eating altogether.

(e) Liquor and other alcoholic beverages are on the taboo list at all times.

(f) Where properly mineralized fresh vegetables are not available, the deficiency should be made up by compounded vitamins. These are available in most drug stores, but they should never be taken without a complete physical analysis by a competent doctor, which will show how many vitamins are required and of what types. Vitamins contain the health-building factors of vegetation. They are the "elan vital" of all vegetation—*the life-giving force.*

There is perhaps not one person in the United States who does not require at one time or another compounded vitamins, of one combination or another, to complete his or her dietary requirements. The wonders the vitamins perform in health building are many. Vitamin A dissolves kidney stones. Vitamin B-1 aids the deaf. Vitamin G softens cataracts. Vitamin C helps to master hay fever and relieves arthritis.

The story of the discovery and use of vitamins reads like the story of Alice in Wonderland! But the best of all sources of vitamins is in their natural state, as they exist in properly mineralized fruits and vegetables. Here they exist, just as Nature intended them, for the benefit of living creatures. Victor Lindlahr, in his book, YOU ARE WHAT YOU EAT, describes a wide variety of fruits, berries, and vegetables, with tables giving the vitamin content of each.

(g) Last, but by no means least, the mind must be conditioned and prepared for eating. One should never eat while angry, or frightened, or worried. Conversation while eating should be of a pleasant nature and not too intense. Family disagreements and discipline should never take place during meal time. Eating should be *a definite form of worship* in which all negative states of mind have been discarded. It should be an expression of gratitude to the Creator for having prepared so great an abundance of the necessities of life for every living creature; not an hour for ugly expressions and negative thinking.

3. RELAXATION:

Relaxation means the complete letting go of both the body and the mind, and particularly the clearing of the mind of all worries, fears, and anxieties. There should be a period of not less than one hour in each day during which the body and the mind are habitually relaxed and *released from all voluntary effort.*

Relaxation for sound health requires an average of eight hours a day for sleep. During sleep the subconscious section of the mind goes to work in earnest, repairing and rebuilding the worn out cells and tuning up the whole body in a general way. One's sleeping time cannot be dissipated or drawn upon for other purposes for any great length of time without serious damage to the physical body.

It is during sleep that the body, by some mysterious method unknown to science, builds up and replenishes its store of bodily resistance—that miraculous energy which keeps disease germs in check and influences the billions of physical cells to do their work.

At least one hour daily should be devoted to some hobby or play, preferably in the open air and the sunshine, to break the rhythm of one's daily routine. Here, as at meal time, the mental attitude should be positive, optimistic and pleasant. A game of golf, or tennis, or volley ball will work wonders for the person whose mind and body are engaged intensely by the demands of his daily occupation.

4. ELIMINATION:

There are four sources of elimination of the waste matter of the body. They are: (1) the lungs, (2) the skin, (3) the kidneys, and (4) the general sewer system known as the alimentary canal. These must be kept in first class working condition at all times, and to make sure that they are in proper condition one should have a complete check-up by a competent doctor at least once every three months.

Of these four sources of elimination the one that gives the greatest amount of trouble is the sewer system! The entire sewer system should be cleansed at least once a week.

The sewer system should be completely detoxified at least once every thirty days. Many doctors are prepared to give detoxifications, which consist of a complete cleansing of the entire alimentary canal with the aid of pure water. These are not to be confused with the enema, or the colonic irrigation, since detoxifications are much more thorough.

Toxic poisoning is almost a national tradition with the American people, due in the main, as we have stated, to the fact that they do not get the right kind of minerals in their food. Those who live in cities and whose occupations are of a sedentary nature, where they get but little physical exercise, are almost universally the victims of toxic poisoning.

Toxic poisoning and good dispositions are never found together!

Toxic poisoning and positive mental attitudes are never found together!

Remember this when that dull headache begins to put you on notice that your sewer system needs attention. Remember it also when your tongue is heavily coated in the morning, and your disposition is one of irritability.

Toxic poisoning kills off enthusiasm.

It undermines the faculty of the imagination.

And it leads to hopelessness and despair.

It also destroys ambition and personal initiative—the two qualities which must precede all personal achievements.

And it provides a favorable spawning place for almost every known physical ailment and disease!

There are danger signals that announce the presence of toxic poisoning, the chief of them being the appearance of a dull headache, followed by the loss of appetite.

The headache is a great blessing.

It is nature's language by which she telegraphs to the brain for assistance, but too often the "assistance" comes, if at all, in the form of a drug which does nothing but cut the line of communication over which the headache is crying out for help.

What the headache really needs is enough plain water to cleanse the entire sewer system!

And the evidence that this is true consists in the fact that the headache usually disappears within thirty minutes after the sewer system has been cleansed.

5. HOPE:

The person who is without hope is temporarily lost! Sound health inspires hope and hope inspires sound health, either way one chooses to look at the matter.

Hope is inspired by a Definite Major Purpose!

It is the natural offspring of the person who is going somewhere in life, knows where he is going, has a plan for getting there, and is busy carrying out that plan. And the man who is filled with the hope of achievement of his major purpose is so happy that he has no place in his mind for fear and worry and doubt. But, make no mistake about this: Hope and toxic poisoning never fraternize. Where one is found the other will be absent!

6. AVOID THE HABIT OF DRUGS:

The first thing one should do, preparatory to the development of a sound health consciousness, is to clean out the medicine chest and throw the entire contents down the sewer!

Sound health does not come in bottles!

Nature provided man with a very good system of health maintenance long before bottles or drugs were invented. Nature uses medicine for the maintenance of sound health, but she stores it in vegetables, and fruits, in the natural state, in the form of more than forty minerals, the more important of which are *calcium, iron* and *phosphorous*.

All of these minerals can be taken in the form of prepared pills and liquid medicines, but they serve nature's purpose much better if they are taken in their natural form, from food that grows from the soil.

Moreover, nature has provided every person with an expert chemist who understands the exact proportion of each of these minerals that is needed for the maintenance of sound health. This is something which no individual can understand. Nature's chemist assimilates the food when it enters the stomach and the alimentary canal, reduces it to a liquid and extracts from it the right combinations which are needed for health; all this, provided the food is grown from properly prepared soil.

Doctors have learned a great deal about the anatomy of the physical body. They have learned much about the maintenance of sound health. But they have not yet learned how to correct the causes of disease as expertly as Nature does the job.

No doctor ever cures any disease. When a cure is effected, it is

Nature that does the curing. The most that any doctor can do is to cooperate with Nature, *and some of the best doctors do this without the use of drugs.*

They are philosophers because they take into consideration both the causes and the effects of all forms of illness, and direct their attention mainly to the *correction of the causes.*

Some of the drug doctors specialize in dealing with the effects of disease, and often prescribe sedatives, which only serve to deaden the pain temporarily.

Physical pain is *Nature's universal language* in which she speaks effectively to every living creature on earth.

Pain is Nature's way of putting an individual on notice that some portion of his body needs attention, and the person who tries to kill pain without endeavoring to determine and correct its cause thereby offers affrontery to man and insult to the Creator. It is the cause of the pain that should be removed.

There are times when one needs professional counsel from a doctor, but it is better to get it *before one becomes ill* than afterward, for here, as in most circumstances, "an ounce of prevention is worth a ton of cure."

Find out how your body functions; study the combinations of food that your particular system and working habits require; acquire moderation in your eating habits; use self-discipline in all your habits. Thus you will express your highest form of gratitude toward your Creator. Everyone has been provided with a *personal doctor* functioning within his own body and skilled in the maintenance of sound health.

Benefit from Cosmic Habitforce

Chapter Seventeen

Before describing the law of Cosmic Habit-force in detail you may be interested in knowing what benefits it offers those who adapt themselves to it.

First of all, you should know that this law is the climax of the entire philosophy of individual achievement. To get a slight degree of understanding of the importance of this law, consider the fact that it is the Master Key to the principles previously described, *and its benefits are available only to those who master and apply the instructions in previous chapters.*

In order that you may approach the study of this chapter with a favorable mental attitude you should be informed at the outset of the promise it offers those who learn how to adapt themselves to the working principle which it presents.

Understanding and application of the law can release you from fears and self-imposed limitations, *thus enabling you to take full possession of your own mind!*

If it offered no further promise this would be sufficient to justify all the time you may devote to its study.

It can help you attain economic freedom for life, provided you follow the instructions in the previous chapters.

It can aid you in eliminating the opposition of others in all your relationships, thus enabling you to negotiate your way through life with a minimum of friction.

It can help you master most, if not all, of the major causes of physical conditions that cause illness and disease.

It can clear your mind of negative conditions, thus paving the way for that state of mind known as faith.

Cosmic Habit-force is the particular application of energy with which nature maintains the existing relationship between the atoms of matter, the stars and planets, the seasons of the year, night and day, sickness and health, life and death, and more important to us right now, it is the medium through which all habits and all human relationships are maintained, the medium through which thought is translated into its physical equivalent.

You, of course, know that nature maintains a perfect balance between all the elements of matter and energy throughout the universe. You can see the stars and planets move with perfect precision, each keeping its own place in Time and Space, year in and year out.

You can see the seasons of the year come and go with perfect regularity.

You can see that night and day follow each other in unending regularity.

You can see that an oak tree grows from an acorn and a pine grows from the seed of its ancestor. An acorn never produces a pine nor does a pine cone ever produce an oak, *and nothing is ever produced that does not have its antecedents in something else* which preceded it.

These are simple facts that anyone can see, but what most people cannot see or understand is the universal law through which nature maintains perfect balance between all matter and energy throughout the universe, forcing every living thing to *reproduce itself*.

A fragmentary glimpse of this great law of nature, which holds our little earth in its proper position and causes all material objects to be attracted toward the center of the earth, was caught when Newton discovered what he called the Law of Gravitation. If Newton had gone a few steps beyond where he stopped perhaps he would have discovered that the same law which holds our little earth in space and relates it to all the other planets in both time and space, *relates human beings to one another in exact conformity with the nature of their own thoughts.*

He would have discovered that the same force which draws all material things toward the center of this earth also builds men's thought habits in varying degrees of permanency. He would have discovered that negative thought habits, of whatever nature, attract to their creator physical manifestations corresponding to their nature, as perfectly as Nature germinates the seed of the acorn and develops it into an oak tree. Also he would have discovered that positive thoughts reach out through the self-same law and attract physical counterparts of their nature.

You are here concerned only with the method by which nature takes a hold on the mind through the operation of the law.

Before going any further here is a brief description of an important function of Cosmic Habit-force through which it controls all human relationships and determines whether an individual will be a success or a failure in his chosen occupation. *Nature uses this law as a medium by which every living thing is forced to take on and become a part of the environment in which it lives and moves daily.*

We are ruled by habits, all of us! Our habits are fastened upon us by repetition of thought and experience. Therefore, we can control our earthly destinies just to the extent that we control our thoughts. It is a profoundly significant fact that over the power of thought a person may have complete control. Everything else is subject to forces outside of one's control.

Nature has given man the privilege of controlling his thoughts, but she has also subjected him to the power of Cosmic Habit-force through which his thoughts are made to clothe themselves in their physical likeness and equivalent.

If a man's dominating thoughts are of poverty, the law translates those thoughts into physical terms of misery and want. If a man's dominating thoughts are of opulence, the law transforms them into their physical counterpart. Man builds the pattern through his thoughts, but Cosmic Habit-force works that pattern into its physical likeness and builds it into permanency.

"But how can a law of nature make something out of nothing?" some will ask. It is but natural that any practical person would want to know the exact manner in which, for example, Cosmic Habit-force could transmute thoughts of opulence into material riches, or thoughts of poverty into material evidences of poverty. We are happy to raise the question and to answer it.

To begin with let us recognize the fact that Cosmic Habit-force is silent, unseen and unfelt and works in complete harmony with all of nature's other forces, such as gravitation, electricity, evolution, etc., but it differs from all other natural forces in that *it is the sole source of their power,* and serves as Nature's Comptroller, through which every form of power and every law of nature must work. *It is the Master Key to the universe,* so great in power that it controls every living thing and every atom of matter, the control being carried out through established habit-force.

The method by which Cosmic Habit-force converts a positive impulse or mental desire into its physical equivalent is simple. It merely intensifies the desire into a state of mind known as Faith which inspires one to create definite plans for the attainment of whatever is desired, the plans being carried out through whatever natural methods the resourcefulness of the individual can command.

Cosmic Habit-force does not undertake to transmute the desires for money directly into bank balances or specie, but it does set into motion the mechanism of imagination through which the most easily available means of converting the desire into money is provided in the form of a definite idea, plan or method of procedure.

This force works no miracles, makes no attempt to create something out of nothing, but it does help an individual—nay, it forces him—to proceed naturally and logically to convert his thoughts into their physical equivalent, by using all the natural media available to him which may serve his purpose.

The force works so quietly that the individual (unless he is of a philosophical trend of mind) does not recognize its relationship to what is happening to him. On one occasion an idea will present itself to his mind in a form which he calls a "hunch," and it will inspire him with such definite faith that he will begin at once to act upon it.

His entire being has been changed from a negative to a positive state of mind, with the result that related ideas flow into his mind more freely, the plans he creates are more definite, and his words have more influence with other people. Because he does not understand the source from which his "hunch" came, he may dismiss the matter and imagine the newly discovered idea or plan with which he achieves success was the creation of his own brain.

The "hunch" is simply a desire that has been given the intensity to enable Cosmic Habit-force to take it over and give it the necessary momentum to convert it into a definite idea or plan of action. From that point on the individual must move on his own, by using such opportunities, human relationships and physical conveniences as may be available to him for carrying out his desire.

At times one is inspired with awe by the "coincidental" combination of favorable circumstances with which he is favored in carrying out his plans, such as voluntary cooperation from unexpected sources, some fortunate transaction in business that provides unexpected money, etc., but always these strange and unexplained things happen *through perfectly natural procedure similar to daily experiences.*

What the individual cannot see or understand is the method by which Cosmic Habit-force gives to one's thoughts that peculiar quality which gives them the power to surmount all difficulties, overcome all resistances, and achieve seemingly unattainable ends through simple but natural procedure.

That is one secret of nature which she has not yet revealed, but neither has she revealed the secret by which she causes a seed of wheat to germinate, grow and reproduce itself, bringing back with it a hundred additional grains for good measure.

The mystery by which nature forces a grain of wheat to reproduce itself is no greater than that by which an individual like Henry Ford can start at scratch, with no working capital and no tools, and convert one simple desire into a huge industrial empire, but the two mysteries have one thing definitely in common— they move in response to the law of Cosmic Habit-force, working on and with the thoughts of man and inherent life in a grain of wheat.

Cosmic Habit-force guided me through an awe-inspiring maze of experiences before revealing itself to me. All through those years of struggle there was one definite purpose uppermost in my mind, the burning desire to organize a philosophy with which the average man can become self-determining. Nature had no alternative but that of yielding to me the working principle of

Cosmic Habit-force, because I unwittingly complied with the law by persistently seeking *the way to its discovery.*

If I had known of the existence of the law, and of its working principle at the beginning of my research I could have organized The Philosophy of American Achievement in a much shorter period of time. It is profoundly significant that the law of Cosmic Habit-force was revealed after a daily contact of minds through the Master Mind principle covering a period of almost two years.

A major portion of this time was devoted to the analysis of problems which had nothing to do with a voluntary search for the law, but the important thing I wish here to emphasize is the fact that *our habit of bringing our minds into rapport for a definite purpose daily* actually had the effect of giving us the benefit of Cosmic Habit-force before we knew of the existence of the law.

Prior to the discovery of this force we had not understood clearly what happens when two or more people bring their minds into rapport and apply the Master Mind principle for the attainment of definite ends.

We knew that this form of harmonious cooperation brought results, but we did not know *how* or *why* our minds were so stimulated during a Master Mind meeting that our thoughts took on an entirely different and more vital quality.

We had observed, prior to discovery of Cosmic Habit-force, that when we went into a Master Mind meeting for the purpose of solving some problem we had little difficulty in supplanting fear with faith; moreover, the mere contacting of our minds for a definite purpose invariably caused a change to take place in our minds which automatically transformed our fears and doubts into confidence and faith.

We understand, now, that the best of all known ways of adapting one's self to the positive influence of Cosmic Habit-force is provided through the Master Mind principle where two or more minds are coordinated in a spirit of perfect harmony for the attainment of a definite purpose. We know that this procedure has the effect of clearing the way for Cosmic Habit-force to act directly upon the thoughts associated with the object of the meeting. We know also something of the manner in which this force operates in carrying out the purpose of the meeting.

In the first place the harmonious contact of two or more minds for a definite purpose fixes the object of the purpose in each mind with greater clarity. This modifies the thoughts of each party to the meeting in such a manner that all doubts and fears associated with the object of the meeting are converted into confidence and faith.

It is a fact that, where any family group or any group of business associates sits down together in a spirit of friendliness for the purpose of analyzing any problem they wish to solve, the mere discussion of the problem generally leads to its solution. When the solution comes it generally comes in the form of a plan or a "hunch" that suddenly presents itself in the mind of one of the group.

Many of these statements concerning the nature of Cosmic Habit-force are abstract, but presently I shall proceed to reduce them to the concrete by describing exactly how this force operates in the daily affairs of men.

I have shown you exactly how it is the determining factor which leads one to success and plenty or to poverty and misery; how it brings harmony and understanding in marriage, or converts that relationship into disappointment and failure.

I realize that merely to say that it is the force with which nature keeps the stars and planets in their place is not enough to be of benefit to the average man who is more concerned with the solution of his daily problems than with electrons, stars, and planets.

I realize that the whole world has passed through economic collapses which have not only reduced millions of people to poverty and want but have tried their very souls as well, and these millions of people who were fighting for the right to live their lives in peace and harmony wanted all the knowledge they could get that would help them. Because you may be faced with a similar situation in your lifetime, I shall describe in the simplest terms possible the most astounding conclusions of my forty years of research into the causes of success and failure.

I wish you to have a bird's-eye view of the relationship between Cosmic Habit-force and three other important principles through which it becomes the most important factor in the lives of men. Two of these principles are associated with the method by which the force operates, and the third is the major principle by which the power of the force can be redirected and converted from positive to negative use by an individual. These four important associated principles are:

(a) Cosmic Habit-force, the principle through which nature forces everyone to take on and become a part of the environmental influences which control his thinking.

(b) Drifting, the habit of mental indifference through which an individual allows chance and circumstance to fasten his environmental influences on him.

(c) Time, the factor with which Cosmic Habit-force weaves together man's dominating thoughts and the influences of his environment, and transforms them into stumbling blocks or stepping stones according to their nature.

(d) Definiteness of Purpose, the only medium under the control of an individual with which Cosmic Habit-force may be controlled.

In the statements to follow you will observe how every success is the result of day-by-day habits of thought. The force may be likened to a great river, one half flowing in one direction, carrying everyone who *drifts* into it to certain failure, and the other half flowing in the opposite direction and carrying to success and power everyone within its reach.

The river is the brain of man, and the force flowing in the two opposite directions is the power of thought, the failure side of the stream being negative thought, the success side being positive thought. The source of power that keeps the river flowing is Cosmic Habit-force.

You will observe that neither success nor failure is the result of luck or chance. I warn you, before you read further, that the knowledge you are about to receive will forever deprive you of the privilege of resorting to alibis to explain away your failures. I warn you, too, that you will never again be privileged to say truthfully that life never gave you an opportunity, for you will know definitely that as long as you have the right to form and express your own thoughts you have the potential power with which to change the circumstances of your life to whatever you wish them to be.

If your life is not what you wish it to be, you can truthfully say that you drifted into your present unhappy condition through the irresistible force of Cosmic Habit-force, but you cannot stop there because you shall know presently that time and Definiteness of Purpose, backed by Cosmic Habit-force, can give you rebirth no matter who you are or what may be your circumstances.

You may be in prison, without friends or money, with a life sentence hanging over you, but you can walk through the front gate and back to the outside world a free man, if you adapt yourself to this force in the proper manner. How do I know this can be done? Because it has been done before. Because your common sense will tell you that it can be done once you understand the working principle and catch the full significance of its relationship to time and Definiteness of Purpose.

You may be suffering with ill health which prevents you from using your mind. In that event, unless your illness is of a nature that can be cured, you may not be able to order your life just as you would have it, but you can make changes that will give you ample compensation for your trouble in living.

You are going to make another outstanding discovery in connection with this force. You are going to learn that "every failure brings with it the seed of an equivalent advantage." You are going to discover, beyond any room for doubt, that every experience, every circumstance of your life is a potential stepping stone or a stumbling block, *due entirely to the manner in which you react to the circumstance in your own mind.*

You are going to discover that your only limitations are those which you set up in your own mind; but more important still, you are going to know that your mind can remove all limitations it establishes. You are going to know that you may be "the master of your fate, the captain of your soul" because you can control your own thoughts.

You are going to learn that failure is one of nature's methods by which she breaks up the grip of Cosmic Habit-force and releases the mind for a new start. You are going to understand that nature breaks the grip of Cosmic Habit-force on human beings through illness that forces them to rest the organs of the body and the brain. You are going to understand, too, that nature breaks the grip of the law on the people of an entire nation through wars and economic collapses known as depressions, thereby breaking up the monopolies on opportunity and reducing all men to substantially the same level.

I have given you a working knowledge of the relationship between Cosmic Habit-force, drifting, time, and Definiteness of Purpose. I have shown you, through illustrations based on actual experience, exactly how and why ninety-eight out of every hundred people are failures.

I want you to know that the failures of life become such because they fall into the habit of drifting on all matters affecting their economic life; that Cosmic Habit-force carries them swiftly along in this drifting path until time fastens the habit permanently, after which there can be no escape except through some circumstance of catastrophe which breaks up their established habits and gives them an opportunity to move with Definiteness of Purpose.

A combination of time and Cosmic Habit-force compels every human being to absorb and become a part of the environment in which he lives and moves daily, just as definitely as time and Cosmic Habit-force create the seasons of the year, follow day with night, and keep the stars and planets in their accustomed places throughout immeasurable periods of distance and time.

By stating and restating the principles by which time and Cosmic Habit-force operate I hope to so clearly fix in your mind the nature of these two irresistible forces that you will recognize their presence and understand the part they play in experiences I shall describe.

I wish you to see that you are where you are and what you are today because of the influences which have reached your mind through your daily environment, plus the state of mind in which you have reacted to these influences. I wish you to see and to understand that you can move with Definiteness of Purpose and make your environment to order, or you can drift with circumstances and allow your environment to control you.

In both cases Cosmic Habit-force is an irresistible force which you cannot evade. It carries you swiftly toward a definite goal *if you have one* and if you are *definitely determined* to reach that goal, or if you have no goal it forces you to drift with time and circumstances until you become the victim of every stray wind of chance that crosses your path.

Everything in life worth having has a definite price upon it. There is no such reality as something for nothing. Having had the full advantage of studying Emerson's conclusions on this subject, plus the advantage of analyzing men and women representing the great successes and the outstanding failures, I am prepared to describe why every desirable thing in life has a price that must be paid. But I cannot pass this information on to the person who is not willing to face facts and admit his own shortcomings. A willingness to look at one's self through unbiased eyes is a part of the price one must pay for the formula which leads to self-determination spiritually, economically and physically.

Every person who succeeds must make use of some combination of the principles of this philosophy. The power which gives life and action to these principles is Cosmic Habit-force. Whenever any combination of the principles has been used successfully, as far as I have been able to determine by my research and personal experience, the law was unconsciously applied. I mean by this that those who have made successful application of the law have done so by mere chance, without recognizing the real source of the power back of their achievements.

Now that the law has been isolated and the principle of its operation understood the fundamental principles of achievements will be treated for their exact value; they will be used as stimuli with which any desired habit may be begun and carried on voluntarily until Cosmic Habit-force picks up the habit and automatically carries it to its logical climax. Observe the importance of the element of time as an essential factor with which the principles of achievement and Cosmic Habit-force become related.

Cosmic Habit-force is so inexorable that it automatically takes over habits and makes them permanent. It is the medium by which the habit of illness known to physicians as hypochondria (suffering from imaginary illness) begins to grow from the very first moment one complains of illness or admits the presence of pain.

If Cosmic Habit-force will—and it most certainly does—crystallize an impulse of thought of illness and pain into a habit, think how much more quickly it will translate into permanency such pleasant sensations as intoxication through liquor, opiates and sex emotion.

Then, push your imagination just one step further and you will quickly recognize what happens when these habits are so presented through clever advertising that the mind of the victim is continuously bombarded with the thought that they are signs of smartness.

Then the forces of advertising become a voluntary and effective ally of the law of Cosmic Habit-force, thus insuring the fixation of the habits in less than one-tenth of the time nature would require if Cosmic Habit-force were the only medium of fixation.

When nature has a message to convey to mankind she does not release it to those who are indulging in dissipation, nor does she hand it over to those who have been pampered and protected from struggle, but she picks as her torch-bearers those who have been seasoned by defeat until they have become self-determining. I could not imagine a WPA worker or a CCC boy becoming an Edison or a Ford. Genius is born of hardship, of deprivation and of toil to surmount difficulties, and not of subsidy.

Keep the Source of All Wealth

You now have a workable understanding of the MASTER KEY to all riches.

It is only natural that you may wish to use the key to unlock the door to material riches. Let us turn, then, to the analysis of the great American System of Free Enterprise, because this is the major source of material riches. It is also the source from which most of our economic leaders have been developed.

Our system of free enterprise is not a quick-growth institution, but it is the product of many decades of evolution during which it has been supported and developed by scientific research as well as by the trial and error method of gathering useful knowledge.

Its birth, development and growth have not been without errors and mistakes, some of which were the result of avarice and greed upon the part of a few who sought quick riches; but most of which were the honest mistakes of men who sincerely sought the way to perfection by the best means that were available through the trial and error method.

Whatever the mistakes of the leaders of our system of free enterprise may have been, whether they were honest or dishonest mistakes, the system stands today as one of the greatest wonders of the industrial world.

This was proved, beyond all reasonable room for doubt, by the astounding job that industry did in providing the necessary materials for the conduct of World War II.

The American system of industry is the envy of the world, due to the fact that it is manned by leaders and workers who coordinate their efforts in a manner which has developed a high degree of industrial economy.

But, there is another reason for its efficiency, and it dates back to the founding of our nation and has its roots in the Constitution which was so written as to provide incentive for the exercise of individual initiative and the right to the benefits of free enterprise popularly known as the "profit motive."

This is the central core of our American industrial efficiency!

It is efficient because the men who run it, the men who own it, and the men who work in it, from the management on down to the humblest worker, all *desire to make a profit.*

No one ever does anything voluntarily without a motive.

The motive of desire for financial gain is one of the three most impelling motives of all mankind, the other two being the motive of love and the motive of sex.

Now consider how wisely the authors of the Constitution wrote into that famous document a system of government which not only provides the humblest citizen with the right to exercise his own personal initiative under our system of free enterprise, but it consists also of a system of checks and balances which protects this right.

It anticipates man's natural desire to govern himself by motives and deliberately provides encouragement for the individual to choose whatever motive he pleases, with the assurance that he will have the power of the government back of him in carrying out his purpose.

Andrew Carnegie, who was recognized as the greatest industrial leader of his time, was so keenly aware of the stimulating effect of the profit motive that he deliberately encouraged his associate workers to make the most of this motive. Some of them began as ordinary laborers but they so related themselves to their fellow workers, under our system of free enterprise, that they accumulated vast personal fortunes.

It was one of these workers, who began as a stake driver at ordinary day wages, who promoted himself until he became the moving spirit in the organization of the great United States Steel Corporation which has added hundreds of millions of dollars of wealth to the nation as a whole, to say nothing of having provided millions of jobs for men and women, directly and indirectly. His name was Charles M. Schwab.

On some occasions Mr. Schwab made such effective use of our

system of free enterprise that he not only earned a salary greater than that of the President of the United States, but an additional bonus of as much as a million dollars in a single year; an achievement that would have been impossible without the friendly co-operation of Mr. Carnegie and the benefits of our system of free enterprise.

When Mr. Carnegie was asked if he could not have availed himself of Mr. Schwab's services without the payment of so huge a bonus he replied, "Oh yes, I could have had his services for less, but *I am in business to make men as well as to make money,* and I have learned that the best way to develop men is to provide them with an incentive to do their best. I have found no incentive which beats that of desire for financial gain!"

So, here is a clear statement by the greatest industrialist this country has ever known, which lays the finger squarely on one of the major advantages of our system of free enterprise. It is a system which develops personal initiative and thereby helps men to do their best; to do it willingly and voluntarily.

This point is emphasized because it turns the spotlight on the greatest of all the assets of the "richest and the freest" nation, and that is the ingenious manner in which the American form of government and the American System of Free Enterprise have been so coordinated that they inspire and encourage every citizen to do his best.

Take away from a man the right to make a profit on his services, and limit his right to exercise his personal initiative in whatever direction he chooses, and you will have destroyed the greatest asset that any man has, no matter what may be the pretense under which this is done.

The desire to accumulate material riches stands near the head of the list of all human desires. It is as fundamental as the Creator could make it, as is evidenced by the fact that it is universal.

We look at the records of such men as Andrew Carnegie, Henry Ford and Thomas A. Edison—men who became eminently successful in the accumulation of material riches—and we marvel at their achievements, not suspecting perhaps that back of these achievements is a plan far more profound than that of the desire for riches.

We seldom stop to wonder whether or not these achievements may be a part of the Creator's plan to urge men onward and upward in civilization's progress, by planting in their minds a strong motive for the exercise of their personal initiative.

But this much we do know: Our country has been blessed—more than the other countries of the world—with the privilege of providing the world with its first system of free enterprise. This system is so ingeniously arranged that it both inspires men to do their best and adequately provides them with a natural motive for doing so.

Surely we are not so bankrupt in our power of thought that we cannot see that back of all these blessings of liberty and freedom and opportunity to accumulate personal wealth, there may be a purpose deeper than that of the mere desires of men.

We sincerely believe it has been the lack of recognition of this Divine purpose which has brought this and all other nations to the very brink of world disaster through spiritual bankruptcy.

The Creator has ingenious methods of carrying out the overall plan of human progress, not the least of which is that by which man is influenced, by natural motives, to do his best.

Take the motives of love and sex, for example, through a combination of which the Creator has provided a system which insures the perpetuation of all human life. These motives have been made so alluring and powerful that it is not of man's choice to respond to them or reject them.

The Creator has seen to it that life on this earth shall continue according to His plans, no matter what man may think he wants, or to what motives he may attribute the results of his activities.

Henry Ford may have believed that he was motivated by a desire for financial gain; or he may have believed that he was motivated by the pride of personal achievement through which he established a great industrial empire that benefitted other people more than it benefitted him; but one thing he may never have known (and it was not essential that he know it) is that through his efforts, millions of men and women are motivated to carry out the Creator's plans by the development of their minds through the exercise of their *personal initiative.*

The human brain develops only through personal initiative!

This is a fact well known to every psychologist, but not everyone recognizes the possibility that back of all expression of personal initiative is the Creator's plan to insure man's mental and spiritual growth through his own endeavors.

The whole of nature and the recognized methods by which all natural laws operate provide inescapable evidence of the soundness of this theory; and recognition of this evidence will remove all odium with which our system of free enterprise has been besmirched by those who would find fault with it without offering the world a better system.

Able thinkers have agreed that it was no mere stroke of chance that has provided the people of this country with unparalleled privileges and opportunities to develop and grow through the expression of their personal initiative.

This privilege outweighs every other privilege we enjoy, for it provides everyone with the opportunity to choose his own motive and to live his own life and accumulate riches in whatever form and quantity he may desire.

Andrew Carnegie recognized that the American people might become over-engrossed in the accumulation of material riches, because he knew, as we all know, that there is such an over abundance of wealth and of opportunity to accumulate wealth in the United States, that there is a danger men may evaluate too lightly that which comes too easily.

He could see the tendency of people to mistake their privileges of opportunity for a license to expect and demand something for nothing—a tendency which now stands out definitely as the greatest danger of our times.

It was Mr. Carnegie's recognition of this danger which influenced him to devise an ingenious plan for the distribution of the greater portion of his personal wealth so that it would influence men to become seekers after knowledge.

And it was his recognition of this danger that inspired him to influence more than five hundred of the leaders of industry to collaborate in the organization of the seventeen principles of the philosophy of individual achievement described in previous chapters.

He well knew that material riches accumulated by a strict application of these seventeen principles could have no other effect than that of enriching the nation as a whole, as well as enriching the individuals who accumulated the riches!

Thus it is clear that Mr. Carnegie understood the benefits of sharing, for he obviously recognized the truth that men are only the temporary custodians of material riches; that riches are a blessing when they are so regarded and so used that they provide opportunities for all men to participate in their use.

"God moves in a mysterious way, His wonders to perform!"

Who, among us, is so blind as not to see that there is something more profound than the mere desire for personal riches, which has made our country the richest and the freest nation of the world?

And who would be so unwise or so blind as to deny that such men as Andrew Carnegie, Henry Ford and Thomas A. Edison have made this a better country than it could have become without their efforts? These men who have added billions of dollars to our wealth and provided an outlet for the talents of tens of millions of men and women!

And who is wise enough to say that the personal initiative of such men is not a part of the overall plan of an all-wise Providence?

The deeper thinker will be more apt to say that what we need is more men of this type, not fewer; that our great system of free enterprise, which provides opportunities for all men seeking an outlet for their talents, is a blessing of major proportions, not a curse.

And the truly wise individual will embrace our system of free enterprise, help to improve it where he can, and relate himself to it harmoniously so it may carry him to the attainment of his personal ambitions.

It was in this spirit that Henry Ford related himself to our system of free enterprise; and while he began without money, with very little schooling, and chose a field of endeavor in which he had to become a pioneer, with the trial and error method as his only guide, he attained results which astounded the entire industrial world.

We know that he struggled tirelessly to perfect the automobile that was destined to make him the directing head of a great industrial empire, working late hours and using all of the talents he possessed.

We know that out of his persistent use of his personal initiative came an industry which provides employment, directly or indirectly, for many millions of men and women whose combined wages amount to many millions of dollars each working day.

All of these facts we know, but what we do not know is the nature of the motive—the real hidden motive—which inspired Mr. Ford to carry on. We may say it was the profit motive, but there are many facts connected with his career which indicate that we shall have to go deeper than the profit motive for the real answer.

Of one thing we may be sure: the American form of government and the American System of Free Enterprise provided aid and encouragement to Mr. Ford, and gave him the hope and the faith necessary to enable him to carry on through many years of struggle. We know also that out of that struggle came a great network of industrial plants, improved highways that cover the entire nation, gasoline filling stations, automobile garages and repair shops, automobile accessory stores and other business enterprises which provide employment for millions of people.

Perhaps Mr. Ford did not have all of these astounding results in mind while he was laboring to perfect his automobile; but whatever his motive may have been, the results were the same.

Surely no one in his right mind would believe that Mr. Ford could have accomplished such stupendous results if in the beginning his personal initiative had been subdued, discouraged, or limited in any manner.

On the other hand, it is obvious that he succeeded because he made intelligent application of the seventeen principles of this philosophy, through which he related himself harmoniously to the great American System of Free Enterprise.

If we combine the results attained by Henry Ford with those attained by the other great industrial leaders of the past several decades, we shall have what is known as the American way of life.

There are many facts connected with the American System of Free Enterprise which require no great amount of analysis in order that we may recognize their benefits. The first of these is the fact that our industrial system provides the greatest source of inspiration for the use of personal initiative. In this respect it is the same today as it was when Henry Ford, Andrew Carnegie and Thomas A. Edison began their careers.

The entire system is one that encourages men to do their best, and appropriately rewards those who, by their superior skill, imagination and personal initiative, render greater service—basing the reward on the *quality* and the *quantity* of the service rendered, plus the mental attitude in which it is rendered.

Our system of free enterprise gives employment to most of the skilled labor and a large portion of the unskilled labor, at wages not equalled in any other country, or during any other period in the history of industry. This same system provides working conditions which are without parallel anywhere else, or at any other time, in the history of the world.

It supplies the income that supports the major portion of all professional service such as that rendered by lawyers, doctors, dentists, architects, and clergymen.

It provides the money which pays for most of the surplus products of agriculture. Therefore, it is no exaggeration to say that it supports the farmers and pays the interest on the farm mortgages, and provides a market for all farm products.

It pays, directly and indirectly, most of the taxes which are necessary for the maintenance of both our State and Federal Governments. It is a partner of Government, and as such it deserves the protection of the Government which was provided by the Constitution.

It provides the machinery and the equipment and the working

capital with which the inventor, such as Thomas A. Edison, may take the products of his ingenuity to the people of the world at a profit.

It has been responsible for the building of every improved highway, and every automobile that travels over these highways, not to mention the stupendous increases in the value of the lands through which the highways have passed.

It provides a ready market for the talents of every person who has a commercially sound idea to market in any field of useful endeavor.

It builds every battleship, every commercial boat used in American shipping, and supplies all needed war materials used in the defense of our nation, which is to say that it is the strong arm of Uncle Sam's fighting forces on both land and sea as well as in the air.

The American System of Free Enterprise and the American System of Government are twin-brothers in fact, for they are inseparable parts of that which we call the American way of life.

The American Constitution was written so as to give the fullest possible measure of protection to our industrial system, and that system has been developed through close coordination with our Government. Therefore, any weakening of one weakens proportionately the other. If the American System of Free Enterprise were destroyed, our American form of Government would go with it.

The man who says "it can't be done" is usually busy trying to keep out of the way of the man who is doing it.

For additional information about Napoleon Hill products, please contact the following locations:

The Napoleon Hill World Learning Center
Purdue University Calumet
2300 173rd Street
Hammond, IN 46323-2094

Judith Williamson, Director
Uriel "Chino" Martinez, Assistant/Graphic Designer

Telephone: 219-989-3173 or 219-989-3166
email: nhf@calumet.purdue.edu

The Napoleon Hill Foundation
University of Virginia-Wise
College Relations Apt. C
1 College Avenue
Wise, VA 24293

Don Green, Executive Director
Annedia Sturgill, Executive Assistant

Telephone: 276-328-6700
email: napoleonhill@uvawise.edu

Website: www.naphill.org